Managing learning

The importance of learning is linked to the current pressures for change facing most, if not all, organizations. Within a stable, unpressured environment, the need for organizational learning on a major scale is seen as unnecessary. In fact, stable environments rarely exist, just environments which are *perceived* as unthreatening where organizations fail to detect the small signs of emerging change and threat or react to them confidentially in terms of established ways of doing things.

The concept of managing learning implies that organizations encourage their staff to be better at recognizing key signals: at analysing data, at seeing possibilities, at thinking the unthought and the unthinkable, at challenging their own and others' assumptions. None of this is new, but the notion of the learning organization seems finally to have come of age. And with maturity come hard questions:

- Can learning actually be managed by an organization or does it just happen?
- Does the definition of competencies clarify or confuse when recruiting, promoting and training staff?
- Why do some organizational norms quench learning, while others promote it as a way of life?
- Do self directed teams represent a long-awaited panacea or a misguided flight from individual accountability?
- How can diversity in the workforce be used to enable, rather than inhibit, learning?

This collection of readings succinctly captures the depth and diversity of the learning literature over the past ten years. Produced as a reader for students on the Open Business School diploma level course 'Managing Development and Change', this book will provide a timely source of reference for DMS and MBA students and any manager concerned with personal, group and corporate learning.

Christopher Mabey is Head of the Centre for Human Resource and Change Management at the Open Business School and is a Chartered Psychologist. He teaches, researches, writes and consults on the subjects of Individual and Organizational Development. **Paul Iles** is Professor of Human Resource Development at Liverpool John Moores University. Also a Chartered Psychologist, he has published widely in the field of Human Resource Management.

This reader is part of an integrated teaching system; the selection is therefore related to other material available to students and is designed to evoke critical understanding. Opinions expressed are not necessarily those of the course team or of the University.

If you would like to study the course to which this reader relates or receive further information about Open Business School courses please write to **The Customer Service Centre,** The Open University, PO Box 222, Walton Hall, Milton Keynes MK7 6YY or telephone 0908 653449/ 652226.

Managing learning

Edited by Christopher Mabey and
Paul Iles
at The Open University

INTERNATIONAL THOMSON BUSINESS PRESS
I (T) P An International Thomson Publishing Company

London • Bonn • Boston • Johannesburg • Madrid • Melbourne • Mexico City • New York • Paris
Singapore • Tokyo • Toronto • Albany, NY • Belmont, CA • Cincinnati, OH • Detroit, MI

Managing Learning

Selection and editorial matter
Copyright ©1994 The Open University

 I(T)P
A division of International Thomson Publishing Inc.
The ITP logo is a trademark under licence

British Library Cataloguing-in-Publication Data
A catalogue record for this book is available from the British Library

First published by Routledge 1994
Simultaneously published in the USA and Canada by Routledge
Reprinted 1995
Reprinted by International Thomson Business Press 1996

Typeset in Garamond by Intype, London
Printed in the UK by Biddles Ltd, Guildford and King's Lynn

ISBN 0-415-11983-7

International Thomson Business Press
Berkshire House
168–173 High Holborn
London WC1V 7AA
UK

International Thomson Business Press
20 Park Plaza
13th Floor
Boston MA 02116
USA

http://www.thomson.com/itbp.html

Contents

Figures

Tables

Introduction

Christopher Mabey and Paul Iles

In the last decade there have been discernible shifts in organizations away from a preoccupation with the methods and technologies for delivering training in organizations, to an emphasis on those approaches and attitudes that encourage learning. Training courses are no longer judged on knowledge and skills acquisition, but knowledge and skills application. Earlier concerns with measuring and assessing have moved to how learning can be interwoven with everyday activities in the workplace. Responsibility for development has been shifting from tutor and trainer to line manager-as-coach and trainee. The development process has overtaken the training event at an individual, group and organization level. The focus is now on learning through reframing workplace problems, self-determined development, unfreezing barriers to learning, and understanding what it means to be a learning organization. It is not that 'learning' has been without its advocates, rather that the message seems finally to have got through that it is an essential strand of commercial flexibility, employee empowerment and personal fulfilment in the work setting. So Peter Senge's chapter, which opens this book, fittingly written at the doorway of the 1990s, both looks back for its inspiration to seminal work on personal and corporate learning (e.g. Argyris and Schon 1978; Mintzberg 1987) and looks forward to a compelling mix of skills, roles and tools that will assist organizational learning in the future. This is followed by some down-to-earth extracts that demonstrate the elusiveness of the learning organization but also some of the pay-offs when organizations finally get it right.

Possibly associated with this gathering interest in learning, the notion of competency has also 'come of age' in the 1990s. There have been other reasons for this attention to competency: a desire to professionalize the previously *ad hoc* world of management training, the ongoing quest for meaningful criteria when assessing workplace performance, and the possibilities of more integrated human resource strategies derived from competency-based frameworks. Yet, the concept and content of competencies remains controversial. Part II of this book reflects some of this crossflow of opinion, but also refers to companies that have successfully harnessed the good that has come from the competency debate.

What can organizations do to encourage their management to take the development of themselves and their staff seriously? On a more pragmatic level, Part III on facilitating development includes a number of shorter extracts that explore a wide range of possibilities from coaching and mentoring through appraisal and developmental assessment centres to the less conventional – though perhaps more natural – approaches like action learning and experiential leaning. Teams and team building deserve a section to themselves (Part IV) because of the unique learning opportunities afforded by working intensively with a small group of individuals, usually not chosen by us. Again, recent writing on self-directed teams, promoting innovation through teams, and the use of teamworking in cultural/structural change programmes are all featured. In each case, practical guidelines are offered as a means of enabling ordinary people to achieve extraordinary outcomes because of the creative synergy they achieve by working effectively together. However, teams are not a panacea for all organizational ills, and those who take a more critical, less sanguine view of team working are also included.

It cannot be assumed that all employees have the same motivation and opportunities to learn in modern organizations: barriers and inhibitors due to race, gender, age and ethnic background can come into play. These may be structural, political, cultural and/or attitudinal in nature. More usually a combination of all these factors conspires against productive working and learning and they go unnoticed by all except those who are discriminated against and made to feel less 'visible' than others. There are also special issues associated with work/non-work balance and learning in and for a multi-cultural setting. The chapters in Part V are not only a reminder to acknowledge but, more importantly, to value difference in the context of learning.

One of the exciting aspects about the concept of managing learning in organizations is the number of disciplines that inform our understanding. Sociologists, anthropologists and psychologists, as well as management theorists themselves, all provide valuable insights on what it is to be a learning organization. This collection of readings seeks to capture something of this diverse heritage although we confess to a slight psychological bias. We have included a range of styles too: from rigorously empirical studies, through case studies and critical essays to the reflections of practitioners. In many cases we have – in the interest of space – edited original extracts heavily, and we are grateful to the contributors for allowing such surgery. Hopefully the resulting selection will serve to stimulate your personal learning in the pursuit of the wider learning of the organizations to which you belong.

Part I

Organizational learning
Christopher Mabey

We start with a chapter by Peter Senge, which draws upon his immensely popular book *The Fifth Discipline: The Art and Practice of the Learning Organization*. In contrast to the traditional concept of the organizational leader as 'charismatic hero' or 'the boss who calls the shots', Senge takes a refreshing look at the new roles and skills required of leaders in organizations and the new tools at their disposal. In fact, most of the concepts referred to are not new, but represent a welcome gathering together of some enduring and enlightening ideas. For instance, the need for systemic diagnosis as against event-driven reactivity, the powerful conception of leader as servant, the need to recognize challenge and defuse defensive routines and the return to 'simple' skills like active listening ('balancing inquiry and advocacy'), avoiding premature conclusions ('seeing leaps of attraction') and recognizing the gap between 'espoused theory and theory in use'. It should be noted that Senge's view of organizations is primarily an optimist one. His creative tension principle tends to assume that individual employees will subscribe to a given organizational vision once it has been clearly articulated and the current reality has been accurately portrayed. His statement that 'negative visions carry a subtle message of powerlessness' may be true, but possibly neglects the incipient plurality of many organizations today in which powerless people cannot (or find it difficult to) create positive visions.

Readers looking for a definitive blueprint for the learning organization, as Margaret Dale's chapter appears to promise, will be disappointed. Certainly the author refers to the work of Pedler, Burgoyne and Boydell in describing what a learning organization might look like and how it might be achieved, but she is at pains to distance the concept from a set of management techniques or behaviours. She goes on helpfully to distinguish the learning organization in the following ways: it is more concerned with how things are done than what is done; with being rather than doing; with learning rather than training; with the unique rather than the universal; with experience rather than exhortation; with sea change rather than first-order change. If application of the learning organization concept still seems somewhat elusive, Dale does give some practical pointers for managing one's own and others' learning. For instance, equipping people to deal with the uncertainty and ambiguity of turbulent change, tolerance of the coexistence of contradictions and opposing views, and working with others – rather than alone – in co-learner communities which encourage a good balance between reflection and action. Dale's contribution is included because of its experiential perspective – describing what it is like to be inside a learning organization.

With Graeme Salaman and Jim Butler's chapter we narrow the focus to management learning, and to the reasons why training courses – in particular – frequently fail to bring about the learning hoped for. In their insightful essay, the authors point out that in this context training and learning, far from being neutral processes, are in fact heavily politicized. This is because such learning pathways cannot be divorced from the wider 'structures of power, reward and evaluation' that exist within a given organizational setting. How an individual or group perceive the value and legitimacy of what they are being taught and how it meshes with their own (sub) cultural loyalties will have as much, if not a greater, influence upon their receptivity and retention of the skills, knowledge and values being imparted as the subject matter itself. This is graphically illustrated with an example of resistance to training in the London Fire Brigade. Dale warns us against the folly of trying to replicate organizational examplars of the learning organization. This is, first, because each organization will have a unique way of developing its learning processes and, second, due to the subsequently rapid demise of some organizations, which had previously been held up as role models.

With these precautions in mind, the fourth and final chapter in this section describes in detail how one organization – the Chaparral steelmill in Texas – became a learning laboratory. Dorothy Leonard-Barton provides an in-depth view into how the company solves problems, gathers and integrates internal and external knowledge and consistently uses this knowledge to challenge the status quo. It is encouraging to note that many of the specific management practices and workplace attitudes accord with those advocated in the earlier chapters. Perhaps the gap between exhortation and actuality is narrowing. The publication of more rigorous learning organization case studies will tell us whether this is so.

Chapter 1

The leader's new work: building learning organizations

Peter M. Senge

The prevailing view of learning organizations emphasizes increased adaptability. Given the accelerating pace of change, or so the standard view goes, "the most successful corporation of the 1990s," according to *Fortune* magazine, "will be something called a learning organization, a consummately adaptive enterprise."[1]

But increasing adaptiveness is only the first stage in moving toward learning organizations. The impulse to learn in children goes deeper than desires to respond and adapt more effectively to environmental change. The impulse to learn, at its heart, is an impulse to be generative, to expand our capability. This is why leading corporations are focusing on generative learning, which is about creating, as well as adaptive learning, which is about coping.[2]

Generative learning, unlike adaptive learning, requires new ways of looking at the world, whether in understanding customers or in understanding how to better manage a business. For years, US manufacturers sought competitive advantage in aggressive controls on inventories, incentives against overproduction, and rigid adherence to production forecasts. Despite these incentives, their performance was eventually eclipsed by Japanese firms who saw the challenges of manufacturing differently. They realized that eliminating delays in the production process was the key to reducing instability and improving cost, productivity, and service. They worked to build networks of relationships with trusted suppliers and to redesign physical production processes so as to reduce delays in materials procurement, production set up, and in-process inventory – a much higher-leverage approach to improving both cost and customer loyalty.

THE LEADER'S NEW WORK

Our traditional view of leaders – as special people who set the direction, make the key decisions, and energize the troops – is deeply rooted in an individualistic and non-systemic world view. Especially in the West, leaders are heroes – great men (and occasionally women) who rise to the fore in times of crisis. So long as such myths prevail, they reinforce a focus on short-term events and charismatic heroes rather than on systemic forces and collective learning.

Leadership in learning organizations centers on subtler and ultimately more important work. In a learning organization, leaders' roles differ dramatically from that of the charismatic decision maker. Leaders are designers, teachers, and stewards. These roles require new skills: the ability to build shared vision, to bring to the surface and challenge prevailing mental models, and to foster more systemic patterns of thinking. In short, leaders in learning organizations are responsible for building organizations where people are continually expanding their capabilities to shape their future – that is, leaders are responsible for learning.

CREATIVE TENSION: THE INTEGRATING PRINCIPLE

Leadership in a learning organization starts with the principle of creative tension.[3] Creative tension comes from seeing clearly where we want to be, our "vision," and telling the truth about where we are, our "current reality." The gap between the two generates a natural tension.

Creative tension can be resolved in two basic ways: by raising current reality toward the vision, or by lowering the vision toward current reality. Individuals, groups, and organizations who learn how to work with creative tension learn how to use the energy it generates to move reality more reliably toward their visions.

The principle of creative tension has long been recognized by leaders. Martin Luther King, Jr., once said, "Just as Socrates felt that it was necessary to create a tension in the mind, so that individuals could rise from the bondage of myths and half truths ... so must we ... create the kind of tension in society that will help men rise from the dark depths of prejudice and racism."[4]

Without vision there is no creative tension. Creative tension cannot be generated from current reality alone. All the analysis in the world will never generate a vision. Many who are otherwise qualified to lead fail to do so because they try to substitute analysis for vision. They believe that, if only people understood current reality, they would surely feel the motivation to change. They are then disappointed to discover that people "resist" the personal and organizational changes that must be made to alter reality. What they never grasp is that the natural energy for changing reality comes from holding a picture of what might be that is more important to people than what is.

But creative tension cannot be generated from vision alone; it demands an accurate picture of current reality as well. Just as King had a dream, so too did he continually strive to "dramatize the shameful conditions" of racism and prejudice so that they could no longer be ignored. Vision without an understanding of current reality will more likely foster cynicism than creativity. The principle of creative tension teaches that an accurate picture of current reality is just as important as a compelling picture of a desired future.

Leading through creative tension is different from solving problems. In problem solving, the energy for change comes from attempting to get away from an aspect of current reality that is undesirable. With creative tension, the energy for change comes from the vision, from what we want to create, juxtaposed with current reality. While the distinction may seem small, the consequences are not. Many people and organizations find themselves motivated to change only when their problems are bad enough to cause them to change. This works for a while, but the change process runs out of steam as soon as the problems driving the change become less pressing. With problem solving, the motivation for change is extrinsic. With creative tension, the motivation is intrinsic. This distinction mirrors the distinction between adaptive and generative learning.

NEW ROLES

The traditional authoritarian image of the leader as "the boss calling the shots" has been recognized as oversimplified and inadequate for some time. According to Edgar Schein, "Leadership is intertwined with culture formation." Building an organization's culture and shaping its evolution is the "unique and essential function" of leadership.[5] In a learning organization, the critical roles of leadership – designer, teacher, and steward – have antecedents in the ways leaders have contributed to building organizations in the past. But each role takes on new meaning in the learning organization and, as will be seen in the following sections, demands new skills and tools.

Leader as designer

Imagine that your organization is an ocean liner and that you are "the leader." What is your role?

I have asked this question of groups of managers many times. The most common answer, not surprisingly, is "the captain." Others say, "The navigator, setting the direction." Still others say, "The helmsman, actually controlling the direction," or, "The engineer down there stoking the fire, providing energy," or, "The social director, making sure everybody's enrolled, involved, and communicating." While these are legitimate leadership roles, there is another which, in many ways, eclipses them all in importance. Yet rarely does anyone mention it.

The neglected leadership role is the designer of the ship. No one has a more sweeping influence than the designer. What good does it do for the captain to say, "Turn starboard 30 degrees," when the designer has built a rudder that will only turn to port, or which takes six hours to turn to starboard? It's fruitless to be the leader in an organization that is poorly designed.

The functions of design, or what some have called "social architecture," are rarely visible; they take place behind the scenes. The consequences that appear today are the result of work done long in the past, and work today will show its benefits far in the future. Those who aspire to lead out of a desire to control, or gain fame, or simply to be at the center of the action, will find little to attract them to the quiet design work of leadership.

But what, specifically, is involved in organizational design? "Organization design is widely misconstrued as moving around boxes and lines," says Hanover's O'Brien. "The first task of organization design concerns designing the governing ideas of purpose, vision, and core values by which people will live." Few acts of leadership have a more enduring impact on an organization than building a foundation of purpose and core values.

In 1982, Johnson & Johnson found itself facing a corporate nightmare when bottles of its best-selling Tylenol were tampered with, resulting in several deaths. The corporation's immediate response was to pull all Tylenol off the shelves of retail outlets. Thirty-one million capsules were destroyed, even though they were tested and found safe. Although the immediate cost was significant, no other action was possible given the firm's credo. Authored almost forty years earlier by president Robert Wood Johnson, Johnson & Johnson's credo states that permanent success is possible only when modern industry realizes that:

• service to its customers comes first;
• service to its employees and management comes second;
• service to its stockholders, last.

Such statements might seem like motherhood and apple pie to those who have not seen the way a clear sense of purpose and values can affect key business decisions. Johnson & Johnson's crisis management in this case was based on that credo. It was simple, it was right, and it worked.

If governing ideas constitute the first design task of leadership, the second design task involves the policies, strategies, and structures that translate guiding ideas into business decisions. Leadership theorist Philip Selznick calls policy and structure the "institutional embodiment of purpose."[6] "Policy making (the rules that guide decisions) ought to be separated from decision making," says Jay Forrester.[7] "Otherwise, short-term pressures will usurp time from policy creation."

Traditionally, writers like Selznick and Forrester have tended to see policy making and implementation as the work of a small number of senior managers. But that view is changing. Both the dynamic business environment and the mandate of the learning organization to engage people at all levels now make it clear that this second design task is more subtle. Henry Mintzberg has argued that strategy is less a rational plan arrived at in the abstract and implemented throughout the organization than an "emergent phenomenon." Successful organizations "craft strategy" according to Mintzberg, as they continually learn about shifting business conditions and balance what is desired and what is possible.[8] The key is not getting the right strategy but fostering strategic thinking. "The choice of individual action is only part of . . . the policymaker's need," according to Mason and Mitroff.[9] "More important is the need to achieve insight into the nature of the complexity and to formulate concepts and world views for coping with it."

Behind appropriate policies, strategies, and structures are effective learning processes; their creation is the third key design responsibility in learning organizations. This does not absolve senior managers of their strategic responsibilities. Actually, it deepens and extends those responsibilities. Now, they are not only responsible for ensuring that an organization has well-developed strategies and policies, but also for ensuring that processes exist whereby these are continually improved.

Leader as teacher

"The first responsibility of a leader," writes retired Herman Miller CEO Max de Pree, "is to define reality."[10] Much of the leverage leaders can actually exert lies in helping people achieve more accurate, more insightful, and more empowering views of reality.

Leader as teacher does not mean leader as authoritarian expert whose job it is to teach people the "correct" view of reality. Rather, it is about helping everyone in the organization, oneself included, to gain more insightful views of current reality. This is in line with a popular emerging view of leaders as coaches, guides, or facilitators.[11] In learning organizations, this teaching role is developed further by virtue of explicit attention to people's mental models and by the influence of the systems perspective.

The role of leader as teacher starts with bringing to the surface people's mental models of important issues. No one carries an organization, a market, or a state of technology in his or her head. What we carry in our heads are assumptions. These mental pictures of how the world works have a significant influence on how we perceive problems and opportunities, identify courses of action, and make choices.

One reason that mental models are so deeply entrenched is that they are largely tacit. Ian Mitroff, in his study of General Motors, argues that an assumption that prevailed for years was that, in the United States, "Cars are status symbols. Styling is therefore more important than quality."[12] The Detroit automakers didn't say, "We have a *mental model* that all people care about is styling." Few actual managers would even say publicly that all people care about is styling. So long as the view remained unexpressed, there was little possibility of challenging its validity or forming more accurate assumptions.

But working with mental models goes beyond revealing hidden assumptions. "Reality," as perceived by most people in most organizations, means pressures that must be borne, crises that must be reacted to, and limitations that must be accepted. Leaders as teachers help people restructure their views of reality to see beyond the superficial conditions and events into the underlying causes of problems – and therefore to see new possibilities for shaping the future.

Specifically, leaders can influence people to view reality at three distinct levels: events, patterns of behavior, and systemic structure.

Systemic Structure
(Generative)
↓
Patterns of Behavior
(Responsive)
↓
Events
(Reactive)

The key question becomes where do leaders predominantly focus their own and their organization's attention?

Contemporary society focuses predominantly on events. The media reinforces this perspective, with almost exclusive attention to short-term, dramatic events. This focus leads naturally to explaining what happens in terms of those events: "The Dow Jones average went up sixteen points because high fourth-quarter profits were announced yesterday."

Pattern-of-behavior explanations are rarer, in contemporary culture, than event explanations, but they do occur. "Trend analysis" is an example of seeing patterns of behavior. A good editorial that interprets a set of current events in the context of long-term historical changes is another example. Systemic, structural explanations go even further by addressing the question, "What causes the patterns of behavior?"

In some sense, all three levels of explanation are equally true. But their usefulness is quite different. Event explanations – who did what to whom – doom their holders to a reactive stance toward change. Pattern-of-behavior explanations focus on identifying long-term trends and assessing their implications. They at least suggest how, over time, we can respond to shifting conditions. Structural explanations are the most powerful. Only they address the underlying causes of behavior at a level such that patterns of behavior can be changed.

By and large, leaders of our current institutions focus their attention on events and patterns of behavior, and, under their influence, their organizations do likewise. That is why contemporary organizations are predominantly reactive, or at best responsive – rarely generative. On the other hand, leaders in learning organizations pay attention to all three levels, but focus especially on systemic structure; largely by example, they teach people throughout the organization to do likewise.

Leader as steward

This is the subtlest role of leadership. Unlike the roles of designer and teacher, it is almost solely a matter of attitude. It is an attitude critical to learning organizations.

While stewardship has long been recognized as an aspect of leadership, its source is still not widely understood. I believe Robert Greenleaf came closest to explaining real stewardship, in his seminal book *Servant Leadership*.[13] There, Greenleaf argues that "The servant leader *is* servant first. . . . It begins with the natural feeling that one wants to serve, to serve *first*. This conscious choice brings one to aspire to lead. That person is sharply different from one who is leader first, perhaps because of the need to assuage an unusual power drive or to acquire material possessions."

Leaders' sense of stewardship operates on two levels: stewardship for the people they lead and stewardship for the larger purpose or mission that underlies the enterprise. The first type arises from a keen appreciation of the impact one's leadership can have on others. People can suffer economically, emotionally, and spiritually under inept leadership. If anything, people in a learning organization are more vulnerable because of their commitment and sense of shared ownership. Appreciating this naturally instills a sense of responsibility in leaders. The second type of stewardship arises from a leader's sense of personal purpose and commitment to the organization's larger mission. People's natural impulse to learn is unleashed when they are engaged in an endeavor they consider worthy of their fullest commitment. Or, as Lawrence Miller puts it, "Achieving return on equity does not, as a goal, mobilize the most noble forces of our soul."[14]

NEW SKILLS

New leadership roles require new leadership skills. These skills can only be developed, in my judgement, through a lifelong commitment. It is not enough for one or two individuals to develop these skills. They must be distributed widely throughout the organization. This is one reason that understanding the disciplines of a learning organization is so important. These disciplines embody the principles and practices that can widely foster leadership development.

Three critical areas of skills (disciplines) are building shared vision, surfacing and challenging mental models, and engaging in systems thinking.[15]

Building shared vision

The skills involved in building shared vision include the following:

Encouraging personal vision

Shared visions emerge from personal visions. It is not that people only care about their own self-interest – in fact, people's values usually include dimensions that concern family, organization, community, and even the world. Rather, it is that people's capacity for caring is personal.

Communicating and asking for support

Leaders must be willing to continually share their own vision, rather than being the official representative of the corporate vision. They also must be prepared to ask, "Is this vision worthy of your commitment?" This can be difficult for a person used to setting goals and presuming compliance.

Visioning as an ongoing process

Building shared vision is a never-ending process. At any one point there will be a particular image of the future that is predominant, but that image will evolve. Today, too many managers want to dispense with the "vision business" by going off and writing the Official Vision Statement. Such statements almost always lack the vitality, freshness, and excitement of a genuine vision that comes from people asking, "What do we really want to achieve?"

Blending extrinsic and intrinsic visions

Many energizing visions are extrinsic – that is, they focus on achieving something relative to an outsider, such as a competitor. But a goal that is limited to defeating an opponent can, once the vision is achieved, easily become a defensive posture. In contrast, intrinsic goals like creating a new type of product, taking an established product to a new level, or setting a new standard for customer satisfaction can call forth a new level of creativity and innovation. Intrinsic and extrinsic visions need to coexist; a vision solely predicated on defeating an adversary will eventually weaken an organization.

Distinguishing positive from negative visions

Many organizations only truly pull together when their survival is threatened. Similarly, most social movements aim at eliminating what people don't want: for example, anti-drugs, anti-smoking, or anti-nuclear arms movements. Negative visions carry a subtle message of powerlessness: people will only pull together when there is sufficient threat. Negative visions also tend to be short term. Two fundamental sources of energy can motivate organizations: fear and aspiration. Fear, the energy source behind negative visions, can produce extraordinary changes in short periods, but aspiration endures as a continuing source of learning and growth.

Surfacing and testing mental models

Many of the best ideas in organizations never get put into practice. One reason is that new insights and initiatives often conflict with established mental models. The leadership task of challenging assumptions without invoking defensiveness requires reflection and inquiry skills possessed by few leaders in traditional controlling organizations.[16]

Seeing leaps of abstraction

Our minds literally move at lightning speed. Ironically, this often slows our learning, because we leap to generalizations so quickly that we never think to test them. We then confuse our generalizations with the observable data upon which they are based, treating the generalizations as if they were data. The frustrated sales rep reports to the home office that "customers don't really care about quality, price is what matters," when what actually happened was that three consecutive large customers refused to place an order unless a larger discount was offered. The sales rep treats her generalization, "customers care only about price," as if it were absolute fact rather than an assumption (very likely an assumption reflecting her own views of customers and the market). This thwarts future learning because she starts to focus on how to offer attractive discounts rather than probing behind the customers' statements. For example, the customers may have been so disgruntled with the firms' delivery or customer service that they are unwilling to purchase again without larger discounts.

Balancing inquiry and advocacy

Most managers are skilled at articulating their views and presenting them persuasively. While important, advocacy skills can become counterproductive as managers rise in responsibility and confront increasingly complex issues that require collaborative learning among different, equally knowledgeable people. Leaders in learning organizations need to have both inquiry and advocacy skills.[17]

Specifically, when advocating a view, they need to be able to:

- explain the reasoning and data that led to their view;
- encourage others to test their view (e.g., Do you see gaps in my reasoning? Do you disagree with the data upon which my view is based?);
- encourage others to provide different views (e.g., Do you have either different data, different conclusions, or both?).

When inquiring into another's views, they need to:

- seek actively to understand the other's view, rather than simply restating their own view and how it differs from the other's view;
- make their attributions about the other and the other's view explicit (e.g., Based on your statement that . . . ; I am assuming that you believe . . . ; Am I representing your views fairly?).

If they reach an impasse (others no longer appear open to inquiry), they need to:

- ask what data or logic might unfreeze the impasse, or if an experiment (or some other inquiry) might be designed to provide new information.

Distinguishing espoused theory from theory in use

We all like to think that we hold certain views, but often our actions reveal deeper views. For example, I may proclaim that people are trustworthy, but never lend friends money and jealously guard my possessions. Obviously, my deeper mental model (my theory in use), differs from my espoused theory. Recognizing gaps between espoused views and theories in use (which often requires the help of others) can be pivotal to deeper learning.

Recognizing and defusing defensive routines

As one CEO in our research program puts it, "Nobody ever talks about an issue at the 8:00 business meeting exactly the same way they talk about it at home that evening or over drinks at the end of the day." The reason is what Chris Argyris calls "defensive routines," entrenched habits used to protect ourselves from the embarrassment and threat that come with exposing our thinking. For most of us, such defenses began to build early in life in response to pressures to have the right answers in school or at home. Organizations add new levels of performance anxiety and thereby amplify and exacerbate this defensiveness. Ironically, this makes it even more difficult to expose hidden mental models, and thereby lessens learning.

The first challenge is to recognize defensive routines, then to inquire into their operation. Those who are best at revealing and defusing defensive routines operate with a high degree of self-disclosure regarding their own defensiveness (e.g., I notice that I am feeling uneasy about how this conversation is going. Perhaps I don't understand it or it is threatening to me in ways I don't yet see. Can you help me see this better?)

Systems thinking

We all know that leaders should help people see the big picture. But the actual skills whereby leaders are supposed to achieve this are not well understood. In my experience, successful leaders often are "systems thinkers" to a considerable extent. They focus less on day-to-day events and more on underlying trends and forces of change. But they do this almost completely intuitively. The consequence is that they are often unable to explain their intuitions to others and feel frustrated that others cannot see the world the way they do.

One of the most significant developments in management science today is the gradual coalescence of managerial systems thinking as a field of study and practice. This field suggests some key skills for future leaders:

Seeing interrelationships, not things, and processes, not snapshots

Most of us have been conditioned throughout our lives to focus on things and to see the world in static images. This leads us to linear explanations of systemic phenomenon. For instance, in an arms race each party is convinced that the other is the cause of problems. They react to each new move as an isolated event, not as part of a process. So long as they fail to see the interrelationships of these actions, they are trapped.

Moving beyond blame

We tend to blame each other or outside circumstances for our problems. But it is poorly designed systems, not incompetent or unmotivated individuals, that cause most organizational problems. Systems thinking shows us that there is no outside – that you and the cause of your problems are part of a single system.

Distinguishing detail complexity from dynamic complexity

Some types of complexity are more important strategically than others. Detail complexity arises when there are many variables. Dynamic complexity arises when cause and effect are distant in time and space, and when the consequences over time of interventions are subtle and not obvious to many participants in the system. The leverage in most management situations lies in understanding dynamic complexity, not detail complexity.

Focusing on areas of high leverage

Some have called systems thinking the "new dismal science" because it teaches that most obvious solutions don't work – at best, they improve matters in the short run, only to make things worse in the long run. But there is another side to the story. Systems thinking also shows that small, well-focused actions can produce significant, enduring improvements, if they are in the right place. Systems thinkers refer to this idea as the principle of "leverage." Tackling a difficult problem is often a matter of seeing where the high leverage lies, where a change – with a minimum of effort – would lead to lasting, significant improvement.

Avoiding symptomatic solutions

The pressures to intervene in management systems that are going awry can be overwhelming. Unfortunately, given the linear thinking that predominates in most organizations, interventions usually focus on symptomatic fixes, not underlying causes. This results in only temporary relief, and it tends to create still more pressures later on for further, low-leverage intervention. If leaders acquiesce to these pressures, they can be sucked into an endless spiral of increasing intervention. Sometimes the most difficult leadership acts are to refrain from intervening through popular quick fixes and to keep the pressure on everyone to identify more enduring solutions.

NEW TOOLS

Developing the skills described above requires new tools – tools that will enhance leaders' conceptual abilities and foster communication and collaborative inquiry. What follows is a sampling of tools starting to find use in learning organizations.

Systems archetypes

One of the insights of the budding managerial systems-thinking field is that certain types of systematic structures recur again and again. Countless systems grow for a period, then encounter problems and cease to grow (or even collapse) well before they have reached intrinsic limits to growth. Many other systems get locked in runaway vicious spirals where every actor has to run faster and faster to stay in the same place. Still others lure individual actors into doing what seems right locally, yet which eventually causes suffering for all.[18]

Some of the system archetypes that have the broadest relevance include the following.

Balancing process with delay

In this archetype, decision makers fail to appreciate the time delays involved as they move toward a goal. As a result, they overshoot the goal and may even produce recurring cycles.

Classic example: Real estate developers who keep starting new projects until the market has gone soft, by which time an eventual glut is guaranteed by the properties still under construction.

Limits to growth

A reinforcing cycle of growth grinds to a halt, and may even reverse itself, as limits are approached. The limits can be resource constraints, or external or internal responses to growth.

Classic examples: Product life cycles that peak prematurely due to poor quality or service, the growth and decline of communication in a management team, and the spread of a new movement.

Shifting the burden

A short-term "solution" is used to correct a problem, with seemingly happy immediate results. As this correction is used more and more, fundamental long-term corrective measures are used less. Over time, the mechanisms of the fundamental solution may atrophy or become disabled, leading to even greater reliance on the symptomatic solution.

Classic example: Using corporate human resource staff to solve local personnel problems, thereby keeping managers from developing their own interpersonal skills.

Eroding goals

When all else fails, lower your standards. This is like "shifting the burden," except that the short-term solution involves letting a fundamental goal, such as quality standards or employee morale standards, atrophy.

Classic example: A company that responds to delivery problems by continually upping its quoted delivery times.

Escalation

Two people or two organizations, who each see their welfare as depending on a relative advantage over the other, continually react to the other's advances. Whenever one side gets ahead, the other is threatened, leading it to act more aggressively to reestablish its advantage, which threatens the first, and so on.

Classic examples: Arms race, gang warfare, price wars.

Tragedy of the commons[19]

Individuals keep intensifying their use of a commonly available but limited resource until all individuals start to experience severely diminishing returns.

Classic examples: Sheepherders who keep increasing their flocks until they overgraze the common pasture; divisions in a firm that share a common salesforce and compete for the use of sales reps by upping their sales targets, until the salesforce burns out from overextension.

Growth and underinvestment

Rapid growth approaches a limit that could be eliminated or pushed into the future, but only by aggressive investment in physical and human capacity. Eroding goals or standards cause investment that is too weak, or too slow, and customers get increasingly unhappy, slowing demand growth and thereby making the needed investment (apparently) unnecessary or impossible.

Classic example: Countless once-successful growth firms that allowed product or service quality to erode, and were unable to generate enough revenues to invest in remedies.

Charting strategic dilemmas

Management teams typically come unglued when confronted with core dilemmas. A classic example was the way US manufacturers faced the low cost-high quality choice. For years, most assumed that it was necessary to choose between the two. Not surprisingly, given the short-term pressures perceived by most managements, the prevailing choice was low cost. Firms that chose high quality usually perceived themselves as aiming exclusively for a high quality, high price market niche. The consequences of this perceived either-or choice have been disastrous, even fatal, as US manufacturers have encountered increasing international competition from firms that have chosen to consistently improve quality and cost.

In a recent book, Charles Hampden-Turner presented a variety of tools for helping management teams confront strategic dilemmas creatively.[20] He summarizes the process in seven steps.

1 Eliciting the Dilemmas. Identifying the opposed values that form the "horns" of the dilemma, for example, cost as opposed to quality, or local initiative as opposed to central coordination and control. Hampden-Turner suggests that humor can be a distinct asset in this process since "the admission that dilemmas even exist tends to be difficult for some companies."
2 Mapping. Locating the opposing values as two axes and helping managers identify where they see themselves, or their organization, along the axes.
3 Processing. Getting rid of nouns to describe the axes of the dilemma. Present participles formed by adding "ing" convert rigid nouns into processes that imply movement. For example, central control versus local control becomes "strengthening national office" and "growing local initiatives." This loosens the bond of implied opposition between the two values. For example, it becomes possible to think of "strengthening national services from which local branches can benefit."
4 Framing/Contextualizing. Further softening the adversarial structure among different values by letting "each side in turn be the frame or context for the other." This shifting of the "figure-ground" relationship undermines any implicit attempts to hold one value as intrinsically superior to the other, and thereby to become mentally closed to creative strategies for continuous improvement of both.
5 Sequencing. Breaking the hold of static thinking. Very often, values like low cost and high quality appear to be in opposition because we think in terms of a point in time, not in terms of an on-going process. For example, a strategy of investing in new process technology and developing a new production-floor culture of worker responsibility may take time and money in the near term, yet reap significant long-term financial rewards.
6 Waving/Cycling. Sometimes the strategic path toward improving both values involves cycles where both values will get 'worse' for a time. Yet, at a deeper level, learning is occurring that will cause the next cycle to be at a higher plateau for both values.
7 Synergizing. Achieving synergy where significant improvement is occurring along all axes of all relevant dilemmas. (This is the ultimate goal, of course.) Synergy, as Hampden-Turner points out, is a uniquely systemic notion, coming from the Greek *syn-ergo* or "work together."

DEVELOPING LEADERS AND LEARNING ORGANIZATIONS

In a recently published retrospective on organization development in the 1980s, Marshall Sashkin and W. Warner Burke observe the return of an emphasis on developing leaders who can develop organizations.[21] They also note Schein's critique that most top executives are not qualified for the task of developing culture.[22] Learning organizations represent a potentially significant evolution of organizational culture. So it should come as no surprise that such organizations will remain a distant vision until the leadership capabilities they demand are developed. "The 1990s may be the period," suggest Sashkin and Burke, "during which organization development and (a new sort of) management development are reconnected."

I believe that this new sort of management development will focus on the roles, skills, and tools for leadership in learning organizations. Undoubtedly, the ideas offered above are only a rough approximation of this new territory. The sooner we begin seriously exploring the territory, the sooner the initial map can be improved – and the sooner we will realize an age-old vision of leadership:

The wicked leader is he who the people despise.
The good leader is he who the people revere.
The great leader is he who the people say,
"We did it ourselves."

NOTES AND REFERENCES

1 B. Domain, *Fortune*, 3 July 1989, pp. 48–62.
2 The distinction between adaptive and generative learning has its roots in the distinction between what Argyris and Schon have called their "single-loop" learning, in which individuals or groups adjust their behavior relative to fixed goals, norms, and assumptions, and "double-loop" learning, in which goals, norms, and assumptions, as well as behavior, are open to change (e.g. see C. Argyris and D. Schon, *Organizational Learning: A Theory-in-Action Perspective* (Reading, Massachusetts: Addison-Wesley, 1978).
3 The principle of creative tension comes from Robert Fritz' work on creativity. See R. Fritz, *The Path of Least Resistance* (New York: Ballantine, 1989) and *Creating* (New York: Ballantine, 1990).
4 M. L. King, Jr., "Letter from Birmingham Jail," *American Visions*, January–February 1986, pp. 52–9.
5 E. Schein, *Organizational Culture and Leadership* (San Francisco: Jossey-Bass, 1985). Similar views have been expressed by many leadership theorists. For example, see: P. Selznick, *Leadership in Administration* (New York: Harper & Row, 1957); W. Bennis and B. Nanus, *Leaders* (New York: Harper & Row, 1985); and N. M. Tichy and M. A. Devanna, *The Transformational Leader* (New York: John Wiley & Sons, 1986).
6 Selznick (1957).
7 J. W. Forrester, "A New Corporate Design," *Sloan Management Review* (formerly *Industrial Management Review*), Fall 1965, pp. 5–17.
8 See, for example, H. Mintzberg, "Crafting Strategy," *Harvard Business Review*, July–August 1987, pp. 66–75.
9 R. Mason and I. Mitroff, *Challenging Strategic Planning Assumptions* (New York: John Wiley & Sons, 1981), p. 16.
10 M. de Pree, *Leadership is an Art* (New York: Doubleday, 1989) p. 9.

11 For example, see T. Peters and N. Austin, *A Passion for Excellence* (New York: Random House, 1985) and J. M. Kouzes and B. Z. Posner, *The Leadership Challenge* (San Francisco: Jossey-Bass, 1987).

12 I. Mitroff, *Break-Away Thinking* (New York: John Wiley & Sons, 1988), pp. 66–7.

13 R. K. Greenleaf, *Servant Leadership: A Journey into the Nature of Legitimate Power and Greatness* (New York: Paulist Press, 1977).

14 L. Miller, *American Spirit: Visions of a New Corporate Culture* (New York: William Morrow, 1984), p. 15.

15 These points are condensed from the practices of the five disciplines examined in Senge (1990).

16 The ideas below are based to a considerable extent on the work of Chris Argyris, Donald Schon, and their Action Science colleagues: C. Argyris and D. Schon, *Organizational Learning: A Theory-in-Action Perspective* (Reading, Massachusetts: Addison-Wesley, 1978); C. Argyris, R. Putnam, and D. Smith, *Action Science* (San Francisco: Jossey-Bass, 1985); C. Argyris, *Strategy, Change, and Defensive Routines* (Boston: Pitman, 1985); and C. Argyris, *Overcoming Organizational Defenses* (Englewood Cliffs, New Jersey: Prentice-Hall, 1990).

17 I am indebted to Diana Smith for the summary points below.

18 The system archetypes are one of several systems diagraming and communication tools. See D. H. Kim, "Toward Learning Organizations: integrating Total Quality Control and Systems Thinking" (Cambridge, Massachusetts: MIT Sloan School of Management, Working Paper No. 3037–89-BPS, June 1989).

19 This archetype is closely associated with the work of ecologist Garrett Hardin, who coined its label: G. Hardin, "The Tragedy of the Commons," *Science*, 13 December 1968.

20 C. Hampden-Turner, *Charting the Corporate Mind* (New York: The Free Press, 1990).

21 M. Sashkin and W. W. Burke, "Organization Development in the 1980s" and "An End-of-the-Eighties Retrospective," in *Advances in Organization Development*, ed. F. Masarik (Norwood, New Jersey: Ablex, 1990).

22 E. Schein (1985).

Chapter 2

Learning organizations

Margaret Dale

WHAT IS A LEARNING ORGANIZATION?

Early work was concerned to find examples of good practice so that the learning organization might be replicated. What happened, however, was that some of the organizations held up as role models were subsequently found to be flawed. Almost as soon as descriptions of their excellence appeared in print, conditions had changed and their performance was no longer outstanding. This has served to diminish the importance of the concept in the eyes of those looking for cook-book solutions. People who are looking for the 'right way' have missed the point of the concept, however. The right way is as elusive as any other idealized state of being – there is no perfect organization, for they are all peopled by fallible human beings; therefore, it is inevitable that organizations make mistakes, get things wrong and suffer setbacks. Mistakes and setbacks are elemental features of development and learning. It is the way in which organizations respond to the normal features of the modern world and the lessons learnt from the experience that qualifies them for the title 'learning organization'. It is not what they do, but how they do it.

Pedler, Boydell and Burgoyne (1988) set out to:

> define and test the feasibility of the idea as an appropriate approach to business and human resource development strategies in the 1990s.

By a process of literature reviews, interviews and other investigations, they were able to produce a working definition of a learning company:

> An organisation which facilitates the learning of all its members and continuously transforms itself.

In their report, Pedler *et al.* take pains to stress the two-sided nature of the definition. A learning company is not one that merely engages in a lot of training. The need for the development of individual skills is embedded in the concept, equal to and part of the need for organizational learning.

Is an organization an entity or a collective?

It is not possible to continue into the investigation of a learning organization without considering whether an organization has an existence of its own which is separate from those of its members, or whether it is simply a sum of the component parts. Organizations are an essential part of the way our society operates. They can be found at all levels of society and are involved in the bulk of the transactions in which we engage with other people.

Gibson, Ivancevich and Donnelly (1988) say:

> Organisations are, however, much more than means of providing goods and services. They create the settings in which most of us spend our lives. In this respect, they have profound influence on our behaviour.

Because of their importance to our everyday lives, the study of behaviour within organizations has become a discipline in its own right, concerning:

> The study of human behaviour, attitudes and performance within an organisational setting; drawing on theory, methods and principles from such disciplines as psychology, sociology and cultural anthropology to learn about *individual* perceptions, values, learning capacities and action while working in *groups* and within the total organisation, analysing the external environment's effect on the *organisation* and its human resources, missions, objectives and strategies.
>
> (Gibson, Ivancevich and Donnelly 1988)

Life within one organization may be similar to life in another, but it will also be different. Each organization is unique. This uniqueness emanates from each organization's culture, which grows and changes during the life of the organization. It is influenced by its original and developing purpose, the people in membership and those with influence on the organization.

If organizations are merely the product of the people in them and their purpose, it would be reasonable to expect that those which are set up for similar purposes would have similar cultures. It would be reasonable to expect this to be especially so in those sectors where people move freely between organizations. In fact, this is not the case. The National Health Service provides an example that shows the opposite. Until recently, each health authority was run according to the same tight guidelines set down by central government. Doctors were trained using a rotation scheme that required the young medics to move between hospitals and specialities. If the argument about cultural commonality were correct, the doctors would have experienced no real difference between health authorities, but this was not so. Each authority had its own distinctive features that made the experience of each novel.

Therefore if each organization is unique and has its own identity manifested in its culture, which develops and changes over time as a result of experience and influence, the organization must be capable of learning. Learning, as defined earlier, is a purposeful activity aimed at the acquisition and development of skills and knowledge and their application. An organization's skills are found in its accepted behaviour patterns and its collective knowledge in its shared assumptions. The organizational attitude exists in the core values. If these can be developed within an individual, there is no reason why this cannot happen for an organization. It is more difficult and will take longer to achieve, but these factors do not reduce the possibility of organizational learning.

Pedler *et al.* say 'a Learning Company is one in which learning and working are synonymous'. They concluded that, as a 'learning company' is really an idealized state, it is not possible to point one out as a visible entity. This is because the definition describes a way of being, which is more than doing. Nevertheless there are some features that can be used to distinguish between a company which is not learning and one which is. Many of these features concern the way in which the organization's members experience the organization and the climate within which they work. Pedler *et al.* give 'glimpses' of a learning company, but as it is more important here to grasp the ideas rather than the actions, no examples will be given. Without the underlying understanding, there is a danger that, as with many other management techniques, the behaviours will be copied incompletely.

What is a learning organization like?

According to Pedler *et al.*:

a Learning Organisation is one which:
- has a climate in which individual members are encouraged to learn and to develop their full potential
- extends this learning culture to include customers, suppliers and other significant stakeholders
- makes human resource development strategy central to business policy
- is in a continuous process of organisational transformation.

The purpose of this process of transformation, as a central activity, is to enable the company to search within and without for new ideas, new problems and new opportunities for learning, to exploit a competitive advantage in an increasingly competitive world.

How to become a learning company

Megginson and Pedler provide a guide to the concept of a learning company. It is:

> an idea or metaphor that can serve as a guiding star. It can help people to think and act together on what such a notion would mean to them now and in the future. Like all visions, it can help to create the condition in which some of the features of a Learning Company could be brought about.

(Megginson and Pedler 1992)

These conditions are:

- learning strategy;
- participative policy-making;
- informating (i.e. information technology is used to inform and empower people to ask questions and take decisions based on available data);
- formative accounting (i.e. control systems are structured to assist learning from decisions);
- internal exchange;
- reward flexibility;
- enabling structures;
- front-line workers as environmental scanners;
- inter-company learning;
- learning climate;
- self-development for all.

Doing all these things would not necessarily mean that an organization is a learning company. To meet the standards of being an 'Investor in People', an organization is assessed by independent assessors. This approach demonstrates the difference between doing and being. The assessors go beyond examining the policy documents, procedures and records – the normal evidence used in quality assurance. Organizations are required to show what they do in practice. This means that they are open to a scrutiny that explores employees' experiences and understanding of training policy and practice. Being a learning company extends well beyond these. All the authors quoted above give systematic training a place within a learning organization, but the concept goes deeper and is more sophisticated. It means, for example, that the learning strategy is much more than a human resource development strategy. In a learning company, this learning is a core part of all operations.

What does organizational transformation mean?

Organizational transformation is different from organizational development. The latter term was in common use in the 1960s and 1970s to describe a process that relied mainly on the intervention of an external consultant. Most of the activities were aimed at exploring and improving the way in which organizational members worked together and responded to change. Techniques used included clarifying goals, negotiating roles, exploring group dynamics and gaining a better understanding of other members of a team, as a way of improving relationships. The economic recessions since then have switched attention from organizational dynamics to task/business requirements and the need to increase and improve skills. There is also a need to control change and to be proactive. Reacting and responding is no longer enough.

Organizational development typically focused on an area or point of time of change. The consultant would work with organizational members helping them work together and cope with change. Now, however, change is a part of normal reality. At one time, organizations moved in stages through periods of change into a steady state, and then again through a period of change. The strength of a bureaucratic organization is its ability to accommodate changes of this nature. What happens is 'first-order' change. The organization does 'more of' or 'less of' the same things, but this sort of response is not good enough. Life is no longer that simple. The changes occurring to organizations are now continuous:

> It is not just new kinds of problems and opportunities that we are facing, but whole new contexts within which these problems and opportunities reside. . . . The ground itself is moving . . . contexts have destabilised to the point where we can no longer assume that the basic structure of the context surrounding a situation will hold still long enough to make a planned course of action feasible. . . . In a destabilised context, you cannot know exactly what your problems are!
>
> Perhaps even the metaphor of permanent white water is not adequate: we are not talking merely about a wild river; we are talking about an unpredictable wild river.
>
> (Vaill 1989)

The rivers have carried us into a world where second-order change is needed. This means 'doing different things'. In this world, there is no one who knows best, no experience of having done it before, and there are no consultants or experts who can show us 'how to do it good'. There is only us, with the untapped, unknown resource of our own potential and creativity. Sadly, the rigidity of most organizations' policies and procedures serve to deny them these resources.

The rational models of decision-making were not put forward as reflections of reality. Being normative theories, they describe how decisions ought to be made. As many organizations say they use the principles of rational decision-making, many people actually believe that decisions are made in this way. The notion of incremental decisions – 'the art of muddling through' – as described by Lindblom (1979) is probably a more accurate representation of what happens in practice. Rational decision-making suggests that an organization decides its long-term goals, works out what needs to happen to get there, and then starts to take action. Muddling through implies that, even if such goals are set, the organization starts from where it is and moves, incrementally onwards – perhaps towards the goals, but not necessarily so. Decisions are made on the grounds of expediency, rather than being goal-orientated.

Examples of both models can be seen to operate within existing organizational realities. The sort of decision-making required for the new reality in the world of permanent white water takes the organization beyond these practices. The term 'sea change' has been used to describe the sort of fundamental shifts that modern conditions impose on organizations, but this notion is still limited to one-off changes. The world of organizations is now iterative; constantly moving and reshaping in unpredictable directions.

What is it like to be part of a learning organization?

Being a member of a learning organization is not necessarily an easy role. In fact it can be distinctly uncomfortable, depending on the individual's views of the world. To those who are excited by learning and development, who actively seek change and growth, the notion of continuous learning is very attractive – the prospect of being involved in a learning company is desirable. To others, the opposite may be true. The idea of change and challenge can be repulsive to those who prefer continuity and routine.

There is a belief among those who are committed to learning and development that this will be beneficial to all. This is not a correct assumption. Some people are content to go to work and do the same job, day in, day out, for the whole of their working lives. They have as much right to take this view as those who believe differently. However, their wish for stability must not lead to stagnation, for stagnation brings death in its wake. As with people, some organizations prefer stability in their cultures and work actively to preserve the status quo. The existence of 'dynamic conservatism' must not be ignored.

The tendency to stagnation can be detected in statements such as: 'We can't do that, we have never done it before', which lead to paralysis and a systemic inability to change. The supposed effect of an ageing working population on organizations has not received much attention. The emphasis, recently, has been given to the positive contribution older people can make. However, there is a general assumption that as people grow older, they tend to be less experimental, becoming more risk averse and preferring the known to the unknown. If this assumption is true, the ageing nature of the workforce may affect organizations' abilities to learn, develop and transform, unless action is taken to counteract its influence. Therefore it will become even more critical for organizations to learn how to learn.

Living with change

Being a part of a learning organization involves living in a state in which questioning and change are normal. Change of this magnitude is much more far-reaching than the stop/start first-order change of the bureaucracy. While changes that involve doing more of or less of something can be traumatic, in comparison to the sea-change implication of second-order changes, they are just storms in teacups. Sea changes involve mental shifts that require people (including those on the edges) to see their world in a totally different way. The term 'sea change' comes from Shakespeare's *The Tempest*:

> Full fathom five thy father lies;
> Of his bones are coral made:
> Those are pearls that were his eyes:
> Nothing of him that doth fade,
> But doth suffer a sea change
> Into something rich and strange.

In other words, even though structures may remain the same, their fabric is altered. While the basic shape stays constant, its very being is different. In terms of organizations, this level of change requires people to do different things and to see the world in different ways. Some of the changes that have occurred in the public sector since the introduction of privatization are examples of sea changes. The same people are working in the same places, providing very similar services as before, but working in totally different ways for new reasons.

Living in an evolving world brings with it high degrees of uncertainty. Staff may know what the vision statement says because care has been taken to share its meaning. But 'what it means to me' may be unclear and likely to remain so until work starts to implement the vision. Even then, the full implications will only be revealed as the plans unfold. But, because the situation is evolving and the people and organization are learning, the plans too will change. The vision, being a long-term dream, will be transformed. As some parts become clearer and move more sharply into focus, other parts will fade. The vision may not change in essence, but how it is seen may. It will be seen by different people from different perspectives at different times and be interpreted in different ways.

The nature of evolution may seem to be contradictory for some of the people involved – hence the cry of shifting goal-posts. However, it is not just the goal-posts that seem to move – the playing field changes into a swimming pool for water polo, to an ice rink for hockey, into an arena for horse-jumping and then to athletics. At least we stay with sporting analogies. Ambiguity to this extent requires managers and their staff to develop special sorts of skills if they are to continue to function effectively. Without these skills people can experience untenable levels of stress. Unchecked, this leads to dysfunctional behaviour or, in extreme examples, breakdown. A learning organization takes action to help its members develop skills of managing in uncertain and ambiguous conditions.

Internal harmony

In the world of permanent white water, the changing nature of the organization brings into question its internal harmony. The traditional view of politics has three strands: the Marxist belief that conflict between the owners or power holders of an organization and its workers is inevitable and unresolvable; the pluralist view that it is possible for multiple agendas to be satisfied; and the unitary view that there is one correct overriding agenda that must be adhered to. None of these definitions hold good in a learning organization. Encouraging questions undermines the unitary view and because there are no experts there is no right and wrong. Without extremes, consensus is possible but the developmental approach encourages healthy conflict as a means of synergizing better, new solutions to new problems. How multiple agendas can coexist and be satisfied when there is one agreed and shared vision is dubious. Another theory is required to describe politics in a learning organization.

Managing diversity

The term 'managing diversity' is increasingly used, mainly in a similar sense to equal opportunities. The new term implies facing up to contradictions and differences and finding ways, not of accommodating them as the pluralist approach would suggest, but of allowing them to exist together, each with equal validity and equal worth. The term implies that each individual has rights and is encouraged to make a unique contribution. The skills needed by those charged with managing in this context are very different from the control skills used in the past for managing groups of staff. Managing diversity brings conflict out into the open. Those used to having a quiet life in waters where the boat is never rocked may find this world of permanent white water a bit too exciting and dangerous.

It is little wonder that modern managers experience an exacting, tiring, stressful existence. The sort of satisfaction that can be obtained from working in these conditions is very different from that previously expected and regarded as normal. To some this sort of life may seem to be un-acceptably pressurized and they may prefer a return to the old ways. However, we are in a new world, and need to find new ways of working with it. There are three ways in which we can respond:

- It will never happen here – the ostrich approach.
- We must work harder – the woodpecker approach.
- We must work smarter – the owl approach.

Sadly for the ostrich and woodpecker, if a pressurized existence is not acceptable, few options are open. The learning company offers a way of achieving the third option, that of 'working smarter'.

WHAT CAN ONE MANAGER DO ALONE?

It is not uncommon to hear senior managers say that they feel powerless to achieve change, and that their opportunities to develop are limited. This is, in part, due to the ease with which they become isolated from the rest of their organization. Status, business, location, size of the organization, different agendas and objectives, the difficulty of the task, perspective, time horizons and the perceptions of others all conspire to drive wedges between an organization's senior managers and the rest of the workforce. As a result, the circle of people with whom senior managers transact is small. Also, and inevitably, they must rely on others to help effect changes and develop the organization and its members.

Much of the attention given recently to management development has focused on the development of individual managers' personal skills and competence. The popular image of a manager is of a person in charge, working and deciding alone on tasks of herculean proportions. Success is possible and can be achieved by long hours, hard work and drive. Mixing metaphors and quotations mercilessly, the manager is a sole actor on the stage delivering a soliloquy to a hostile audience; the lone agent. This picture, of course, is false. The real role of a manager is to work with and through others, on objectives that are far too big for one person to achieve alone. This is done by the use of appropriate processes and techniques – and by treating colleagues and staff as respected individuals who each have a distinct and valued contribution to make.

If managers see themselves in terms of the popular image, it can be of little surprise to find them feeling disempowered and unable to achieve. The learning company philosophy provides a way of empowering oneself and others within the organization. The term contains two concepts. The first, obviously, is that of learning; the second is not so apparent. Pedler, Boydell and Burgoyne (1988) do not use the word 'company' in its business sense. They are not describing a legal entity. Rather, they use the word in its older meaning – a group of companions, associates, friends, united by a commonality of purpose.

Developing this form of community is a means of reducing the sense of disempowerment and the overwhelming magnitude of the task. To mis-quote Benazir Bhutto 'the only way to eat an elephant is to chop it into small pieces'; sharing the task, by separating and distributing its elements reduces the strain on the individual. It can also improve the quality of the process of work and the outcome achieved. Involvement of appropriate others in appropriate ways can have a number of predictable outcomes:

- Group working avoids tram-line thinking.
- Individual assumptions are questioned by concerned others.
- Debate stimulates the creation of new ideas.
- Group members help each other stand back from the problem to reframe it.
- The available experience, knowledge, skills and brain capacity is increased.
- The vision or purpose can be restated and revalidated as a result of group discussion, challenge and debate.
- Group members can mentor and coach each other, and providing 'moral' support and encouragement.
- People are essentially social creatures and generally function better when working with others in conducive settings.

Thus, a group working on a common problem can produce better solutions than one person working alone. In the learning company, managers are not sole individuals. They are members of a professional community of co-learners, who help each other and provide support when the going gets tough. Collectively, they act as reflective practitioners, complementing each other, moving between action and thought as appropriate.

Vaill (1989) describes the Chinese concept of Wu-wei – the art of non-action. This, he says, is about learning how to go with the flow, or follow the grain (of the wild river). This concept does not counsel passivity. It is a powerful idea and a way to learn the art of judgement, knowing when to intervene and when to leave well alone. Too many managers, led on by the decisive, driving 'I'm in charge' model, rush in, often making matters worse than they already are. Wu-wei suggests stepping back, examining what is happening, gathering ideas, listening to others' perspectives, con-sidering options, thinking about the situation and, only then, deciding what action, if any, to take.

Stepping back in this way sometimes requires existing (preferred) approaches and ideas to be left to one side. It also means that assumptions and beliefs have to be abandoned while they are checked out with others. To be able to question one's assumptions and thought processes in this way requires a degree of self-doubt. However, to continue to function

10085

effectively, managers need to retain some confidence. The learning company provides the networks and trustworthy companions, which help the process of questioning and reframing. It provides the context that allows this degree of risky self-challenge to be carried out in safety.

SHAPE OF A LEARNING COMPANY

It is not possible to construct a diagram of a learning company. There is no predetermined structure that can be laid out on a page. Neither is there a flow chart of systems and processes, which can act as a formula for other organizations to replicate. Learning companies are not like that. Pedler, Burgoyne and Boydell (1986) give some glimpses of organizational and managerial behaviour they have seen that fulfil the requirements of being called a learning company. It may be easier to draw a picture of a learning company than to show its structure. A picture can communicate feel as well as give form to an organism, for a learning company is more than doing; it is being. It is important that managers who want to develop such an organization appreciate that they need to believe. To become a learning company an organization must be more than one with a policy. Commitment and beliefs only become real when they are translated into the actions and approaches taken by the organization's managers and others with leadership or power roles. These people need to base their actions on the belief that people throughout the organization have the right to be treated in a developmental way.

A total organization can be a learning company. Alternatively it is possible for a small section of a larger organization to become a learning company, even though the rest of the wider organization would not meet the conditions. This is because the actions and approaches taken by individual managers can foster and nurture a developmental climate. Equally, they can inhibit one. Even in an organization striving to be a learning company, an individual manager can sabotage the intent by the attitudes adopted and actions taken towards other staff. Being a developmental manager requires determination, commitment, effort and belief. Being a contra-developmental manager is easy. You expect nothing, give nothing and get nothing.

REFERENCES

Gibson, J. L., Ivancevich, J. M. and Donnelly, J. H. (1988) *Organizations*, Business Publications Inc, Homewood, Ill.

Lindblom, C. (1979) 'Still muddling, not yet through' in *Decision Making: approaches and analysis* (eds A. G. McGrew and M. J. Wilson) (1982) Manchester University Press, Manchester.

Megginson, D. and Pedler, M. (1992) *Self-development: a facilitator's guide*, McGraw-Hill, Maidenhead.

Pedler, M., Boydell, T. and Burgoyne, J. (1988) *Learning Company Project Report*, Training Agency, Sheffield.

Pedler, M., Burgoyne, J. G. and Boydell, T. H. (1986) *A Manager's Guide to Self-development* (second edn), McGraw-Hill, Maidenhead.

Vaill, P. B. (1989) *Managing as a Performing Art: new ideas for a world of chaotic change*, Jossey-Bass, San Francisco, Calif.

Chapter 3

Why managers won't learn

Graeme Salaman and Jim Butler

Times are changing. 'New times' do not just affect social and political life, they also have a major impact on organizations and those who work for them. The certainties of the past disintegrate: 'all that is solid melts into air'. Markets are changing – diversifying and differentiating; levels and forms of competitive pressure are changing; in many industries government-induced regulation is disappearing. Information technology increases the speed of communication and enables incredibly detailed control of work operations, thus in turn generating product differentiation. Organizations themselves are changing – and the ways they are changing are changing.

For the new certainty is change, and organizations and their employees must now be prepared to change and be able to change. In order to change appropriately they must be able to analyse themselves, their processes, structures and their environments, be able to identify preferred and appropriate responses, and be able to implement them. In a word, organizations must be able to learn, and to learn from their learning. On the basis of this learning, choices will be made: choices of structure, of process, of organization, of product, of market, relationship with staff, with subcontractors and with clients. And these choices themselves must be the subject of constant review and revision. A barrier to learning is thus a barrier to survival.

Within organizations today form does not follow function, if it ever did; structure does not follow strategy. For survival, both strategy and structure (in the widest sense) must be carefully analysed and chosen to ensure mutual support. Increasingly, all this is known to and accepted by managers at all levels, not least because of the sheer volume of exhortation from management gurus and consultants. But the pervasiveness of the acceptability and inevitability of change may mask a paradox: much change seems highly imitative, simply the application of the currently accepted nostrums and solutions, many of them derived in some form from the 'excellence' literature. If every organization changes in the same direction, where is competitive advantage? Second, despite the current emphasis on change, and indeed the apparent evidence that change is going on around us, we also know that change is difficult and that an organization's ability thoroughly to review, monitor, evaluate and replan (i.e. to learn) is systematically influenced by the fact of organization itself, with its inbuilt tendency to develop or encourage sectionalism, careerism and defensiveness. If 'new times' place a premium on organizational learning, and on consequent change, then barriers to that learning assume even greater importance. This chapter is about these barriers.

MANAGEMENT LEARNING

Suddenly, management learning is hot news. We know that British managers are seriously undertrained and educated; only 15 per cent of British managers have a degree or equivalent. Only about 12,000 of the 90,000 people who start managerial careers every year are receiving any form of education or training in management. The 2,500,000 managers in Britain currently receive the equivalent of one day's training per year.

There is general concern about this situation. Recent reviews of management training education and development contrasted the British situation with that of the USA, Japan, West Germany and France. Their call for radical change resulted in the establishment of the Council for Management Education and Development in 1987.

We also know that managers have a lot of new things to learn. There are various lists of what must be learnt. Peters talks about responsiveness, innovation, participation of all employees, leadership for change and simplified support systems (Peters 1987). Wickens talks of the tripod of teamworking, quality and flexibility (Wickens 1987). These behaviours are seen as required by significant changes in organizational environments: 'growing "turbulence" and complexity, growing competition, increasingly international markets' (Prospect Centre 1988).

These new forms of behaviour are regarded as essential to corporate survival: 'Turning outwards to face an increasingly turbulent environment, (successful companies) have developed strategies based on quality, innovation and responsiveness to their customers' (Prospect Centre 1988: 1). New situations require new responses.

But all the necessary behaviours and attitudes have to be learnt. Managers must be able and willing to shift their focus from the operational to the strategic, they must learn about, and possibly modify their management styles, or their team roles; they may need to learn about a new form of corporate culture. They must learn to manage in ways which encourage innovation and participation and ensure quality. The message then is: learn, learn, learn. Hence our interest in management learning. Management learning is important because managers are underqualified and must be more exposed to relevant learning, at a time when circumstances demand that there are many new things that they have to learn – even those who are qualified. But what has to be learnt is inherently new; because of environmental 'turbulence' managers cannot learn a set formula with which to cope with rapid change, for any new approach or technique will soon be obsolete. They must learn to be adaptive. They must now learn to learn.

HOW AND WHY MANAGERS LEARN

Traditionally interest in how managers learn has centred on the possibility – often unspoken, but evidently implicit – that managers may resist learning, or may learn in peculiar ways. Could there be something inherent in the role of the manager that might predispose against or structure the form of management learning? This is important. Could managers, by virtue of their roles, be trained and rewarded in ways which obstruct or restrict their capacity to learn?

A related argument is the suggestion that experience of managing within different sorts of organizational and discipline environments might shape managers' learning styles. This suggestion has obvious practical significance for trainers. But it also has theoretical importance in that it argues, first, that people's willingness and capacity to learn may differ in form and cannot be assumed and, second, that learning style may be affected by work and organizational experience.

Trainers, consultants and business school lecturers have for practical reasons always been concerned with how managers learn. Consciously or not, they have assumed that to be a manager has definite implications for how, indeed for if, managers learn. The conventional assumption is that managers learn best through doing, through experience, whenever possible. When the subject matter is highly theoretical or knowledge-based it must be built around worked examples, case-studies or project work. Most of all, it is assumed that managers will only learn when the subject has obvious and immediate practical application: the words 'theory', 'academic', 'model', are usually seen as negative, even pejorative. What is valued is certainly, tied to prescription.

This view of managers' needs and limitations is interesting in itself, and goes largely unchallenged. It is, of course, tied to a conception of management consultants and trainers that places responsibility for the success of a course session of the trainer/performer as much, if not more than on the material itself. It defines the trainers as performers, absolutely central to the delivery and success of the material, and rewards them appropriately. Form may be as important as content in a milieu where success – and reemployment – depends on audience appraisal and a high need for certainty and technique.

This view of what managers want may be correct. It may also be self-fulfilling. The interesting point, however, is that this view of learning applies solely and specifically to managers qua managers (it would not apply to managers attending a course or conference in their specialist discipline capacity, as engineer, personnel, production). It argues, implicitly, that to be a manager means one is trained and rewarded to learn only under very restricted conditions: lots of variety, short input sessions, powerful 'professional' and immediate presentation, lots of activities and exercises, obvious relevance to learners' own experience, maximum emphasis on practical technique or recommendation (certainty), with theory and conceptual elements reduced (uncertainty).

Paradoxically, while in some sense this could be seen as active in that it involves doing things, and practical in that it involves examples and case studies, it is also in a sense passive in that it involves little effort on the part of the learner to see for him/herself the relevance, application, practicability of general propositions to personal situations or problems. This is done for them (it is also of interest that when related to pedagogic models used in the education of young people, this model would appear to be closer to the primary school than to the university).

Although trainers offering material designed to appeal to these audience requirements may not know it, may even deny it vehemently, when they design their course in this way, they are in effect in the grip of a theory. The theory asserts that some aspects of managers' roles cause them to be able to absorb new information or new techniques successfully only in the way described. As university students, managers presumably learnt in the conventional academic manner. But once they become managers, they put away these methods and learn new ways to learn, and learn to reject old ways.

One might wonder what it is about being a manager that has this effect, and whether the effect is as marked in other societies, or in all organizations within one society. Presumably it would be held that this orientation towards learning was a result of the location of the manager within hierarchic structures, and within cultures which explicitly rewarded forms of behaviour (and discouraged, even penalized others). And these value/reward systems had the result of structuring how, possibly if, managers learn. This is in fact highly plausible.

Thus, management structures and cultures probably have serious implications for management learning. One further implication of this is that the success of training and development programmes could well be sorely limited by the impact of the value/reward structures delegates come from. Thus not only may management structures define how managers learn. They may also establish managers' resistance to learning.

RESISTANCE TO LEARNING

Such resistance may derive from various sources – from different levels of the organization. It may derive from the organization's structure and culture, from the way the organization is differentiated into specialisms, from pathologies of teamwork, and even from individuals themselves. At the organizational level, the most significant factor concerns the way in which power is exercised, and the behaviours that are rewarded and penalized.

If it is necessary for organizations to change drastically to meet the challenge of today's environment and if one way such changes as listed by Peters (1987) (most of which require radically new behaviour on the part of managers) are to be achieved is via training courses, then an immediate paradox occurs. The course is only necessary because the required behaviours are not a normal outcome of existing practice and procedures, otherwise there would be no need to develop them in courses. Yet if they are not a normal part of organizational procedure, managers may sense a disjuncture between course content and everyday organizational life, and be cynical about course exhortation.

For example, there may be conflict between a value being advocated in formal training and the structure and culture of the organization. An example of this could be the discussion, and encouragement, in a session on human resource development, of the value of management innovation, creativity and risk-taking, on a course where delegates come from a highly hierarchic organizational structure where success is defined in terms of compliance with established procedures, where authority is highly centralized, where lower level authority is minimal, and where the dominant culture values compliance and deference. Under such circumstances managers learn that to survive they must avoid deviating from established and safe practice.

The point is, of course, that managers learn all the time even when they are not on courses – especially when they aren't on courses. If they hadn't learnt so much away from courses they would be more willing to learn on courses. They learn how to survive, how to operate within their organizational milieu. And this learning may be in tension with, even in opposition to formal learning. The problem thus is not that managers won't learn, or that they resist learning but that they have learnt too much and too well. They have 'learnt the ropes' and these lessons about how their organization works may obstruct their openness to further learning.

These days we are used to seeing organizations as strategic phenomena. Strategic thinking attempts to reduce uncertainty, achieve consistency, aid understanding and achieve efficiency (Mintzberg 1987: 28–9). We may be less used to the realization that organization employees also think strategically, not least with respect to their willingness to learn.

Managers, since they exist within structures of power, reward and evaluation will probably only learn when they can see that what they are learning will be valuable and legitimate within their organizational setting; when they can see that what they are learning will help them do what they are rewarded for doing in ways which will be valued. They would be mad, and soon redundant, if they did anything else.

THE IMPORTANCE OF ORGANIZATIONAL STRUCTURE

Some support for this argument comes from a study of how Japanese electronics companies successfully encourage their engineers to manage and to implement technological development in an innovative manner which argues that the way in which elite engineers are rewarded and located within these companies is of great significance: engineers are developed to become highly placed, highly honoured, key figures in the development of the organization. Achieving the desired behaviour in others is as much a result of how they are treated and rewarded as it is a result of how they are exhorted (Werksey 1987).

But this is not the only way in which organizational structures may have implications for managers' willingness to learn. Recent sociological research experience suggests another possibility. Some of the main organizational characteristics intended to achieve efficiency and rationality may actually serve to obstruct them, partly at least by reducing employees' willingness to learn. It is not just the hierarchic structure of rewards and values which have consequences for management learning, so also has the fact that organizations are essentially and irredeemably political structures. This political element derives from the fact that organizations are differentiated into specialisms, departments, sub-groups of various kinds, within a structure of hierarchy where power, resources, prestige and reward are differentially distributed. These specialisms breed differences of perspective, priority, interest. Within structures of power individuals seek to defend and advance their interests. As individual members of organizations compete for scarce rewards, so departments, sections and specialisms tend to seek to defend their share of budget, their interests, their view of the organization's 'real' priorities (which strangely often tend to be closely related to their departmental goals and activities), their skill and discipline base. Have you known trainers who insist on the irrelevance of training, accountants who admit finance is overemphasised, marketeers who argue that marketing is largely guesswork, and irrelevant? And are these specialists often to be seen insisting that their budget is too large, their allocation of staff too generous, that other departments should receive from their share?

A consequence of the inevitable sectionalism of large organizations is that information becomes a resource useful to protect or advance sectional interests; change (which is often associated with learning) becomes potentially threatening. 'Each service, each division, indeed every sub-unit, becomes a guardian of its own mission, standards and skills; lines of organization become lines of loyalty and secrecy. In industry, the personnel department defends its control over selection and training; accounting, its standards of reporting; production, its schedules of output; sales, its interests in product design and customer service – each restricting information that might advance the competing interests of the others' (Wilensky 1967: 48).

Managers may resist certain planned innovations and their associated training for two related reasons: because they fear the change as having implications for their sectional position, and because they are suspicious of those who initiate the change whom they see as distinct from themselves – as 'them' in contrast to 'us'. Under these common conditions, learning may thus cease to be a neutral process where individual recipients have no resistance to absorbing new knowledge or skills save their individual capacity or 'learning style', and becomes a politicized process where new knowledge, systems and techniques are viewed suspiciously, even rejected because they are seen to represent the priorities of others whose priorities are distinct and possibly opposed, or to result in a reallocation of organizational resources, or a weakening of a section's traditional power-base.

For example, in the bad old days of quantified psychometric appraisal schemes, when department managers were asked by the personnel office to complete appraisal forms on their staff, allocating grades, ticking boxes or ranking them against each other, many managers, when undergoing training, showed a marked reluctance (to put it mildly) to learning the new procedures, or developing the skills of appraisal interviewing. Their resistance was nothing to do with capacity to learn or willingness to learn. It was based on their conviction that this sort of performance appraisal would damage their relations with their subordinates, would reduce their ability to seek the best for their people, would result in them losing control over their staff, to personnel's advantage. Personnel were seen as having their own properties and values, which were to do with spreading personnel systems, formalizing procedures. Managers, therefore, often rejected learning about the systems and their procedures because they saw them as carrying significant implications for the control of their staff, and thus for the distribution of power within the organization. These managers knew that information about their staff's performance was politically significant. As a result they saw the information in the training course as representing interests – personnel priorities over departmental management priorities. So they rejected it. And they rejected these appraisal systems too.

During the course of a series of seminars held with station officers within the London Fire Brigade, designed to identify and when necessary modify attitudes towards the introduction of non-white and non-male firefighters, a similar pattern of resistance was evident. The station officers were markedly unsympathetic to the messages of the seminars. They frequently denied the truth of the explanation of the nature and purpose of equal opportunities (EO) legislation, and refused to accept the validity of the arguments presented in the seminar – a severe case of refusal to learn.

Initially, the temptation was to explain this resistance in terms of the conservatism or the possible racism/sexism of the officers. It looked like that. But reflection suggested that an explanation solely in terms of the existence of a strong, white, male organizational culture was inadequate, not least because of its circularity: station officers' refusal to accept the messages of the EO seminar was a result of their organizational culture. The racism of the organizational culture was seen to be revealed in officers' resistance to the EO programme.

A more plausible explanation for station officers' refusal to learn was developed, which tried to locate their attitudes towards the EO programme within the context of officers' conviction that the programme represented a significant reduction in the traditional authority of firestation personnel to intervene in recruitment/selection, and to allocate advantage in these processes to applicants from among their own family and friends. The application of EO procedures immediately eliminated this informal labour market and replaced it with a formalized, open system. It was this aspect of the change as much as the openness towards previously barred categories of applicant which accounted for much of the resistance.

Also relevant was the fracturing of the management structure: station officers were based with the watch at the firestation. They worked shifts and spent their days and nights with the firefighters. When a call came, the station officers went with the crew of the engine. Inevitably they developed close relations with members of the watch, and shared a world composed of danger and boredom, a world of jokes, memories and myths. The next layer of management was spatially and temporally separated: they worked office hours, were based in regional offices, and were seen to inhabit a different and more bureaucratic world far from the realities of actual firefighting. A marked 'them' and 'us' perspective developed and it was in this context of insiders and outsiders that resistance flourished. For it was 'their' policies that were seen to be represented in the EO policy and to conflict with the traditional 'rights' of the ordinary fireman.

Thus organizational structures and cultures, and the common internal differentiation (formal or informal) into specialisms and subgroups, may generate conceptions of interest and in-group loyalty, out-group resistance, which seriously gets in the way of managers' willingness to learn. Actually this has been remarked on before, although the full implications may have been missed. Janis in his important work *Victims of Groupthink* (1972) argues that when a small group of people develop strong bonds of loyalty and cohesion, and develop an interest in a particular policy or point of view (deriving usually from the group leader), they become victims of what he calls 'groupthink'. The elements of the condition are fully described and illustrated by Janis. They refer to a condition where loyalty to the group and to the emerging group decision blinds the group to evidence which would reveal the inadequacies of the favoured line, leads members to overlook the deficiencies in their analysis, and the likely implications of their preferred solution.

In short, Janis argues that excessive group solidarity can lead to a condition where the group becomes entirely unable to learn: where all its energies go into finding grounds for supporting its preferred solution rather than into thorough and open analysis of all possibilities and their implications. The group becomes so convinced that it is right, that when finally the unexpected happens members frequently refuse to believe it – it 'couldn't happen'.

SUMMARY

This chapter argues that some cases of management resistance to learning should be explained not in terms of the individual attitudes or learning style or 'openness' of managers but in terms of the nature of the organizational structures within which they live and work, and what these structures may teach managers. It has been argued that when training involves an attempt to change management practice significantly (as is apparently required for organizations to be able to cope with today's environments) resistance to learning may derive from what managers have already learnt from their organizational experience. This has obvious implications for management training for it suggests some organizational limits to training, and implies that managers can only learn successfully when there exists a complementarity between training messages and organizational experience, or when they are entirely convinced that the training content represents a genuine intention to implement change on the part of the senior executives.

REFERENCES

Janis, I. (1972) *Victims of Groupthink*, Houghton Mifflin, Boston.
Mintzberg, H. (1987) *Harvard Business Review*, July–Aug.
Peters, T. (1987) *Thriving on Chaos: handbook for a management revolution*, Macmillan, London.
Prospect Centre (1988) *Strategies and People*, Prospect Centre, Kingston.
Werksey, G. (1987) *Training for Innovation. How Japanese Electronics Companies Develop their Elite Managers*, General Electric Co., London.
Wickens, P. (1987) *The Road to Nissan, Flexibility, Quality, Teamwork*, Macmillan, London.
Wilensky, H. (1967) *Organisational Intelligence*, Basic Books, New York.

Chapter 4

The factory as a learning laboratory

Dorothy Leonard-Barton

A learning laboratory is an organization dedicated to knowledge creation, collection, and control. Contribution to knowledge is a key criterion for all activities, albeit not the only one. In a learning laboratory, tremendous amounts of knowledge and skill are embedded in physical equipment and processes and embodied in people. More important, however, are the nontechnical aspects, the managerial practices and underlying values that constantly renew and support the knowledge bases.

In this chapter I put Chaparral Steel under the microscope as an example of a highly successful learning laboratory; its leadership has put tremendous effort into creating a consistent learning system. Many of Chaparral's practices are found piecemeal (often experimentally) in other U.S. organizations. As my references suggest, scholars studying best practices among Japanese manufacturers have made strikingly parallel observations, and Chaparral's policies are consistent with prescriptions by organizational learning theorists. Whether you are managing a fabrication shop or claims processing in an insurance office, Chaparral's management system offers a potentially useful model.

TAKING AN ORGANIC SYSTEM VIEW

Chaparral is the tenth largest U.S. steel producer. Its high-quality standards have been rewarded by the market, and it consistently sets records for productivity, compared to both U.S. and Asian competitors. Clearly, whatever it is doing works.

A close look at the company reveals an organic learning system so tightly integrated that Forward (the CEO) says he can tour competitors through the plant, show them almost "*everything*, and we will be giving away *nothing* because they can't take it home with them." His confidence derives from the fact that the learning laboratory cannot be constructed piecemeal. It is comprehensible only as an organic whole; close scrutiny is required to appreciate its delicacy. To complicate matters, such a corporate ecosystem is in continuous flux, constantly regenerating itself. Even if a competitor identifies important elements of the system, emulation will require time.

A learning laboratory does not occur spontaneously but is designed, created, and maintained through constant managerial attention to communicating the underlying values, checking the management systems' smallest details for consistency, and adapting any inharmonious elements. Thus managers designing a learning laboratory need to adopt holistic, systems thinking. They will have to acknowledge the practical utility and bottom-line impact of corporate values. They may have to confront chronic underestimation of the interdependence between incentive and education systems and corporate strategy. Moreover, such systems thinking must permeate the organization's every level. Everyone in the firm must appreciate the self-reinforcing nature of knowledge-creating activities. Only by comprehending the whole system can one understand why, when a fragment of the learning laboratory is pulled out to be examined (a particular project, a specific learning activity), it comes out vinelike, trailing roots back to deeply held values and widely observed management practices. It is this intense interconnectedness that makes such systems difficult to imitate and fragile – but effective.[1]

Learning requires creation and control of both external and internal knowledge for both current and future operations. Therefore, four distinguishing activities are critical to a learning laboratory:

1 problem solving (in current operations);
2 internal knowledge integration (across functions and projects);
3 innovation and experimentation (to build for the future);
4 integration of external information flows.[2]

Each activity is the operational expression of an underlying value and is strongly supported by a compatible managerial system of procedures and incentives. Thus each activity, value, and managerial system functions as an internally consistent subsystem. Although I will describe each subsystem separately, the four are mutually aligned and interrelated; that is, values and managerial systems underlying one subsystem also support the other there. An in-depth look at the four subsystems at Chaparral suggests some of the principles that distinguish a learning laboratory.[3]

Subsystem One: Owning the problem and solving it

The first critical learning subsystem is the triad of

1 the independent problem solving required for continuous improvement of current processes;
2 egalitarianism as an underlying value;
3 shared rewards as the reinforcing incentives system.

Empowered individuals, who command respect in the organization and who feel ownership in the system, have the self-confidence, freedom, and motivation to continuously solve problems. The principle involved here turns the old production saw of "if it ain't broke, don't fix it" on its head and maintains: "if it ain't being fixed continuously, it's broke."

Activity: Independent problem solving

Learning starts with empowered individuals who can identify and solve problems independently because they have a clear sense of operating objectives.

In a learning environment, progress has to be everyone's business – not just that of a few specialists. At Chaparral, who owns a production problem and responsibility for its solution? An incident during the first few weeks of operating the near net-shape caster, when cooling hoses were bursting, provides some insight. "When something like that comes up, and there seems no immediate solution," explains a senior operator, "you go see what the problem is. You don't say, 'That's not my area,' or 'I don't know that much about it.' You just show up." In this case, a group of operators, a welder, some foremen, and a buyer spontaneously gathered to discuss the problem and just as spontaneously scattered to seek solutions. "Everybody telephoned some person they thought might know how to fix the problem – vendors, experts – and within three to four hours we were getting calls back," says the senior operator. "Service people were showing up, and we worked the problem out. If it had been just one guy, probably a foreman, and everyone walked out . . . it would have taken him ten times longer to find a solution."

Value: Egalitarianism and respect for the individual

A learning environment is premised on egalitarianism, the assumption that all individuals have potential to contribute to the joint enterprise (if they are willing to develop competence). Forward has observed, "We figured that if we could tap the egos of everyone in the company, we could move mountains."[4] Outward symbols of values are important because they convey meaningful messages to all employees. At Chaparral there are no assigned parking places, no different colored hard hats or uniforms reflecting title or position, and the company dining-room is a local diner. More unusual, a scant two levels separate the CEO from operators in the rolling mill; a visitor is surprised when an operator stops Forward on a walk through the plant to discuss a new product's problems.

Managerial system: performance rewards

Positive thinking and slogans alone cannot create genuine employee investment in innovation and in identifying and solving problems.[5] Chaparral
has taken unusual steps to ensure that performance and incentive systems
back up management's belief in egalitarianism. In 1986–1987, when employment leveled off, and management confronted potential stagnation, the
pay structure was overhauled to reward accumulation of skills as well as
performance. Even more radical (especially for a steel mill) was the switch
from hourly wages to salary for everyone. There are no time clocks at
Chaparral. Forward explains, "When I am ill, I get a day off. Why shouldn't
everyone else?" He is fond of saying that the management system was
designed for the 97 per cent who are "conscientious people who want to
put in a full day's work." The 3 per cent who abused the system were let
go.

Subsystem Two: Garnering and integrating knowledge

The second subsystem revolves around knowledge accrual. In the learning
laboratory, knowledge is highly and visibly valued. Management invests in
educating the whole person, not just the technical side, and knowledge
flows freely across boundaries. The principle is this: every day, in every
project, add to the knowledge resources.

Activity: Integrating internal knowledge

In a learning laboratory, one would expect to see visible embodiment of
knowledge creation and control in highly innovative physical systems.
Chaparral boasts of such cutting-edge equipment as an automobile shredder
that they believe is the fastest and most efficient in the world, a horizontal
(instead of vertical) caster, and some of the most advanced digital furnace
controls anywhere. Because of the constant push to improve production,
Chaparral managers have to design what they need, rather than purchase
the best available equipment off-the-shelf. Why design in-house? "To
keep the knowledge here," a mill manager explains.

Information flow at Chaparral is obviously aided by its size, deliberately
held to under a thousand employees. An individual garnering knowledge
on a trip, at a conference, or from an experiment can readily transmit it,
as all employees are located in the same place and know each other. The
company was also designed to facilitate knowledge flows by encouraging
as many accidental meetings as possible. The plant layout accommodates
the hands-on style of management favored at Chaparral; even Forward's
office is just steps away from the furnaces and mills. The locker room is
located here also, so that at least once a day employees cycle through the

one-storey headquarters building.[6] Consequently, meetings are as likely to be held in the halls as in the conference rooms. Since many decisions go unrecorded and memos are anathema, it is important that people see each other frequently.

Hierarchical boundaries are minimal. This is a do-it-yourself company with no acknowledged staff positions and only a few positions that seem stafflike, such as personnel. There are fifty graduate engineers and technicians, all with line duties. In fact, everyone has line responsibilities, most of them tied directly to steel production, and decision-making is pushed down to the lowest possible supervisory level, "where the knowledge is."

Managerial system: Apprenticeships and education

An organization that values knowledge must provide mechanisms for continuous learning. Chaparral management has sent some employees to school to obtain advanced degrees, but it also invests heavily in an unusual formal apprenticeship program for everyone in the plant, which it developed with the Bureau of Apprenticeship and Training in the U.S. Department of Labor. (Most apprenticeships are run by unions.) As Forward notes, "Expertise must be in the hands of the people that make the product."

One unusual aspect is the instructors. Selected foremen rotate in from the factory floor to teach. "It creates a lot of credibility for the education program on the factory floor," explains one instructor. "What's more," he adds wryly, "I have to live with what I teach. So I'd better do a good job."

Subsystem Three: Challenging the status quo

The third subsystem in a learning laboratory involves constantly pushing knowledge frontiers. The company must select employees for their desire to challenge their own and others' thinking. They must see risk as positive, because it comes with the experimentation critical to innovation. The company must select suppliers for their superior capabilities – and for their willingness to be pushed beyond the bounds of their current knowledge. The principle involved is this: always reach beyond your grasp.

Activity: Continuous experimentation

Learning requires constant pushing beyond the known, and Chaparral employees are skilled experimenters. A visitor was surprised to find that extensive overhead slides explaining the formal Taguchi experimental designs that were guiding the development of the horizontal caster had been prepared for the board of directors. This extremely technical presentation was to help directors understand the methodical knowledge-creation process, enable them to identify critical decision points, and thereby better equip them to evaluate the risk.

The operating rule is this: if you have an idea, try it. Line managers authorize tens of thousands of dollars for experiments without higher authority. Hunt explains, "We use products to do research. We can close the feedback loop between researchers and users by using new methods and new materials within our own facility."

Value: Positive risk

In a research laboratory, risk is accepted as the norm, since the cutting edge is always fraught with uncertainty. In contrast, risk is usually anathema in a production environment. Managers of a learning factory must tolerate, even welcome, a certain amount of risk as a concomitant of knowledge acquisition. Chaparral managers avoid riskless projects because a "sure thing" holds no promise of competitive advantage – no opportunity to outlearn competitors. Says Forward, "We look at risk differently from other people. We always ask what is the risk of doing *nothing*. We don't bet the company, but if we're not taking some calculated risks, if we stop growing, we may die."

This positive attitude toward risk permeates the company. If everyone experiments, learns, and innovates, then neither success nor failure can be heavily personalized. If individuals are singled out for praise, then they have an incentive to protect ideas as intellectual property rather than seek embellishment from friendly critics and codevelopers. If individuals are singled out for blame, then the risk of failure may overwhelm the impulse to innovate.

Managerial system: Hiring practices and career paths

The most important managerial system in a learning laboratory is selecting and retaining the right employees. Because employees must be innovators, constantly challenging the status quo, they are selected as much for their potential, their attitude toward learning, and their enthusiasm as for a specific background.

Chaparral's original applicants went through six weeks of intensive training with daily evaluations and faced stiff competition. Top performers were given their choice of jobs and an immediate 20 per cent pay raise. Highly selective hiring procedures continue to reflect concern that new employees fit into the Chaparral culture, that at least one supervisor be personally committed to their training and progress, and that the team have a stake in their success. Although personnel does some preliminary screening, current applicants undergo one or more days of demanding interviews with at least five employees, including two foremen, before they join Chaparral. Only one out of ten applicants selected for interviews can expect to be hired, and the final decision belongs to the foreman with direct responsibility. These very cautious, resource-intensive selection practices may account in part for the extremely dedicated workforce, which boasts an absentee rate about one-fourth that represented by the National Association of Manufacturers.

Subsystem Four: Creating a virtual research organization through networking

A learning laboratory obviously needs access to the latest knowledge, embodied in the best minds and best equipment available. However, not all companies can afford an internal research organization. Moreover, no company can cover all the technological advances, worldwide, they may affect its future. Therefore the principle behind the fourth and final subsystem is this: create a virtual research organization through extensive networking and alliances – for learning and for economic reasons.

Activity: Integrating external knowledge

At Chaparral, employees constantly scan the world for technical expertise that others have already invested in. Managers never hesitate to invent when necessary but only after assuring themselves through extensive searches that no available system will suit their needs. While building the horizontal caster, they made repeated trips to the few other world sites that had somewhat similar equipment. Chaparral also constantly benchmarks its capabilities, not just against immediate competitors but also against best-of-class companies, even those from totally different industries. Three on-site laboratories support production through chemical and physical product analysis, but the company has created a virtual research organization through extensive networking and alliances. Information obtained externally is rapidly incorporated through development projects, flowing through the created network almost as readily as it does inside the walls of the learning laboratory, because in both cases people working directly in production transmit the knowledge.

Value: Openness to knowledge from outside

Knowledge garnered through such networks can flourish only in an environment that rejects the "not invented here" mentality. At Chaparral, "not *reinvented* here" is the operative slogan. There is no value in recreating something – only in building on the best existing knowledge. People in a learning laboratory value the capability to absorb and use knowledge as much as to create it. They understand that all invention is a process of synthesis. As its practices suggest, a key Chaparral value is global outreach – openness to innovation, whatever its origin. Knowledge is valued not so much for the pedigree of its source but for its usefulness.

Managerial system: Resources for alliances and networks

To support information gathering and reinforce global outreach, the company invests heavily in employee travel (and regards the expenses as just that – investments), often sending a team, including foremen and technical staff as well as vice presidents and operators, to investigate a new technology or to benchmark against competitors. Newly acquired knowledge need not filter down through the ranks, because the people who absorbed it are the ones who will apply it. In 1990, 78 people from production, several of them operators, visited a customer site at least once. They also visit other minimills.

This constant dispersal of mixed employee teams to customers, competitors, and suppliers throughout the world serves a dual purpose. The visits are regarded as learning sabbaticals that keep life "exciting" for employees. They are a source of information for the company as a whole. "We want them to . . . come back with new ideas about how to make improvements or new ways to understand the problem."[7]

CONCLUSION

The factory, in fact any backroom operation, is not usually regarded as an arena for experimentation and learning. Chaparral Steel challenges this concept of operations. Factories *can* function as learning laboratories (see Table 4.1). The most important characteristic of such organizations is that they are totally integrated systems. They are difficult to imitate because every employee, from CEO to line operator, is technically capable and interested in learning. Moreover, the whole organization is designed around the creation and control of knowledge. The four subsystems described above are not only internally linked but tremendously dependent upon each other. Continuous education depends upon the careful selection of willing learners. Sending workers throughout the world to garner ideas is cost effective only if they are empowered to apply what they've learned. The organization is unlikely to be open to outside knowledge if it does not place a strong value on sharing knowledge or does not give rewards for bettering the whole company's performance. Thus continuous learning depends upon the sense of ownership derived from the incentive systems, upon the pride of accomplishment derived from special educational systems, upon values embedded in policies and managerial practices, as well as upon specific technical skills. The line operator appears to take the same

Table 4.1 Comparison of traditional factory with factory as learning laboratory

	Traditional factory	Learning laboratory
1 Research and development function	Separate and distant from production	Merged with production (everyone does development)
2 Experimentation on factory floor	Rare, feared	Constant, welcomed
3 Innovation	Exclusive province of engineers	Everyone's business (but their own methods)
4 Equipment and processes	If it works, don't fix it	Design your own; constantly improve
5 New technology	Reject: not invented here	Never reinvent here

perspective on the conduct of daily activities as the CEO. Chaparral is tremendously consistent.

Paradoxically, the system's interdependence is also a potential weakness, as competencies often are.[8] A learning laboratory may have trouble recreating itself. Any organization is likely to be somewhat limited by its "congenital knowledge" and by the stamp placed upon it by its founders.[9] A significant challenge for Chaparral is how to grow. Forward has noted that "to stand still is to fall behind," and the company's credo to provide growth for its skilled people requires some forward momentum. Therefore, it must either grow larger where it is or clone itself in a new location. How will it transplant the deep worker knowledge, the motivation, the commitment, and the informal systems of knowledge sharing?

For other companies interested in creating factories as learning laboratories, the questions are: Can it be done in a plant within a large corporation, where many of the managerial systems have already been set corporatewide and therefore are not at the plant manager's discretion? Can an existing plant be transformed when plant managers may not have the luxury of selecting people as freely as Chaparral did? Can a company less geographically isolated hope to reap returns on investing in its employees' intellectual advancement, or will they be lured away by other companies?

Similar questions were raised a decade ago when U.S. manufacturers first began to understand how Japanese companies were competing on the basis of quality. Initially overwhelmed by the difference in activities, values, and managerial systems implied by the total quality approach, many U.S. managers were pessimistic about their ability to change their operations to the extent needed and reluctant to invest in employee education. Yet today, many U.S.-based factories achieve quality levels never even aspired to in 1980.[10]

For many of these improvements, the Japanese were our teachers, having learned from Deming and Juran.[11] According to some researchers, Japanese managers may also be ahead of their U.S. counterparts in creating learning laboratories, since "Japanese companies are usually adept at organizational learning."[12] As the references at the end of this article suggest, many of Chaparral's managerial practices and values also characterize best practices in Japan, such as investing extensively in formal and informal education; searching worldwide for the best technology and methods and absorbing that knowledge into home operations; and valuing employee empowerment, problem solving, and risk taking.[13] Apparently, such learning systems are not uniquely Japanese.

Of course, creating a learning laboratory in a "green-field" site is easier than in an existing plant. As not all U.S. factories can start up from scratch, creating a learning laboratory implies big changes. But do we really have any choice? No financial formulas, corporate reshuffling of departments, or exhortations by corporate management to integrate across functions will foster the creativity and productivity needed for international competition.

Experts on change management suggest that three critical elements are required for altering current practices:

1 dissatisfaction with the status quo;
2 a clear model of what the changed organization will look like;
3 a process for reaching that model, that vision of the future.[14]

Examples such as Chaparral can aid all three. One way of stimulating dissatisfaction with current practices and hence motivation to change is to observe other companies where an alternative management style appears to be yielding superior results. By benchmarking against such companies, managers can derive principles to incorporate into their own particular visions. Chaparral offers a model of a factory as a learning laboratory, and if the specifics are not transferable, the principles underlying the Chaparral vision are.

The precise process for implementing these principles will differ markedly from company to company. It is possible to interrupt a factory's current systems by introducing new equipment, new learning skills and activities, new knowledge-creating management systems, or new values. But interrupting a current system is only the first step. As the Chaparral example demonstrates, learning skills, management procedures, and values are interrelated. Values unsupported by management systems are vapid; management systems that run counter to values are likely to be sabotaged; learning activities unsupported by values and management practices will be short-lived. If a learning capability is to be developed, the whole system must eventually be addressed.

NOTES AND REFERENCES

1 Senge argues persuasively that successful leaders are systems thinkers, able to see "interrelationships, not things, and processes, not snapshots." See: P. Senge, "The leader's new work: building learning organizations," *Sloan Management Review*, Fall 1990, pp. 7–23.

   Other theorists similarly note how interrelated are strategy, structure, and culture in creating learning environments. See: C. M. Fiol and M. A. Lyles, "Organizational learning," *Academy of Management Review* 10 (1985): 803–13.

2 I assume that learning occurs if "through its processing of information, the range of [an organization's] potential behaviors is changed." See: G. Huber, "Organizational learning: the contributing processes and the literatures," *Organizational Science* 2 (1991): 89.

   That is, beyond contributing to an accumulation of formal knowledge bases, learning creates "capacities . . . for intelligent action." See: G. Morgan and R. Ramirez, "Action learning: a holographic metaphor for guiding social change," *Human Relations 37* (1983): 21.

   A growing literature on the topic emphasizes that organizational learning is more than an aggregation of individual learning. See, for instance: B. Hedberg, "How organizations learn and unlearn," in *Handbook of Organizational Design*, eds. P. Nystrom and W. Starbuck (New York: Oxford University Press, 1981), pp. 3–27.

   While the four critical activities proposed here have not been previously combined into a framework, each has been identified as characteristic of a learning organization. On problem identification and solving, see: E. Hutchins, "Organizing work by adaptation," *Organization Science 2* (1991): 14–39.

   On integration of internal information, see: R. Duncan and A. Weiss, 'Organizational learning: implications for organizational design,' *Research in Organizational Behavior* 1 (1979): 75–123.

   On experimentation, see: R. Bohn, "Learning by experimentation in manufacturing," (Cambridge, Massachusetts: Harvard Business School, Working Paper No. 88–001, 1988).

   On acquisition and use of external information, see: Huber (1991), pp. 88–115.

3 Chaparral managers have verified the accuracy of the descriptions of activities and events offered here, but they are not responsible for the characterization of learning laboratories in general or for the way I have analyzed their organizational culture.

4 Quoted by B. Dumaine, "Chaparral Steel: unleash workers and cut costs," *Fortune*, 18 May 1992, p. 88.

5 Argyris and Schon point out that "espoused theory" does not always influence behavior, "theory in practice" does. See: C. Argyris and D. Schon, *Organizational Learning* (Reading, Massachusetts: Addison-Wesley, 1978). See also: S. Kett, "On the folly of rewarding A, while hoping for B," *Academy of Management Journal*, December 1975, pp. 769–83.

6 For an understanding of the impact on communication patterns of physical proximity and centrally located common facilities, see: T. Allen, *Managing the Flow of Technology* (Cambridge, Massachusetts: the MIT Press, 1977), ch. 8.

7 G. Forward interviewed by A. M. Kantrow, "Wide-open management at Chaparral Steel," *Harvard Business Review*, May–June 1986, p. 101.

8 I have argued that core capabilities almost inevitably have a flip side, core rigidities, that hamper nontraditional projects and can hobble an organization in moving to new competencies. See: D. Leonard-Barton, "Core capabilities

and core rigidities in new product development," *Strategic Management Journal* 13 (1992): 111–26.

9 Huber (1991) discusses this limitation. See also: J. Kimberly, 'Issues in the creation of organizations: initiation, innovation, and institutionalization,' *Academy of Management Journal* 22 (1979): 437–57.

10 This includes Japanese transplants such as New United Motor Manufacturing, Inc., whose employees are mostly rehires from the same United Auto Workers workforce that had one of the industry's worst labor records. See: R. Rehder, 'The Japanese transplant: a new management model for Detroit,' *Business Horizons*, January–February 1988, pp. 52–61.

11 See the profiles of these two men in: O. Port, "Dueling pioneers," *Business Week*, 25 October 1991, p. 17.

12 I. Nonaka and J. Johansson, 'Japanese management: what about the hard skills?' *Academy of Management Review* 10 (1985): 184. In fact, some management practices now being imported into the United States were advocated by younger U.S. contemporaries of Deming such as Chris Argyris, whose early books were translated into Japanese within a year of their publication in the United States. See: C. Argyris, *Personality and organization* (New York: Harper Brothers, 1957) and *Integrating the Individual* (New York: John Wiley & Sons, 1964).

13 See, for example, R. Rehder and H. Finston, "How is Detroit responding to Japanese and Swedish organization and management systems?" *Industrial Management* 33 (1991): 6–8, 17–21; R. T. Pascale, *Managing on the Edge* (New York: Simon & Schuster, 1990), ch. 9; and G. Shibata, D. Tse, I. Vertinsky, and D. Wehrung, "Do norms of decision-making styles, organizational design, and management affect performance of Japanese firms? An exploratory study of medium and large firms," *Managerial and Decision Economics* 12 (1991): 135–46.

14 See, for example, M. Beer, *Organization Change and Development* (Santa Monica, California: Goodyear Publishing Company, 1980), ch. 3.

Part II

Assessing and developing competency

Christopher Mabey

A key component of learning is finding ways of accurately determining an individual's competencies and then devising appropriate development activities to build on their strengths and address their weaknesses. Views vary on how such competencies might be derived and operationalized, how they might be addressed in the workplace, who should take primary responsibility for subsequent development and where such learning should take place. The four chapters in this section are intended to reflect some of this diversity of opinion.

The original publication of the chapter by Paul Sparrow and Mario Bognanno was extremely timely for a number of reasons. Some of the disquiet concerning the concept of competencies in the context of human resource (HR) management has been caused by a confusion between generic standards of competence, typified by the Management Charter Initiative in the UK, and competencies derived in a specific and tailored way by different organizations. The authors helpfully distinguish the two approaches and outline a number of advantages of organizationally specific, competency-based HR strategy – not least the possibility of horizontal integration (of discrete HR policies) and vertical integration (of the HR plan with the strategic objectives of the organization). One criticism of conventional competency approaches is their static and/or retrospective focus when being formulated. Sparrow and Bognanno propose some ways of overcoming these problems with reference to the derivation of competencies in BP, with the additional challenge of making them cross culturally relevant.

Tony Cockerill, in his account of how competencies were defined and used by the UK bank National Westminster, also addresses the need to identify future dimensions of job performance. Cockerill argues that the eleven high-performance managerial competencies capture the sorts of skills needed by the bank in a time of rapid competitive and technological change and that they also encompass the 'softer' behavioural repertoires, like 'impact' and 'concept formation'. The National Westminster experience suggests that these competencies can be reliably measured by observers at an assessment centre. This centre then provides full and accurate diagnostic data from which development activities can be planned. It is questionable whether an individual's heightened self-awareness of strengths and weaknesses always proves to be catalytic for their development and – more broadly – for the organization's learning, but Cockerill offers some guidelines to overcome some of the common pitfalls of management assessment and development.

Alan Mumford's contribution to this section deliberately shifts the focus away from the organization to the individual learner and from formal training and assessment programmes to everyday learning opportunities. Mumford's message is simple but important: more account needs to be taken of individual learning styles. Too much development relies on off-the-job training courses and planned job moves – which in reality reap very little in the way of predictable learning outcomes. More thought should be given to real-time action learning opportunities on-the-job, which are often poorly designed and usually remain unreviewed. Finally, in their enthusiasm for transformational, double-loop learning, organizations should not neglect learning that is derived from incremental single-loop learning which is far more commonplace.

The chapter by Gratton and Pearson is somewhat different from most others in this edited collection. It reports the detailed results of research (into the perceived strengths and weaknesses of fast-track executives) conducted in a large multinational company. The debate about what strengths and weaknesses, or 'competencies' constitute effective management has been raging for some time now, frequently peppered by competing prescriptive lists of what differentiates excellent from mediocre performance. This research article has been included because it offers an empirical rather than a normative view. It focuses on empowering behaviours (which would seem to be crucial to a learning organization), and it assesses the incidence of this empowering style with reference to boss, peer and subordinate perceptions, rather than relying on spurious self-report. Perhaps predictably, empowering capabilities are among the most frequently cited development needs and this view is held most strongly by subordinates of their bosses!

Chapter 5

Competency requirement forecasting: issues for international selection and assessment

Paul R. Sparrow and Mario Bognanno

WHY HAVE COMPETENCIES BECOME SO IMPORTANT?

Human resource management (HRM) implies two processes of integration: vertical integration to link HRM policies and practices with business strategies, and horizontal integration to create consistency, coherence and mutual reinforcement across and within HRM policies and practices. When all such activities have been integrated and mobilized, their effect on the behaviour of individuals in their efforts to formulate and implement the strategic needs of the business may be considered as strategic human resource management (Schuler 1992). Typically, organizations choose a number of pathways as they develop a human resource strategy.

Competency-based approaches represent only one out of a number of HRM programmes that may together comprise a human resource strategy. However, over recent years, this approach has been a rising star. Throughout the late 1980s, many organizations began to focus a wider range of their HRM policies and practices around a defined set of management 'competences' or 'competencies'.

A number of developments have fuelled this rise of competency-based approaches. Strategic change has increasingly been appreciated as a learning process in which the ability to learn faster than a competitor – and therefore reconstruct and adapt the knowledge base of the organization – is a key to competitive success. This realization has been supported by the recent move away in the academic literature from external market-driven concepts of strategy towards a greater focus on internal resources and capabilities of organizations. Research into strategic change in the late 1980s demonstrated a clear link between business performance and skills development, and also the failure of many large-scale change programmes to achieve desired results. This was largely because they only created representational learning (i.e. new words, language and symbols) as opposed to behavioural learning (i.e. sustained change in what people actually do). To ensure more strategic HRM interventions, managers needed a 'management integration technology' that was:

- couched in behaviours (what people actually do, not what they say they do);
- sensitive to the sharp end of the business as well as the strategic direction;
- demonstrably linked to effective business performance.

WHAT EXACTLY ARE COMPETENCIES?

Competencies seemed to fit the bill nicely. Despite a range of methodologies being available to practitioners, there appeared to be a common focus on identifying 'outputs', couched in terms of what an individual achieves and produces from a situation by managing it effectively. This achievement of outputs was operationalized as a series of overt manifest behavioural indicators, frequently evidenced by positive and negative indicators. Importantly, the behaviours associated with some predefined criterion of effectiveness or performance were identified first, and only then were they clustered and interpreted into underlying dimensions of competency. In his pioneering work, Boyatzis (1982) recognized that such a *post hoc* labelling process meant that competencies drew upon a variety of individual attributes such as personality traits, skills and abilities. Unfortunately, therein lay a source of confusion. Over the 1980s, a number of competing models identifying 'competence' or 'competencies' (terms frequently used interchangeably) emerged.

Table 5.1 contrasts two variants that have emerged along several dimensions in an effort to clarify the differing assumptions and concepts. The left-hand column reflects the approach taken in the UK as part of the Management Charter Initiative, while the right-hand column reflects the approach taken by organizations who identify their own competencies. It can be seen that the two approaches contain within them very different concepts. This chapter focuses on developments in the second framework (i.e. organizationally specific competencies used as part of a human resource strategy).

To make matters more confusing, some organizations adopt both frameworks or systems, applying them to different levels within the organization or developing in-house variations on a theme. It is not surprising that competencies have for many become a confusing and ambiguous concept and that there is continuing debate about their underlying nature (Arnold and Davey 1992). Are they general personality traits, general ability traits, transferable skills, knowledge and behaviour, or organization-specific skills, knowledge and behaviour? The truth is that they draw upon all these psychological attributes. This is a major strength, but also provides potential for misinterpretation.

Table 5.1 Distinctions between common definitions of competences and competencies

Element of definition	What are competences?	What are competencies?
DESCRIBE	Knowledge, skills and attitudes (with some personal behaviours).	Behavioural repertoires which people input to a job, role or organization context.
IDENTIFIED THROUGH	Functional analysis of job roles and responsibilities.	Behavioural event investigation techniques.
FOCUS ON	Task-centred job analysis techniques that reflect expectations of workplace performance.	Person-centred job analysis techniques that reflect effectiveness.
INDICATE	Areas of competence (fields of knowledge) which a person must perform effectively.	What people need to bring to a role to perform to the required level.
PERFORMANCE CRITERION	Entry (threshold) standard (i.e. wide reach into broad range of management).	Characteristics of superior (excellent) individual performance (i.e. more senior management levels).
APPLICATION	Generic VET standards across organizations and occupations (i.e. common denominators).	Tailored excellent behaviour unique to the organization (i.e. distinguishing characteristics).
LEVEL OF ANALYSIS	Occupation and sector based on sample of key jobs.	Job level, or management hierarchy.
OWNERSHIP	Competence owned by institutions or organization and granted to the individual.	Competency held by the individual and brought to the organization.
ASSESSMENT ONUS	Selection in order to grant professional status	Identification of potential in order to ensure best internal resourcing decisions.
INDIVIDUAL MOTIVATION	Transferable achievement.	Promotable achievement.

USE OF COMPETENCIES TO INTEGRATE PERSONNEL SYSTEMS

Despite such criticism, organization-specific, competency-based approaches have been used successfully to create horizontally integrated HRM policy areas. Through the creation of a core set of effective behaviours that can be used to create a large range of assessment tools (such as behavioural ladders to facilitate rankings in performance appraisal; assessor observation guidelines for group exercises, role plays and presentations; training needs analysis checklists; and job descriptions to inform choice of psychometric tests), competencies encourage mutual behavioural reinforcement across a number of HRM policy areas and create multiple pressure points for change. Considerable benefits have therefore been reported in four areas of HRM: recruitment and selection; career development; performance management; and the management of change (Boam and Sparrow 1992).

Feltham (1992) identified the main benefits brought to recruitment and selection by competency-based approaches as being the creation of shared understandings of the kinds of people needed for new systems, more informed resourcing options, agreed standards and more systematic recruitment processes, realistic job previews and identification of the most appropriate assessment methods. Similar benefits apply to the use of competencies for career development. Career planning decisions are made on the basis of likely performance at the next level, enabling more meaningful, planned and effective decisions (Craig 1992). The approach has potential in performance management settings and can be used to resolve problems in the effective operation of performance-related pay schemes by creating a common language for talking about performance, a framework for setting objectives for appraisal schemes and for the appraisee, and improving the quality of appraisal interviews (Torrington and Blandamer 1992).

Finally, organizations are beginning to appreciate that the process of labelling behavioural indicators into organizationally meaningful titles provides a language and a forum for capturing cultural changes (Iles 1992). Applications in this arena are fewer. A review of the literature indicates that six organizations have used the approach in this manner. British Petroleum, for instance, have made efforts to link executive competencies to a cultural competency model (Bognanno 1990, 1992; Quinn Mills and Friesen 1992); Digital Equipment Europe Ltd created a business-oriented human resource strategy around competencies (Smith and Verran 1992); Bass plc used competencies to streamline, restructure and recruit in order to build a new company culture (Probert 1992); Rank Xerox have defined boardroom competencies for Facilitating Directors (Coulson-Thomas 1990); National Westminster Bank plc accelerated change in personnel practices and business performance by defining competencies (Francis 1992); and a medium-sized accountancy organization used competencies to articulate a changing business market (Shackleton 1992).

WHAT IS IN A NAME?

In short, it has proved to be an attractive technology and is being used increasingly to deliver not just horizontal integration across HRM practices, but also vertical integration with the strategy. When considered as a

Table 5.2 Strengths and weaknesses of competency-based approaches to
human resource management

Strengths of the competency approach	Weaknesses of the competency approach
Identifies the requirement for potential managers.	Competing frameworks for competences and competencies that result in very different application.
Enables recruitment of people for the present and future.	Variable practitioner skill in focusing competencies around clearly described behavioural outputs.
Improves and broadens the selection process.	Concentration of effort at the job-person fit level rather than organizational effectiveness level.
Improves the inter-rater reliability of assessment of potential.	Heavy reliance on job analysis techniques that are retrospective, not forward-looking.
Enables a clearer focus in the performance review or appraisal process.	Competency identification techniques limited by the existing imagination of employees and managers.
Provides a common language system to convey the nature of effective performance.	Values-led identification of competencies leads to charges of behavioural engineering or cloning.
Facilitates self-assessment and development.	Application focused strongly in US and UK organizations. Limited intenational transfer.
Acts as a basis for coaching and training.	Specification of effectiveness in terms of behaviours may limit the cross-cultural transfer of the technique.
Provides a tool for developing the business culture.	
Provides a method for identifying the implications of changes in job or organizational design.	

strategic HRM practice, there are a number of clear strengths and weaknesses associated with competency-based approaches. See Table 5.2.

Competencies represent a simple concept, i.e. behavioural repertoires that have been identified as relevant to a particular organizational context such as effective performance at the level of a job, across a career stream, or in the context of an organization's strategy), that some people can perform better than others. Confusion arises from the limited scrutiny given to how competencies are identified and labelled. Identification relies on one or more of a range of job analysis techniques (such as repertory grids, critical incidents, structured skills questionnaires, observations, diaries and behavioural event interviews) used to gather data from a neutral (blind) or values-driven stance (Kandola and Pearn 1992). It is the relevance of the behaviours identified and the quality and consistency of the rules applied to govern the way they are expressed in a written profile that provides the power of the approach. The labels used to make the list of behaviours more palatable (and more traditionally assessable by psychologists) are of less importance.

The labelling process is a *post hoc* tool for reducing potentially hundreds of effective behaviours into simpler groupings usually based on three options: mathematical clustering; interpretation by trained psychologists; or allocation of behaviours to labels that have some other purpose or meaning within the organization, such as statements of culture or mission. All three approaches create difficulties in interpretation. Mathematical clustering does not guarantee that linked behaviours make common or, indeed, psychological sense. Asking psychologists to group behaviours together carries the danger of reverting to traditional thinking ('this behaviour is more to do with a personality trait', 'this one is an analytical skill') and simply rehashing current job descriptions that the competency approach was intended to bypass. It also tends to leave a clutch of less easily classified behaviours (probably the most interesting ones!) that have to be put somewhere. Finally, using already established labels linked on ongoing HRM programmes begs the question that some effective behaviours undoubtedly do not fit into the convenient descriptions of culture or mission that have been adopted elsewhere. It is a mistake, however, to assume that it is the competency labels that need to be assessed. It is the behavioural indicators, in all their complexity and with all their multiple psychological roots, that need to be commented on. What is needed is a competency framework that allows both valid comment about the behaviours and a basis for informed decisions about where to focus assessment effort. The next section summarizes the British Petroleum (BP) experience to exemplify how some organizations may take the competency approach forward.

The British Petroleum experience: ensuring cross-cultural validity of behavioural indicators

BP are one of the few organizations to use a competency-based approach as part of a human resource strategy. The learning from their experience centres around the selection of a competency-based approach to implement the corporate strategy, and the attempts made to address the impact of diverse national cultures on the behaviours associated with effective implementation.

The strategic problems faced by BP were ominous. In the 1970s, it consisted of 11 businesses and 70 national affiliates. It diversified into minerals and coal production, consumer products and information systems. To manage such diversity, it created a strong matrix organization around a series of business streams and national associates. Rather than creating the intended decentralization, the structure resulted in enormous additional complexity. At the same time, a major acquisition programme was undertaken and the organization was privatized. An internal analysis of the organization by the incoming (and now departed) chairman (called Project 1990) revealed that BP had to reduce complexity throughout the corporation, redesign the central organization and reposition the management style and culture. There followed a period of intense activity as BP attempted to fundamentally change its structure, management processes and organizational culture, and a human resource strategy to develop Project 1990 emerged. It became apparent that there was a gap between the Chairman's Vision and Value Statement (based on espoused values of openness, care, teamwork and empowerment) and practice, which required the reduction of management layers and costs. A series of culture change workshops allowed managers to express their concerns: what exactly is the new culture? What does it look like? What do I do differently? Do we need a single corporate culture?

To answer the managers' concerns, BP chose to create a corporate-wide competency framework. It was appreciated that the process of decentralization and downsizing meant that implementation strategies would vary across businesses and countries. The performance criterion against which competencies were to be established, therefore, was the ability to enable change to happen (whatever that change might prove to be). A competency model was developed with consultants by comparing BP to other multinationals on their database and creating appropriate behavioural indicators that reinforced the culture and would enable Project 1990 to be implemented. It was essentially a desk-top exercise and the labels chosen to group the 67 identified essential behaviours were the same ones that had been used in relation to Project 1990 (i.e. Open Thinking, Personal Impact, Empowering and Networking (OPEN)).

Over a period of several months, the model was tested and validated internally and was then communicated throughout the business as awareness of the new competency model grew amongst senior managers. It then had to be devolved across all the national businesses. The challenge was that the OPEN competencies (and the 67 behaviours that evidenced them) had been designed to express BP's organizational culture, yet had to be adapted to suit a wide range of national cultures. The cross-cultural validity of the essential behaviours was challenged by non-British or non-American managers. They had been developed by a team of Anglo-Americans. Were they transferable to other countries?

BP conducted its investigation using a two-pronged approach: consultation of experts in the field of cultural diversity and the use of Focus Groups using non-Anglo-American employees. The expert reviews conducted by external academics and consultants sampled twelve countries. It was concluded that the competencies (i.e. the essential behaviours) were capable of cross-cultural implementation and represented a cogent statement of the shift in management behaviour required. However, the behavioural anchors used to describe specific competencies were, in some instances, unnecessarily directive and contained a culturally provocative bias. The greatest challenge came from competencies contained in the Personal Impact (Bias for Action, Knows What Makes Others Tick, Concern for Impact and Self-Confidence) and Empowerment (Coaching and Developing, Building Team Success and Motivating) clusters. The recommendation was that BP step back from the behavioural detail of the proposed OPEN competencies and encourage people in different countries to offer their own illustrations of how they might change behaviours and culture. The process demonstrated that the OPEN competencies were capable of crossing cultural barriers in their essential meaning and purpose (reinforcing their use as a 'corporate glue' to integrate human resource policies and practices), but also that their implementation and assessment would require greater effort in order to customize and translate the behavioural indicators to fit the culturally different groups involved. The customization process, however, had to avoid any misinterpretation or fundamental change to the meaning of the competencies.

BP ran a series of Focus Groups in France and Germany, in which it presented the intended objective of the behaviour contained within the competency and the intended meaning behind the English words. The Focus Groups each contained ten to twelve national employees who spoke English as a second language. Meetings were held in the local language and were facilitated by consultants operating in the area of cross-cultural management and fluent in English, French and German. Each group was able to flex the behavioural indicators around each competency so that they were appropriate for their culture and organization. The feared barriers to cross-cultural implementation did not materialize.

Local business trainers and facilitators were then given instruction on how to present the OPEN competencies as part of change programmes being carried out in Europe and Asia-Pacific. It was found that it was better to instruct local trainers on the meaning and purpose behind the competencies and then let them fashion the actual training process used to introduce the competencies themselves.

Finally, role plays were run as part of Awareness Building Workshops in which managers who would be responsible for assessing the competencies enacted them out in role plays. Further lessons were learned about the behavioural enactment of specific competencies across the national cultures.

From this lengthy process, BP was confident that the OPEN competencies could be applied throughout the organization. The final step was to formalize the OPEN behaviours through other HRM practices. A variety of applications of the competency model followed as part of awareness and communication exercises and workshops, the performance appraisal process (including upward evaluation of supervisors using the essential behaviours), an international development programme, graduate recruitment procedures, training and development offerings, an executive competency model, and employee surveys used to monitor the change in behaviour against the competencies.

A life-cycle perspective

The BP experience demonstrates the use of competency-based approaches to facilitate strategic change, as well as the potential of these approaches to achieve cross-cultural transfer. However, the identification of competencies at BP was based around a broad concept of 'enabling change to happen'. In many cases, organizations will want a more specific and focused set of future-orientated competencies.

In linking organizational level competencies to behaviours observed at the individual level, there is a critical distinction between identifying competencies for change and analysing changing competencies. Organizations take a dynamic and changing view about what constitutes effective performance and, as they move through different business environments, or themselves mature, the relevance of any one competency is bound to alter. They need a flexible framework to reflect the changing relevance of competencies in the present and future. Rather than create generic lists of competencies associated with 'coping with change' or 'making change happen' (such as the BP approach), organizations will need to develop an even more sophisticated picture of competencies that allows them to analyse how the relevance of any competency to the organization as a whole (or to a career stream, or individual job) waxes and wanes. Standing in the present and looking out to the future, organizations should expect to see four different categories of competency (see Figure 5.1). The actual competencies that fall within these categories – and the behavioural indicators in particular – will, of course, vary from organization to organization and across industrial sectors.

Some competencies may be termed *emerging*. These competencies may not be particularly relevant to the organization and its jobs at present, but the particular strategic path the organization is pursuing will undoubtedly place greater emphasis on them in the future. In other cases the opposite applies.

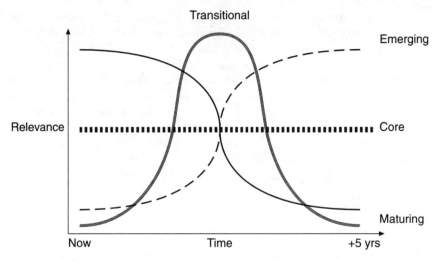

Figure 5.1 A life-cycle perspective for organizational competencies

Competencies may be *maturing* when they have formed an important part of organizational life (and the jobs within it) in the past, but are becoming less and less relevant in the future. The projected drop in relevance may be due to a shift in strategy, or the designing out of the competency through technology or work structuring.

A third category of competency may be termed *transitional*. These competencies are not currently important, nor indeed are they implied by the strategic plan, yet the change can only be achieved or managed smoothly by placing greater emphasis on these competencies. The 'competencies for change' identified by organizations such as British Petroleum, Cadbury Schweppes, National Westminster and Shell should really be viewed as transitional competencies. They represent an integral part of the change process and so are highly relevant. At the individual level, the requirement to demonstrate a high capacity to live with uncertainty, to manage stress, to cope with pressure and manage conflict may also be viewed or identified as transitional competencies.

Finally, a fourth category of competency may be termed *stable* or *core*. These are enduring competencies that will remain as important tomorrow as they are today. They lie at the heart of effective performance, despite the current or forthcoming flavour of the business plan or strategic direction. We are in danger of becoming obsessed with change, improvement and transformation at the expense of those competencies needed for continuity and implementation. Reasoning or analytical ability are likely to be core competencies in most settings. Other core competencies may relate to the way business is carried out in the particular industrial sector the organization is in.

In thinking about – and classifying – competencies as being stable, emerging, declining or transitional, it becomes easier to understand the need to attach a 'shelf life' to any competency profile. Clearly, the relative focus or weighting that can be given to a competency will change in proportion to the speed of change within the business environment and nature of the job. However, the more forward-looking the profile is, the longer its shelf life. It is impossible to put a finite figure in years, months and days on any profile, but experience indicates that organizations only need to reidentify and reclassify competencies every two to three years or so.

There is a need to develop a flexible package of competency requirement forecasting techniques that overcome the methodological flaws described above. In extending the shelf-life of a competency profile and moving beyond generic 'competencies for change', we need to help organizations create powerful distillations of 'effective behaviours'. This requires careful definition and manipulation of what 'effective' performance really is in an organizational and strategic context. It also requires forecasting techniques to incorporate defensible hypotheses about the organization's future, incorporate an educative and broadening process, yet still be able to identify the behaviours that are relevant in such a context. Sparrow and Boam (1992) have articulated some of the most fruitful techniques that may serve this purpose, but much more development is required.

Challenges to the selection paradigm

Finally, as organizations like BP continue to develop and pursue corporate-wide competency programmes, psychologists will find that there is a significant challenge to their selection paradigm. Many of their traditional selection tools and techniques (as well as much of their acquired wisdom and technology) will be put to the test as they attempt to match recent developments and priorities in organizational practice. The focus of selection approaches on job-person fit has carried an implicit criterion of selecting for performance on a variety of tasks. Considerable analysis and review has shown that the single most valid and reliable predictor of task performance is general intelligence, with the 'Big Five' personality factors adding some additional information. Intelligence tests form the bedrock of many advanced selection and assessment systems.

With competency-based systems, this need not be the case, particularly when they are derived from corporate-wide or culturally determined criteria. Here, the focus is on the actual behaviour, regardless of the task. Analysis of typical behavioural indicators that constitute a competency profile identified at the career stream, cross management or organization level leads to a number of observations. Although most competency profiles involve a range of analytical and reasoning-linked competencies, the actual behavioural indicators, while clearly linked to underlying general intelligence, are extremely specific and also demonstrate considerable variety between organizations.

General tests of intelligence, with their measures of verbal, numerical and spatial reasoning, may not always pick up the real behavioural context implied by the competency. More sophisticated and targeted measures of analytical competencies are required. Moreover, by the very breadth of behaviour specified in competency profiles, far more is being looked at by organizations than general intelligence. While intelligence is a good predictor of task flexibility, it is of little relevance to behavioural flexibility, which lies at the heart of most competency profiles. Few organizations can afford to develop the comprehensive assessment centre approaches that can cope with a broad range of competencies throughout their selection systems and, once intelligence and personality tests are taken out from such approaches, the reliability and validity of the other typical assessment tools is not impressive. Psychologists will, in the end, need to become more inventive in designing reliable and valid non-test forms of behavioural assessment if they are to facilitate the behavioural engineering that is implied by competency-based human resource strategies.

REFERENCES

Arnold, J. and Davey, K. M. (1992) 'Self-ratings and supervisor ratings of graduate employees' competences during early career', *Journal of Occupational and Organizational Psychology*, 65, 235–50.

Boam, R. and Sparrow, P. (1992) 'The rise and rationale of competency-based approaches', in R. Boam and P. Sparrow (eds), *Designing and Achieving Competency: a competency-based approach to managing people and organizations*, McGraw-Hill, London.

Bognanno, M. (1990) 'Facilitating cultural change by identifying the new competencies required and formulating a strategy to develop such competencies', *Conference on identifying and applying competencies within your organization*, 6 November, Resource Ltd, London.

Bognanno, M. (1992) 'Linking executive competences to a cultural competency model', *Conference on the latest developments in identifying, measuring and applying competences*, 28–29 January 1992, IIR Ltd, London.

Boyatzis, R. (1982) *The Competent Manager*, Wiley, New York.

Coulson-Thomas, C. (1990) 'Developing directors', *European Management Journal*, 8(4), 488–99.

Craig, S. (1992) 'Using competencies in career development', in R. Boam and P. Sparrow (eds), *Designing and Achieving Competency: a competency-based approach to managing people and organizations*, McGraw-Hill, London.

Feltham, R. (1992) 'Using competencies in recruitment and selection', in R. Boam and P. Sparrow (eds), *Designing and Achieving Competency: a competency-based approach to managing people and organizations*, McGraw-Hill, London.

Francis, K. (1992) 'Using a competency approach to achieve higher business performance and the acceleration of change in personnel practices: a line manager's story', *Conference on the latest developments in identifying, measuring and applying competences*, 28–29 January 1992, IIR Ltd, London.

Iles, P. (1992) 'Centres of excellence? Assessment and development centres, managerial, competence and human resource strategies', *British Journal of Management*, 3(2), 79–90.

Kandola, R. and Pearn, M. (1992) 'Identifying competencies', in R. Boam and P. Sparrow (eds), *Designing and Achieving Competency: a competency-based approach to managing people and organizations*, McGraw-Hill, London.

Quinn Mills, D. and Friesen, B. (1992) 'The learning organization', *European Management Journal*, 10(2), 146–56.

Probert, P. (1992) 'Using a competency model to streamline, restructure, recruit and build a new company culture with the aim of competitive advantage', *Conference on the latest developments in identifying, measuring and applying competences*, 28–29 January 1992, IIR Ltd, London.

Schuler, R. (1992) 'Strategic human resource management: linking the people with the strategic needs of the business', *Organizational Dynamics*, Summer 1992.

Shackleton, V. (1992) 'Using a competency approach in a business change setting', in R. Boam and P. Sparrow (eds), *Designing and Achieving Competency: a competency-based approach to managing people and organizations*, McGraw-Hill, London.

Smith, B. and Verran, M. (1992) 'Business-oriented human resource development', *Conference on the latest developments in identifying, measuring and applying competences*, 28–29 January 1992, IIR Ltd, London.

Sparrow, P. and Boam, R. (1992) 'Strengths and weaknesses of existing competency-based approaches: where do we go from here?' in R. Boam and P. Sparrow (eds), *Designing and Achieving Competency: a competency-based approach to managing people and organizations*, McGraw-Hill, London.

Torrington, D. and Blandamer, W. (1992) 'Competency, pay and performance management', in R. Boam and P. Sparrow (eds), *Designing and Achieving Competency: a competency-based approach to managing people and organizations*, McGraw-Hill, London.

Chapter 6

The kind of competence for rapid change

Tony Cockerill

In 1963 Tom Burns pointed out that most organizations operated in a relatively stable environment which favoured bureaucratic structures, but that increasing environmental change signalled the need for more flexible, organic organizational designs.[1] Few people now doubt the wisdom of Burns' analysis: organizations in nearly every sector of the economy are facing increases in the rate of environmental change, and managers are making major structural changes in order that their organizations are better adapted to the new conditions. Increased global competition, technological innovation, and more sophisticated customers with a wider range of needs, are just some of the forces which have made the financial services environment in particular more turbulent and which have led firms such as NatWest to become more adaptable to changing conditions.

NEW ROLES AND SKILLS FOR MANAGERS

Experience of working in more flexible organizations, and studies like those by Rosabeth Moss Kanter, show that the role of managers changes considerably as organizations become more organic and less mechanistic.[2] In bureaucracies the high level of predictability leads to a heavy emphasis on planning, organizing and monitoring. The segmentation of work makes the co-ordination of relatively independent units essential. The recurrence of similar issues results in the emergence of rules, regulations and precedents, which make work heavily programmed so that managers must consistently and efficiently apply these rules to solve problems and must direct and control subordinates to ensure they do the same.

In organic structures change means that managers must continually gather new information, form ideas about what is happening and have several well-evaluated options available, because they are unsure of the circumstances that will emerge. Managers need to build and develop fluid networks and teams that span across organizational boundaries, and they need to develop staff to take on the greater responsibilities that flatter structures imply. In addition, managers must take, justify and be confident in the success of decisions when a 'right' solution does not exist; they must present these decisions clearly and get political support for them. Also, managers must make things happen; they must introduce change. This change must improve the performance of the organization, and it must be introduced on or within the target date.

As the role of managers changes, so do the skills that managers need to use in order to be successful. Nevertheless, in my view most managerial assessment centres have been designed to evaluate skills such as planning, organizing, monitoring, co-ordinating, directing and controlling, which are most relevant to bureaucracies in stable environments. As Robin Jacobs pointed out few assessment centres are designed to assess the additional competencies which become important as environments get more dynamic.[3] Furthermore, while the use of promotion, salary increase and boss ratings as criteria to judge the validity of assessment centres has shown that they can predict career advancement, these criteria do not demonstrate that assessment centres predict the performance of bureaucratic organizations, let alone any other type.

Many validation studies are examples of a sterile, closed loop of research. Techniques such as repertory grids are used to elicit 'effective' dimensions of behaviour from the minds of managers; managers, often the same ones, assess participants against these dimensions at an assessment centre; managers are then asked to validate the assessment centre by using the same or similar dimensions of behaviour to rate the 'job performance' of participants. This method tells us more about the reliability with which managers can rate the same dimensions of behaviour in different settings than it does about the relationship between these dimensions and organizational performance. Additionally, this approach can formalize the self-perpetuation of a cadre of managers who, consciously or not, are using the process to select in their own image when circumstances have changed and when they have no evidence to demonstrate that this image is significantly related to organizational performance. (The term 'organizational performance' is used throughout this chapter to mean the performance of the unit run by the manager in question.)

Need for new selection and development approach

Dynamic environments in which organizational success is harder to achieve and resources are scarcer mean that we must use approaches to the selection and development of managers which have a demonstrable link to organizational performance. The advent of more flexible structural forms means we need to use additional assessment centre dimensions.

At NatWest the belief that the environment will become more dynamic and turbulent in the future, and the implications that this has for organizational design and managerial jobs, led in September 1985 to a four-year research programme to identify managerial behaviour which results in outstanding performance under these circumstances. We have also explored how this sort of behaviour can be used to select and develop managerial staff. Our approach, therefore, has recognized fully the limitations which accompany the exclusive use of bureaucratic assumptions to design management development programmes, and has been focused deliberately on the creation of programmes which are future oriented, and which should therefore raise organizational performance as the rate of environmental change increases.

A thorough review of the literature and of management development practices across the world revealed that very little work had been undertaken to prepare managers for more dynamic environments. However, one initiative did seem to be far ahead of everything else: that led by Harry Schroder,[4] former professor of psychology at Princeton and now professor of management at the University of South Florida. He has drawn on several areas of research to identify and test the validity of eleven 'high-performance managerial competencies' (see Table 6.1), and subsequent research in NatWest to test his findings strongly indicates that high levels of performance are achieved in changing circumstances when managers use the competencies.

I should make it clear that the eleven competencies are not concerned with mere 'competence' – with sufficiency or adequacy; rather they are forms of managerial behaviour which will raise performance beyond adequacy to excellence.

Furthermore, the competencies include behaviour which Robin Jacobs has called 'soft' and which he regards as 'difficult to measure under any circumstances and virtually impossible under simulated conditions.' Both Schroder's work and my own show that each of the eleven competencies can be measured (with a very high degree of consistency between assessors) under simulated assessment centre conditions or through the direct observation of managers at work.[5]

The belief that interpersonal skills, such as 'impact', or cognitive skills, such as 'concept formation', cannot be measured reliably by behavioural observation is a popular fallacy. For example, the three cognitive competencies (information search, concept formation and conceptual flexibility) are derived primarily from a 15-year research programme into human information processing at Princeton University which used complex simulations to identify and validate behaviourally observable cognitive skills that result in high levels of performance when the environment is uncertain, rapidly changing and turbulent.[6]

Nor does our experience bear out Jacobs' view that simulations cannot take into account the extent to which organizations depend on mutual support and collaboration between colleagues operating in groups and teams. At NatWest we use simulations which successfully create these

Table 6.1 Eleven high-performance managerial competencies

Information search	Gathers many different kinds of information and uses a wide variety of sources to build a rich informational environment in preparation for decision-making in the organization.
Concept formation	Builds frameworks or models or forms concepts, hypotheses or ideas on the basis of information; becomes aware of patterns, trends and cause/effect relations by linking disparate information.
Conceptual flexibility	Identifies feasible alternatives or multiple options in planning and decision-making; holds different options in focus simultaneously and evaluates their pros and cons.
Interpersonal search	Uses open and probing questions, summaries, paraphrasing etc to understand the ideas, concepts and feelings of another; can comprehend events, issues, problems, opportunities from the viewpoint of another person.
Managing interaction	Involves others and is able to build cooperative teams in which group members feel valued and empowered and have shared goals.
Developmental orientation	Creates a positive climate in which individuals increase the accuracy of their awareness of their own strengths and limitations and provides coaching, training and developmental resources to improve performance.
Impact	Uses a variety of methods (e.g. persuasive arguments, modelling behaviour, inventing symbols, forming alliances and appealing to the interest of others) to gain support for ideas, strategies and values.
Self-confidence	States own 'stand' or position on issues; unhesitatingly takes decisions when required and commits self and others accordingly; expresses confidence in the future success of the actions to be taken.
Presentation	Presents ideas clearly, with ease and interest so that the other person (or audience) understands what is being communicated; uses technical, symbolic, non-verbal and visual aids effectively.
Proactive orientation	Structures the task for the team; implements plans and ideas; takes responsibility for all aspects of the situation.
Achievement orientation	Possesses high internal work standards and sets ambitious yet attainable goals; wants to do things better, to improve, to be more effective and efficient; measures progress against targets.

conditions and which make it possible, to assess competencies such as 'managing interaction'.

MANAGERIAL COMPETENCIES AT NATWEST

In summary, our work at NatWest has enabled us to identify high-performance managerial competencies, relevant to rapidly changing environments and flexible forms of organization, which can be reliably measured and which two validity studies have shown to be significantly related to measures of performance. We are now using them as a basis for development.

It seems to me that the pillar on which personal development rests is self awareness. I have found two types of information to be valuable to my own development and to that of others. The first type of information relates to preferences (e.g. what each of us does or does not value, what we like or dislike doing). At NatWest we have found that self-report inventories (like the Myers-Briggs Type Indicator), guided interviews between course participants (using the 'career anchors' approach of Ed Schein) and group discussions are all valuable and well-received ways of enabling staff to gain insight into their own preferences and to value others with similar or different preferences.

The second type of information concerns capacities (i.e. what each of us is good or not good at doing). Managerial competence is a 'capacity' as it refers to a level of performance. A variety of methods exists to provide individuals with information about their competencies. At NatWest we have used information from assessment centres as well as boss, peer, subordinate and self-ratings, gathered by means of questionnaires designed to measure the high-performance managerial competencies.

Each type of information has its strengths and limitations. For example, in his study Schroder found that assessment centre ratings were much more reliable and highly related to measures of performance than were boss, subordinate and self-ratings. Furthermore, in line with other research, he found that boss, subordinate and self-ratings were lenient and undifferentiated (i.e. all competencies tended to be rated the same). Nevertheless, ratings of this kind are capable of providing people with a picture of how they are perceived by others in their organization, which in itself is valuable feedback.

Thus, in my experience assessment centres can provide individuals with very valuable information on their competence to manage in dynamic conditions; other sources of information also have their place. The critical thing to do when providing individuals with feedback on their competence is to explain the relative validity, reliability and usefulness of the different types of information. This enables them to make an accurate assessment not only of their strengths, adequacies and limitations but also of how they are perceived by others.

Once individuals have accurately identified their strengths, adequacies and limitations, development can take place. At NatWest we have found three strategies of development to be particularly valuable. First, staff devise a plan to make a better contribution to the organization with their strengths. Our experience supports Kotter's notion that managers do not have a clear perception of their strengths;[7] the first benefit of self-insight is that it gives individuals a clear idea of their strengths. Even when staff are aware of their strengths, we find that they do not make full use of them; for instance, an individual will gather information very well from a customer in a one-to-one situation but will not be effective at doing this in a group meeting. Staff therefore plan how to use their strengths consistently in different situations and across a fuller range of activities.

Second, staff create a plan to compensate for their limitations. Schroder's research in the USA and the UK has found that, on average, managers tend to have three high-performance competencies as strengths. These results help to debunk the popular macho belief that managers must be good at everything. We find it comes as quite a relief to staff when they find that they do not have to be supermen or superwomen and that it makes sense to learn how to work co-operatively with others who have different strengths.

This approach also highlights the importance of building managerial teams with individuals who have complementary strengths, so that the team as a whole possesses the full range of competencies that are needed for high performance.

Third, staff devise a plan to develop one or two competencies which are limitations into strengths. All three plans include ways of measuring whether development is occurring and whether this is raising the level of organizational performance. The plans are implemented in the workplace using the principles of action learning. The relevance and practicality of these plans avoids a problem which is the Achilles heel of many management courses – how to transfer learning back to the workplace.

In conclusion, I have tried to highlight the danger of two extremes. The first uses traditional competencies exclusively and does not take into account the additional competencies needed when environments are changing rapidly. The second denies the value of assessment centres and managerial competencies when environments are rapidly changing. I have also tried to show that these are high-performance managerial competencies that can be reliably measured by a variety of means, especially assessment centres, which appear to be relevant to modern conditions and which can be used in a practical, cost-effective way to select and develop managers.

Competency-bashing is a popular blood sport at present. However, in our experience this new approach to management development has a high and demonstrable payback for the investment it requires, is relevant to the challenges of the present and the future, is based on behaviour that managers use and that can be clearly observed, rather than surrounding itself in mysticism, and is welcomed by managers.

Furthermore, it is my belief that the insistence – by the initiators of the high-performance managerial competencies approach – on combining research with practical application means that this is one of the few ways of undertaking management development which will contribute to and change our understanding of organizational behaviour and effectiveness.

For all of these reasons, I believe it is shortsighted to reject the approach I have described; willingness to experiment with innovation – as NatWest has done – is the only way, in my view, that organizations are going to achieve a durable competitive advantage through management development. The need to do this is pressing because the emergence of more dynamic environments means that organizational performance is more heavily dependent on the quality of managers than it has ever been before.

REFERENCES

1 Burns, T. 'Industry in a new age', *New Society*, 31 January 1963.
2 Kanter, R. M. *The Change Masters*, Allen and Unwin, 1984.
3 Jacobs, R. 'Getting the measure of management competence', *Personnel Management*, June 1989.
4 Schroder, H. M. *Managerial Competence: the key to excellence*, Kendall/Hunt, Iowa, 1989.
5 Cockerill, A. P., 'Managerial competence as a determinant of organizational performance', doctoral research at the London Business School.
6 Schroder, H. M., Driver, M. J. and Streufert, S. *Human Information Processing*, Holt, Rinehart Winston, New York 1967.
7 Kotter, J. P. *The General Managers*, The Free Press, New York, 1982.

Chapter 7

Individual and organizational learning: the pursuit of change

Alan Mumford

THE NEED FOR BALANCE

The discussion of 'the learning organization' is receiving increased attention, and indeed even perhaps some analytical research, in both the UK[1] and the USA.[2] I will show later why I believe some of that attention is rather unhelpfully focused and defined. At this point I want to state fairly starkly what I regard the appropriate balance of attention to be. It is simply stated. We all know of individuals who manage to learn with little or no contribution from 'the organization'. It is, however, impossible to conceive of a learning organization, however defined, which exists without individual learners. The learning organization depends absolutely on the skills, approaches and commitment of individuals of their own learning.

Clearly, however, the individual learner can be helped or hindered by the organization in which he or she works; the environment may not be absolutely fundamental but it can be a powerful influence, which ought to be properly defined and directed. In that sense attention to 'the learning organization as environment' is certainly desirable. The extent to which it is necessary or useful to move from the helpful organization, to a view of the organization as in some sense a corporate body possessed of learning attributes, is discussed later.

AN EFFECTIVE LEARNING PROCESS

The most powerfully influential figures in the world of management education and training have been Malcolm Knowles,[3] with his assertion that adult learning crucially depends on interest in resolving relevant problems, and David Kolb with his vital identification of individual learning styles as a major feature to accompany his version of a learning cycle.[4] In the as yet brief history of understanding about management learning, the significance of relevance and individuality, as compared with the characteristic pedagogic forms of teaching are landmarks. The fact that at least in the UK management education institutions are stumbling at last towards relevance, though not sadly yet to individuality, shows that it sometimes takes only twenty years for institutions apparently dedicated to knowledge, to make use of that knowledge!

The Kolb version of the learning cycle is now relatively familiar. It is particularly helpful in encouraging educators and trainers to consider how to design learning experiences effectively so that they embrace all aspects of the cycle at some stage in the experience. While still using my own version of the cycle for that purpose, it has become increasingly clear to me that the totally enclosed learning cycle represents better the design of structured learning events than it does the possible routes or progress of the individual learner. My new version (see Figure 7.1) attempts to indicate that after any completed particular learning cycle an individual may veer away from the straightforward repetition of the cycle; the next learning step may not be to engage in a new activity or experience, but for example to revisit an experience already undertaken and to collect more facts about it. For example, an individual might be encouraged to go and get more information about a meeting from someone else who has participated in it. Or the appropriate step in the learning cycle may not be even to revisit an achieved experience, but to amend the conclusions drawn from it. It is one of the defects of drawing the cycle flat on the page that it is impossible to represent properly the alternative directions of such learning thought processes. In addition this version gives emphasis and literally direction to the concept of continuous learning, in which learning is now treated as a series of structured but not separate events.

THE INDIVIDUAL LEARNER

The idea that individuals will choose differently what additional learning they may pursue after any learning experience can be explained by a number of different factors. David Kolb's revelatory contribution – learning styles – has already been mentioned. As with Kolb, Peter Honey and I developed our diagnostic instrument from the view that individuals would choose often to focus more on one stage of the learning cycle than on

Figure 7.1 The progressive learning cycle

another; while the designer of learning experiences can use the idea of the learning cycle, the cycle and learning styles instruments can be used to assist the individual learner to identify and make better use of any kind of learning experiences – designed or accidental. The two Honey and Mumford publications are complementary in providing for this enhancement of learning effectiveness.[5,6] It is interesting to note that no alternatives to the Honey and Mumford learning styles work have appeared in the UK in the nine years since we first published it – although in the USA there are a number of alternatives to Kolb's Learning Styles Inventory (LSI) and our Learning Styles Questionnaire (LSQ).

Of course not all trainers and educators are convinced that a diagnostic instrument is the best approach to the individual learner, and useful indications of different aspects of the learner are given for example by Pedler, Cunningham and Snell.

Whichever approach is adopted, the crucial issue is that not only of identifying individual differences in the ways in which individuals learn, but the provision of action based on those differences. Just as a version of the learning cycle will help to create the awareness of actions necessary to encourage continuity of learning, so learning styles information can be the best focus for 'learning how to learn'. This latter issue is so important because it enables individuals to make more effective use of those experiences that actually predominate in their lives. It is not courses, nor even often planned job moves and job experiences which create the quantity of learning experiences – or indeed often the quality of learning experience. Learning on and through the job is and will remain the prime occasion for learning for managers. But the intensity and variety of work experiences are too often not planned and directed at all, or if planned are not effectively used.

The argument has so far focused on the preferences of the individual learner, we must look now at the context in which the learner learns.

THE LEARNING ORGANIZATION

The relatively recent attention to the learning organization is potentially a powerful aid to effective learning. As presently stated, however, I find some problems with the conceptual statements in terms of their ability to secure action. First, they contain much of the flavour of the Organization Development (OD) movement of the 1970s; there is nothing necessarily wrong with that, except that one might hope that people essentially proposing the same ideas fifteen years later would have reviewed and made use of learning from the OD movement. That learning seems to me to include the unwillingness of most managers to engage with high-level statements containing a sense of moral purpose, their lack of acceptance of the values usually held by OD practitioners (openness, trust, confrontation) and an apparently overwhelming concern for personal development as the essential focus for organizational purpose.

The best feature for current concerns about organizational learning is the recognition that there is much more to effective management development than a computerized data system, regular meetings to discuss succession plans, and a high volume of training. The explicit recognition that learning occurs in and around the job is a substantial move forward. Many of the current writers however are longer on description of desirable states than they are on processes for achieving those states. In terms of tools for practising training and management development officers, there is too little that is helpful. The necessary position, which admittedly might be seen to be an intermediate one, is to set out the situations and practices that need to exist for there to be a benign environment for learning. What actions actually need to be taken by line managers to secure for themselves and to provide for others effective learning experiences?

RECOGNIZING AND USING LEARNING OPPORTUNITIES

The basic components of management development in most organizations are:

- A review of existing resources, and the extent to which these meet organizational needs.
- A process for moving people around the organization with the conscious objective of providing different learning opportunities.
- The use of internal and external courses.

In the UK, this view was captured by the Training Services Agency in 1977: 'An attempt to improve managerial effectiveness through a planned and deliberate learning process.' I have argued that the problem with this definition is that it excludes from 'management development' that huge volume of unplanned and relatively unconscious learning and development actually achieved by managers.[7] My definition therefore takes out 'planned and deliberate' from that definition – which I otherwise still like because of its use of the phrases 'managerial effectiveness' and 'learning process'. This interpretation of the reality of management development is significant for a number of different reasons. In this section the particular significance is the question of the extent to which opportunities, especially on and through the job, are planned, designed and effectively implemented.

The picture here is designed to illustrate what I call 'big O' and 'small Os'. Management development systems, and powerful individuals within it, when describing a potential job move to an individual often set it out as 'a big opportunity for you'. They will describe it in terms of the different experience that the individual will garner from moving from one function to another. The organization and powerful people in it often see themselves as actually participating in an effective learning organization – they are after all providing the opportunities necessary for personal growth and for later organizational effectiveness. My research and experience both show what a feeble actuality is contained within this glowing presentation. Very rarely are the specific opportunities for particular learning identified in advance, reviewed with individuals, subsequently reviewed and discussed. The fact is that even within the formal processes of management development, managers are most frequently in effect 'dumped' into a new situation with the pious hope that they will learn from it – a hope that, because managers are intelligent, thrustful and relatively thoughtful, is often partially achieved.

Yet this is the 'planned and deliberate' element of management development! Most on-the-job experiences are essentially accidental deriving from the particular circumstances of a job on any day or week of the manager's working life.

It is crucial that we manage to improve the capacity of individuals to recognize and take advantage of learning opportunities, both those planned on a grand scale and those which occur intimately on a smaller scale. Only when we achieve this – which I am happy to describe as the intermediate, position for a learning organization – can we really begin to think about the larger values and purposes set out in the statements about the learning organization given at the beginning of this section. This will be achieved if we begin to define smaller opportunities contained with 'O'. Figures 7.2 and 7.3 present the metaphor. The metaphor is explicit in that what in management development is described as 'O' for opportunity, can be experienced as 'O' for zero in terms of achieved development.

One way of creating more effective use of opportunities is expressed in the idea of the learning contract or learning agreement. Originally developed in the USA as a relationship between a tutor and a trainee, the idea has been more recently taken up in the UK as a more total relationship between an employee and employer, in terms of the kind of learning opportunity which will be presented and committed to by both parties. In many ways close to the better versions of the consequences of an appraisal system, perhaps the most useful aspect is the philosophy of joint agreement. However, this process, while at least advancing the idea of the review of achievement of learning objectives, may still leave some opportunities underused, and may still focus too much on formally created opportunities, particularly courses.

What is necessary whether as part of a learning agreement, or as a stand-alone feature, is some process for helping people to recognize and take advantage of a variety of learning opportunities. Partly because of their necessary and quite proper focus on achieving work objectives, managers are not usually geared to recognize beforehand, and only partly able to recognize afterwards, the learning opportunities open to them within and

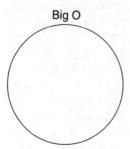

Figure 7.2 Big O

Figure 7.3 Big O and smaller Os

around the job. So they need some help in this. This needs to be expressed in much more explicit detail than the familiar catalogue of training courses, list of possible job opportunities provided within many formal management development systems. We need to provide for much more self-examination, much more detail for self-analysis. The earlier work of Pedler and his colleagues[8] provides for some aspects of this, within the context of the self-development philosophy. The continued and deserved popularity of their book shows that this can be a very successful route.

An alternative approach, which gives rather more emphasis to the environment in which the individual can 'self-develop' is provided in Honey and Mumford,[9] again accompanied by a personal workbook.[10] This manual provides for several of the requirements mentioned above, particularly the definition and effective use of learning opportunities.

PROVIDING HELP

While we have long moved away from the proposition that a manager has primary responsibility for developing subordinates, of course we still recognize the major and powerful influence any boss has on the opportunities offered to subordinates, their willingness to take them up, and their ability to do so. One of the consequences of interested attention to learning through the job is necessarily that we have to look again at the capacity and willingness of those surrounding the individual learner to assist in the effectiveness of achieved learning. For the purpose of this chapter the obviously significant role of trainers, educators and management development advisers has deliberately been omitted.

There is a certain paradox in this, since clearly most of the things set out here will only be achieved through the initial design and subsequent collaboration of management development specialists and trainers with line managers. The focus here is on the line manager. After all, the natural but not inevitable consequence of the argument deployed in this chapter is that managers need to be better equipped to help themselves and others learn, and not to leave it to professionals who cannot be in contact with the day-to-day realities of each individual's working life. If the argument of this chapter is accepted, for example management developers and trainers will have to think about the priorities, not only within the total management development system, but within those parts of it on which they have the strongest influence. Are there guidebooks provided to help managers not merely do an effective appraisal, but to discuss learning objectives and learning achievement? Is there a guidebook or training course available on the different kinds of help which managers at different levels should be able to offer? There are very few workshops on 'Helping Managers Learn to Learn', compared with large numbers on 'Interpersonal Skills', let alone 'Finance for Non-financial Managers'. Particularly we need to help identify the different roles of potential helpers in development. A list of different helpers on the job includes:

- Boss
- Grand boss
- Mentors
- Colleagues
- Subordinates
- Clients for projects

There is altogether too little available to assist people in recognizing these different roles – and subsequently to make use of them. What exactly do we expect individuals to do when they are holding the roles? What is the difference between acting as a boss-helper and a mentor-helper?

It will surely be readily recognized that the issues of the kind of help and helpers available within the organization are those which will in fact determine whether an organization is a learning organization or not. The reality of managerial life determines the nature and effectiveness of any development process – and those realities consist of achieving managerial objectives and specific tasks primarily, not achieving the development of others (or even oneself). Unless our management development system provides a counterweight to the dedication to task achievement, there is no prospect of achieving a learning organization.

USING REAL-TIME MANAGEMENT EXPERIENCE

Although one might not think so from reading some books on management development, the question is not whether we should use real-time managerial experience for learning, but how we do so more effectively. That proposition has been partly examined earlier. Three aspects of it require further discussion.

The first is that experience can be a leaden weight, a negative and frustrating feature inhibiting learning. Experience can teach individuals that 'you can't' just as frequently as it teaches them 'you can'. In addition, too frequently experience is badly examined. While failure and its causes can be assessed in detail, success and its causes are not. While continuing to emphasise that experience is the essential basis for effective management development, we have to avoid any temptation by individuals or organizations to idealize that experience – by not examining it properly, by creating subsequent failures through the misapplication of misperceived success. Explicitly we need to enhance the capacity of individuals and organizations to evaluate their understanding of experience, not just to extrapolate it.

While clearly I am an enthusiast for the more effective use of learning on the job, I am also a believer in well designed and integrated off-the-job experiences. While the phrase 'well designed' might be taken for granted by educators and trainers, both that phrase and 'integrated' need further explanation.

First, it is clear that effective design includes the principles of the learning cycle, the use of individual learning styles, and the encouragement of learning to learn processes. To encounter two-year MBA programmes in prestigious business schools that pay no explicit attention to any of these is to recognize how far we have to go. If in our major programmes we do not attempt to enable individuals to learn more effectively, we are missing the major opportunity which most of the participants will ever have to improve their skills in this, as programmes normally intend to help them to improve on decision making, the use of management information systems, and awareness of the economic environment.

Second, we need to ensure that our real-time processes are integrated. The argument earlier has been that we need to examine large-scale on-the-job opportunities to convert them into smaller successfully achieved learning experiences. On the job, that will only be achieved by successfully integrating task and learning. In off-the-job situations, the same proposition carries a different element. Here we must ensure that our carefully designed processes actually integrate with the real world. This is not simply a question of throwing in some practical exercises, using illustrative case studies, providing simulations or on the course or outdoor training as an element in it. It is the fundamental proposition of constantly enabling individuals to undertake real work as part of an off-the-job experience by taking them back into the real world – and then enabling them to use the experience and techniques for reviewing that experience on further opportunities which will not be part of the formal programme.

The most developed version of this is of course action learning. In its best versions, action learning provides precisely that integration between task and learning which effectively matches the motivation and therefore potential commitment of managers. In its best versions it also provides the dynamic and engine for change – not only personal but organizational. It therefore, and because of its explicit association with defined organizational needs, represents potentially the most appropriate vehicle in many organizations for the concept of the learning organization. However, not all versions of action learning meet these potential goals. Throwing in a project as 'an integrative exercise in business management', or as an external consultancy exercise for bright managers is not to provide the best form of action learning.

The four Is in work-centred learning

These are:

1 Interaction – with colleagues, boss, mentors.
2 Implementation – accountability not consultancy.
3 Integration – off-the-job designed to aid on-the-job.
4 Integration – continuous learning through conscious use of further opportunities.

It is of course easier to set out these principles than it is necessarily to apply them in practice. Over the last few years I have had the opportunity of doing this with a group usually regarded as the most unlikely candidates for training – directors in organizations. It is of course precisely because the 'Four Is' clearly place a value on their experience and on the use of their real problems that these programmes have been designed and implemented.[11]

EMPOWERMENT

The concept of empowerment is increasingly entering the vocabulary of people talking about organizational systems, management styles and relationships within managerial hierarchies. One argument for the more effective deployment and use of learning opportunities is that only by this process will organizations enable themselves to change and continue to function effectively in a turbulent environment. A final issue worthy of discussion is the question of whether learning processes are to a greater or lesser degree intended to enable individuals to challenge the environment in which they work. One version or understanding of the word could well be focused on the concept of challenge. Indeed the definitions of organizational learning given earlier by Pedler[1] and Senge[2] focus on that.

I am not happy with a view of personal or organizational learning which implies a total or indeed even a substantial emphasis on transformation. My view of learning opportunities is that they can be incremental (rather like Chris Argyris's single-loop learning) or can be transformational. For most of us most of the time our learning is going to be the former and not the latter. Sometimes this could, of course, be a matter of concern. Often it need not be. It is my belief, based of course on experience, that improvement of the capacity to learn at incremental level is worthy in its own right, as well as because without it leaps into the transformational mode apparently expected by some organizational learning theorists are quite unattainable. The vision I have projected in this chapter – focused on events, situations and people – is closer to actuality than the more distant higher-level images of some versions of organizational learning. To me, however, the same virtues of empowerment arise. If we provide individuals with a greater capacity to learn from the widest possible variety of opportunities, we are empowering that individual to be in greater command of his or her personal destiny. That is a vision which is surely acceptable to the value system of all trainers and educators, and one which many of us have the capacity to pursue more effectively than we are doing at the moment.

REFERENCES

1 Pedler, M., Boydell, T. and Burgoyne, J., 'Towards the Learning Company', *Management Education and Development*, 20, Part 1, 1989.
2 Senge, P., *The Fifth Discipline: the art and practice of the learning organization*, Doubleday, New York, 1990.
3 Knowles, M., *Andragogy in Action*, Jossey-Bass, London, 1985.
4 Kolb, D., *Experiential Learning*, Prentice-Hall, Englewood Cliffs, NJ, 1984.
5 Honey, P. and Mumford, A., *The Manual of Learning Styles*, Honey, Maidenhead, 1986.
6 Honey, P. and Mumford, A., *Using your Learning Styles*, Honey, Maidenhead, 1986.
7 Mumford, A., *Management Development: strategies for action*, IPM, 1989.
8 Pedler, M., Boydell, T. and Burgoyne, J., *Self Development for Managers*, McGraw-Hill, Maidenhead, 1986.
9 Honey, P. and Mumford, A., *The Manual of Learning Opportunities*, Honey, Maidenhead, 1989.
10 Honey, P. and Mumford, A., *The Opportunist Learner*, Honey, Maidenhead, 1990.
11 Mumford, A., 'Developing the top team', *Journal of Management Development*, 10, 5, 1991.

Chapter 8

Empowering leaders: are they being developed?

Lynda Gratton and Jill Pearson

INTRODUCTION

An increasing number of firms are moving from a production-line process (Levitt 1972) to one in which employees are empowered and involved (Lawler, Ledford and Mohrman 1989). This has been achieved through a variety of employee involvement practices, which have included quality circles, participation groups, self-managing work teams, suggestion involvement and job involvement (Bowen and Lawler 1992). These schemes have been accompanied by significant changes in organizational form and management behaviours. Empowerment processes have been achieved by a movement from hierarchical layers to team-based activities; from narrow, single-task jobs to whole-process, multiple tasks; from a management role of directing and controlling to one of coaching and facilitation; from top-down leadership to sharing with the team; and from job processes based on management planning and control to team planning and learning. Some commentators (e.g. Torbet 1976) have gone even further describing an increasing emphasis in organizations on a 'community of enquiry' characterized by a shared discourse on mission and goals, with employees capable of openness and interpersonal disclosure. He has argued that it is this shared and collaboratively derived understanding of the context of the organization which will lead to informed, team-based decision-making.

The empowering characteristics

The facilitation of empowering processes and employee involvement requires executives capable of using a wide repertoire of skills. These empowering characteristics can be clustered into six areas: management style, delegation and involvement, giving recognition and feedback, interpersonal empathy, communication style and ability to communicate a vision.

Management style

The management style of empowering executives is characterized by their open and collaborative approach to management tasks (Drath 1990). They work to foster opportunities for the subordinates to engage in decision-making (Conger and Kanungo 1988) and create a team who are joined in a common purpose (Bennis 1989). They ensure that employees have the knowledge and understanding to contribute to organizational performance (Bowen and Lawler 1992).

Delegation and involvement

Central to the concept of empowerment is the process by which the executives share their power with subordinates. Empowering executives work hard to enable rather than simply to delegate; they ensure their team members have autonomy from bureaucratic constraints (Conger and Kanungo 1988).

Giving recognition and feedback

A major theme is the relationship between the executive and significant others. They motivate their team by expressing confidence in their team members (Conger and Kanungo 1988), by ensuring that employees are made to feel they make a difference (Bennis 1989) and by rewarding followers informally with personal recognition (Burke 1986).

Interpersonal empathy

Empowering executives demonstrate interpersonal empathy and an ability to build relationships with many kinds of people (Kotter 1986). In demonstrating empathy, they are able to deal with the emotional side through humour and symbolism (Tichy and Devanna 1986). It has been argued that this development of personal power, courage and values is derived from a highly mature stage of personal and emotional development (Nielsen 1986; Drath 1990).

Communication

Kotter (1986) has argued that the executive's understanding and use of power are central. Empowerment arises through executives capable of managing complex interdependencies, who are networked into relevant parties in the organization and have established credible communication channels with their boss, peers and subordinates.

Vision

They have a vision and are able to develop and articulate a set of values (Burke 1986) and create inspirational and meaningful goals (Bennis and Nanus 1985).

Current management capabilities

For those firms committed to gaining competitive advantage through involvement, a key question for them is around the capability of their current executives to sustain and support employee involvement by using empowering and participative behaviours. As Bowen and Lawler (1992) have argued, if the management ranks are filled with people who believe that employees only do their best work when closely supervized, then it will be very difficult to introduce or support team-based, empowering initiatives.

When considering the likely empowering characteristics of current executives, it must be remembered that most will have developed in hierarchical organizations very different from the organizational forms their companies are moving towards. Many have flourished in bureaucratic structures with highly specified roles and an 'accountability hierarchy' (Jaques 1989). They have been motivated and rewarded as highly autonomous individuals pursuing their ambitions, need for achievement and personal enhancement. The involvement, delegation style and interpersonal empathy required of empowerment are unlikely to have been appraised, rewarded or actively developed.

The question of the empowering characteristics of executives has been examined in a range of studies. These have used a variety of methodologies, from observational studies of executive activity (Mintzberg 1973, 1975; Kotter 1982; Luthans *et al.* 1985) to in-depth biographical studies of career histories and motivational patterns (Kofodimos 1989). The general evidence from these studies suggests that while the empowering characteristics of communication and networking are likely to be prevalent, other characteristics, particularly those which involve giving recognition and feedback, and interpersonal empathy may be areas of executive weakness rather than strength.

More specifically, a key finding of the observational studies has been the considerable amount of time executives spend communicating, interacting with others and networking (Mintzberg 1973, 1975; Kotter 1982). The importance of these networking and communication activities to success is reinforced by Luthans *et al.* (1985). In this study the authors report that more rapidly promoted executives are significantly more involved in networking activities and interacting with outsiders than those with flatter promotion curves. Clearly, communication and networking are key aspects of executive success in many organizations, and within the changing paradigm of empowerment will continue to be.

However, while executives may communicate and network, the evidence is mixed about their ability to show recognition and give feedback. Hall (1976) has argued that more successful executives have participative and coaching styles and are concerned with the needs and development of subordinates. However, Luthans *et al.* (1985) in their observational study report that rapidly promoted executives spend significantly less time performing activities classified as motivating, reinforcing and giving credit.

There is strong evidence that of all the empowering characteristics, it is in the area of interpersonal sensitivity that executives are the weakest. For example, Drath (1990) reports that the executives he studied scored low in the area of 'confronting others skilfully' or 'dealing with problem subordinates' and concludes that they are not able to operate constructively through intense, immediate emotion. In an earlier study of British senior executives, Norburn and Schurz (1984) found that executives were more likely to be authoritarian, and did not consider that social adaptability or concern for others were likely to be behaviours which would enhance their success. Finally, from in-depth biographical studies, Kofodimos (1989) reports that some of the executives she observed could be hyper-active, impatient, callous, insensitive and self-serving.

It could be argued that this lack of interpersonal empathy is simply an acceptable negative aspect of the critical executive motivation of striving for mastery, power, achievement and self assertion (Bakan 1966). In effect, this objectifying of feelings increases the executive's ability to make effective interpersonal relationships by creating a persona which allows them to generate respect in a hierarchy, be tough and objective in decision-making, and create working relationships based on mutual respect and performance of duty (Gabarro 1979, 1987). While this behaviour may be well adapted for hierarchical, command control organizations, it could be argued that when interpersonal feelings become personal and less task-based, as they do in team-based organizations, executives run away from conflict or deal with it aggressively. This dilemma is perhaps best summarized by Drath (1990) when he wrote: 'Many of today's managers are in a bind. They are being asked to behave towards subordinates in ways that run counter to what has made them successful.'

Based on these findings we propose the following hypotheses: When colleagues comment on executives' strengths and development needs:

1.1 Empowering characteristics will not be amongst the most frequently cited strengths.

1.2 Empowering characteristics will be amongst the most frequently cited development needs.

1.3 In particular, interpersonal empathy will be amongst the most frequently cited development needs.

METHOD

Subjects

Data were collected from 1074 employees of a large multinational company. Target executives (n=109) represented 60 per cent of the company's 'fast-track' programme. All target executives attended a one-day workshop in which they were introduced to a programme of personal development planning. The collegiate review process, together with a number of psychometric instruments was used as a vehicle for enhancing self-awareness and hence career development. In the months following the workshops, all 'fast-trackers' were required to prepare personal development plans. Although their use and choice of diagnostics was optional, they were strongly encouraged to use the collegiate review. The target executives in this study were randomly selected from the 85 per cent who used the collegiate review.

'Fast-track'

The company's 'fast-track' programme was designed to accelerate the career development of those employees deemed to have the potential to reach senior executive positions. Selection into the 'fast-track' was rigorous. Most were nominated into the group only after successfully completing an assessment centre which contained standard intelligence tests, measures of motivational traits and a series of work-related simulations. The performance of group members was monitored periodically and only those who maintained the expected standards were kept on the 'fast-track'.

Target executives

The average age of the target executives was 35.7 (SD = 3.4); 96 were male and 13 were female. The majority of the group was British (n=65); 25 were American, 12 were continental European and 7 were Australian/Asian. Eighty-five per cent were educated to degree level and 23 per cent had additional post-graduate qualifications. All target executives had worked in more than one functional area and had international work experience.

Colleagues

The target executives were asked to complete one questionnaire on their own performance and to distribute copies to approximately 10 colleagues. They were encouraged to select colleagues from a variety of levels (i.e. subordinates, peers and superiors) and from those who had knowledge of their performance. Demographic data were not collected on these colleagues. In total, the 109 target executives sent questionnaires to 1038 colleagues, with a 93.6 per cent response rate. Including self-assessments, completed questionnaires were received from an average of 9.85 raters (SD = 2.11) per target executive.

Empowerment measures

The 92 categories were then scrutinized and compared with descriptions of empowering behaviours developed in the literature. Of the 92 categories, 25 emerged relating directly to empowering characteristics. The 25 categories are shown in Table 8.1. The table includes the category headings followed by typical comments made on target executives' strengths and development needs. For ease of interpretation the categories have been clustered into the six themes which emerged from the literature.

Table 8.1 The classification of empowerment measures

Empowering category	Strengths	Development needs
Management style		
1.1 Management of people	'Fair, compassionate, views people as peers'	'Poor at managing people generally'
1.2 Expectations of others	'Sets high standards for self and others'	'Expects too much, impatient'
1.3 Joint problem-solving	'Good at involving others in the decision-making process'	'Fails to take on board the views of others when making important decisions'
1.4 Team player/ builder	'A real team-player: sensitive to the strengths and weaknesses of individuals in the team'	'Doesn't take others with him; must replace the "yapping terrier" with a more team-based approach'
1.5 Leadership skills	'Leads from the front'	'Fails to integrate individual tasks or explain to staff how it will come together'

Table 8.1 Continued

Empowering category	Strengths	Development needs
1.6 Autocratic style	'Isn't autocratic in his approach'	'Won't "back off" in team discussions, wants to win every battle'
1.7 Flexibility of style	'He's very flexible'	'Not good in unstructured, ambiguous situations, isn't flexible, needs clear objectives'

Delegation and involvement

2.1 Propensity to delegate	'Prepared to delegate and take the risks'	'Does not have the ability to work through others, does the key tasks himself'
2.2 Delegates too much	'Is willing to get involved when we're under pressure even if it means doing things he could delegate'	'Won't roll up her sleeve. Delegates everything; always passes jobs on to others'
2.3 Delegation of responsibility	'Adopts a "hands-off" approach, allows team to pursue own objectives'	'Delegates on a "bitty" basis, not letting go of the interesting tasks'
2.4 Defends against frivolous tasks	'Defends us from frivolous requests'	'Allows our team to be inundated with purposeless jobs'

Giving recognition, feedback and developing

3.1 Motivation and encouragement	'Effectively motivates people'	'Must develop a more relaxed managerial style which has stronger motivational appeal'
3.2 Feedback	'Very good at communicating and giving feedback to subordinates'	'I never know whether I've done a good job or not. No feedback'
3.3 Recognizing and rewarding effort	'Recognizes individual and team efforts and rewards it'	'Fails to recognize the effort her team makes'

Table 8.1 Continued

Empowering category	Strengths	Development needs
3.4 Giving credit	'Champions subordinates' achievements'	'Suffers from "I" strain; seldom gives credit to anyone but himself'
3.5 Developing employees	'Keen to develop staff'	'Fails to develop staff or understand their training needs'
Interpersonal empathy		
4.1 Understanding others' needs	'Has respect for others' attitudes and sensibilities'	'Doesn't recognize that people have different needs and concerns which should be addressed'
4.2 Listening skills	'Sympathetic and constructive listener'	'Doesn't listen'
4.3 Interpersonal skills	'Gets on well with colleagues'	'Must develop the ability to interact with a wide range of personalities'
4.4 Pleasant v. Abrasive	'Nice guy, delightful sense of humour'	'Abrasive and aggressive'
Communication		
5.1 Informs others and shares information	'Prepared to share ideas and thoughts'	'Rarely gives her colleagues the whole picture'
5.2 Establishes channels of communication	'Very effective communication to all levels'	'Needs to use broader communication channels'
5.3 Networks	'Works hard at developing networks, relationships'	'Must develop networks further into the organization'
Vision		
6.1 Links objectives to strategy	'Able to link team objectives to corporate strategy'	'Needs to provide clearer direction on goals and strategy'
6.2 Communicates vision	'Communicates his vision clearly'	'Does not share his vision of the future with his direct reports'

RESULTS

Hypothesis 1

1 Empowering characteristics will not be amongst the most frequently cited strengths.
2 Empowering characteristics will be amongst the most frequently cited development needs.
3 In particular, interpersonal empathy will be amongst the most frequently cited development needs.

We found strong initial support for the first two parts of Hypothesis 1. With regard to item 1, almost half (46.8 per cent) of all development needs pertained to empowering characteristics. In contrast, and in support of 2, only a quarter (26.9 per cent) of all strengths referred to empowering characteristics.

To illustrate the difference more clearly, we examined the 15 most frequently cited strengths and development needs in more detail. Table 8.2 lists these top categories in rank order. Fifteen categories were selected because they represent approximately half of all comments made (51.8 per cent of strengths, 46.5 per cent of development needs).

The frequency of the top categories shows that a number of colleagues did in fact see these target executives as having empowering characteristics as strengths. Four of the empowering categories were ranked in the top 15: *1.4 Team player/Builder; 4.4 Pleasant v Abrasive; 4.3 Interpersonal skills; and 1.3 Joint problem-solving.* As shown in the last two columns of the table, a large portion of these executives were told by their colleagues that these empowering characteristics are part of their strengths. For example, over 80 per cent of target executives were told by at least one colleague that they were good *Team players or Builders* while over 50 per cent were told by two or more colleagues.

However, to gain a perspective on the frequency of these top empowering strengths, it is important to view them in the context of the 11 other most frequently cited strengths. The majority of comments on these managers' strengths were not about their ability to empower. These managers are clearly, however, a hard-working, determined, intelligent group with good communication and analytical skills.

Turning to the development needs also puts the empowering strengths into perspective. Of the top 15 categories, 10 were empowering characteristics. A large portion of these target executives were described as having unreasonably *1.2 High expectations of others*, as being *4.4 Abrasive, not pleasant*, as not utilizing *1.3 Joint problem-solving* and as not *5.1 Informing others or sharing information*. These four empowering development needs ranked in the top five. Again, the last two columns of Table 8.2 show the percentage of target executives who received this feedback from one or more colleagues.

The final part of Hypothesis 1 looks specifically at interpersonal empathy which is the fourth cluster from Table 8.1. It includes: *4.1 Understanding others' needs; 4.2 Listening skills; 4.3 Interpersonal skills*; and *4.4 Pleasant v. abrasive*. As can be seen in Table 8.2, *4.4 Pleasant v. abrasive* and *4.3 Interpersonal skills* were amongst the most frequently cited strengths. They ranked ninth and twelfth respectively. However, an examination of the top development needs puts this into perspective. All four interpersonal empathy categories ranked in the top 15 development needs and *4.4 Pleasant v. abrasive* was ranked second. It is clear that interpersonal empathy is a developmental area frequently commented on by the target executives' colleagues.

It appears that there is support for all three parts of Hypothesis 1. Empowering comments represented a significantly smaller portion of the most frequently cited strengths than development needs. They also represented a smaller portion of the total number of comments on strengths than on development needs. Interpersonal empathy in particular seemed to be a major developmental area for these target executives.

Hypothesis 2

2.1 The frequency with which the boss cites empowering characteristics as strengths or development needs will be significantly less than the frequency of citation by subordinates.
2.2 The subordinate will be more likely than the other rater groups to observe and comment on interpersonal empathy as a development need.

For the first part of this hypothesis, strengths and development needs were collapsed into one category. In other words, we were interested in the frequency with which the rater groups made comments on empowering characteristics regardless of whether they were strengths or development needs.

To understand better where the rater groups differed in their use of empowering comments, the most frequent empowering categories have been explored in further detail. Figure 8.1 illustrates group differences in the frequencies of the top 10 empowering strengths and Figure 8.2 illustrates the top 10 development needs. These figures graphically illustrate a cross-tabulation analysis of the top empowering categories. The categories are presented in rank order and show the percentage of each rater group who used the category to describe a target executive. The lines across each set of bars represent the percentage of all raters who used the category. That is, they represent the expected frequency for the category. When the bar extends beyond the line, the rater group made more comments on the category than expected and conversely, when the bar falls short of the line, fewer than expected comments were made. Significance levels are indicated next to the category label.

With regard to Hypothesis 2.2, we looked specifically at the four inter-personal empathy categories: *4.1 Understanding others' needs; 4.2 Listening skills; 4.3 Interpersonal skills* and *4.4 Pleasant v. Abrasive.* As can be seen from Figure 8.2, the group differences on development needs, subordinates cited these categories as often expected for *4.2 Listening skills* and more often than expected for the other three categories. In fact, in all but two of the top empowering development needs, the subordinates had as high or higher frequencies than expected.

Although we did not hypothesise that subordinates would comment on interpersonal empathy as a strength more often than the other groups, we did look at this. Three of the four interpersonal empathy categories ranked in the top ten and are therefore shown in Figure 8.1. From this figure it can be seen that subordinates cited *4.4 Pleasant v. Abrasive* and *4.2 Listening Skills* more often than expected, but cited *4.3 Interpersonal skills* less often than expected.

These two figures show that there is a complex pattern of results in how frequently the various rater groups commented on empowering strengths and development needs. What is clear, however, is that empowering charac-teristics were commented on most by subordinates. Subordinates appear to be particularly sensitive to the interpersonal empathy of their bosses. Not only were they more likely than expected to comment on it as a development need, but also in some cases as a strength.

DISCUSSION

The findings reported in this study raise a number of issues and challenges for the continuing research agenda and for practitioners. However, before debating these issues, perhaps the first question we must address is whether the findings can be generalized outside this research population. Do these findings simply reflect the idiosyncrasies of the company and its manage-ment cadre, or do they illustrate a trend in managerial behaviours which would be repeated in other companies? We are currently repeating the study in other companies and the initial findings suggest that what we are seeing here is illustrative of a wider trend. But even without these repeat studies, a case could be made for some level of generalizing. The company from which the cadre were drawn is a typical multinational, which has provided the range of career experiences, reward mechanisms and job placements found in many other multinationals.

Further, with regard to generalization, the study supports the find-ings from a number of other commentators (Norburn and Schurz 1984;

Table 8.2 Rank order of the fifteen most frequent strengths and development needs

Rank	No.[1]	Category Description	Strengths Frequency[2]	Percentage Raters[3]	Percentage Comments[4]	% target managers >=1	% target managers >=2
1		Drive/energy	286	26.6	6.5	84.4	66.1
2		Analytical	246	22.9	5.6	83.5	57.8
3	1.4	**Team player/Builder**	190	17.7	4.3	80.7	52.3
4		Intelligent	169	15.7	3.8	69.7	42.2
5		Communication skills	159	14.8	3.6	66.1	39.4
6		Determination	157	14.6	3.6	64.2	36.7
7		Action-oriented	152	14.2	3.4	74.3	46.8
8		Isolates key issues	140	13.0	3.2	71.6	36.7
9	4.4	**Pleasant v. Abrasive**	138	12.8	3.1	64.2	33.0
10		Strategic think	128	11.9	2.9	56.0	30.3
11		Organizational skills	117	10.9	2.6	56.0	29.4
12	4.3	**Interpersonal skills**	116	10.8	2.6	57.8	29.4
13		Decision-making	105	9.8	2.4	55.0	24.8
14	1.3	**Joint problem-solving**	95	8.8	2.1	53.2	22.9
15		Enthusiasm	94	8.8	2.1	47.7	22.2

% total comments made: 51.8%

Development needs

Rank	No.[1]	Description	Frequency[2]	Percentage Raters[3]	Percentage Comments[4]	% target managers[5] >= 1	% target managers[5] >= 2
1	1.2	**Expectations of others**	143	13.3	5.0	56.0	38.5
2	4.4	**Pleasant v. Abrasive**	117	10.9	4.1	48.6	23.9
3	1.3	**Joint problem-solving**	112	10.4	3.9	54.1	26.6
4		Management experience	104	9.7	3.6	50.5	24.8
5	5.1	Informs/Shares information	94	8.8	3.3	49.5	20.2
6	1.4	**Team player/builder**	89	8.3	3.1	53.2	25.7
7		Impact	88	8.2	3.1	44.0	19.3
8		Business experience	84	7.8	2.9	44.0	21.1
9	2.1	**Delegation**	77	7.2	2.7	42.2	15.6
10		Functional experience	76	7.1	2.6	43.1	20.2
11	1.1	**Management of people**	75	7.0	2.6	46.8	14.7
12		Influencing skills	74	6.9	2.6	44.0	16.5
13	4.2	**Listening skills**	73	6.8	2.5	33.0	15.6
14	4.3	**Interpersonal skills**	67	6.2	2.3	35.8	15.6
15	4.1	**Understanding others' needs**	66	6.1	2.3	43.1	13.8

% total comments made: 46.5%

Notes:

[1] Category numbers from Table 8.1.
[2] Total number of comments classified under the category.
[3] Percentage of 1074 raters who made comments classified under the category.
[4] Percentage of 4421 comments on strengths and 2880 comments on development needs classified under the category.
[5] Percentage of Target Managers who received comments classified under the category from at least one rater (> = 1) and from two or more raters (> = 2).

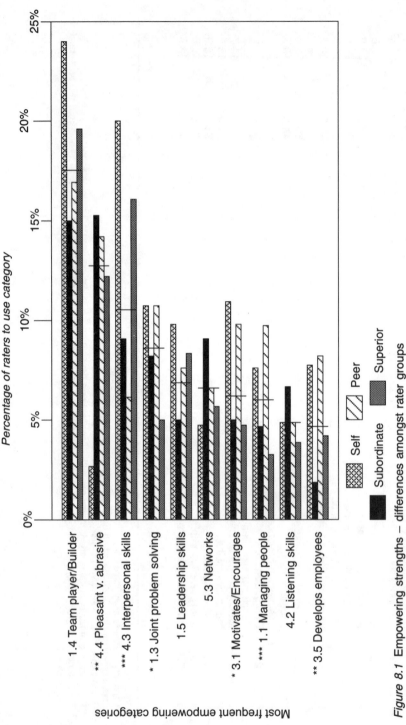

Figure 8.1 Empowering strengths – differences amongst rater groups

Notes: This figure graphically illustrates the cross-tabulation analysis of the top empowering strengths. The line across each set of bars represents the frequency with which the total set of raters made comments classified under the category.

Key: * = p<.05 ** = p<.01 *** = p<.001

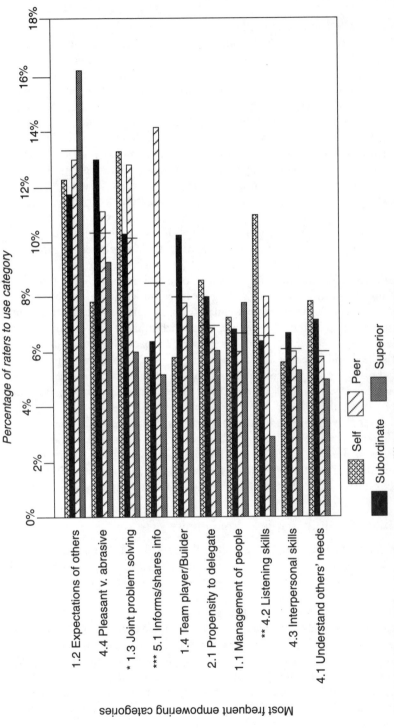

Percentage of raters to use category

Most frequent empowering categories

- 1.2 Expectations of others
- 4.4 Pleasant v. abrasive
- * 1.3 Joint problem solving
- *** 5.1 Informs/shares info
- 1.4 Team player/Builder
- 2.1 Propensity to delegate
- 1.1 Management of people
- ** 4.2 Listening skills
- 4.3 Interpersonal skills
- 4.1 Understand others' needs

Self Peer Subordinate Superior

Figure 8.2 Empowering development needs – differences amongst rater groups

Notes: This figure graphically illustrates the cross-tabulation analysis of the top empowering development needs. The line across each set of bars represents the frequency with which the total set of raters made comments classified under the category.

Key: $* = p<.05$ $** = p<.01$ $*** = p<.001$

Kofodimos 1989; Luthans *et al.*, 1985; Drath 1990). With reference to Table 8.2, the characteristics of this group are very similar to those managers described by Kegan (1982) as at the institutional stage of development. The majority of these high-potential executives are good at communicating, are hard-working and are determined to see through their agenda. When many of the group describe their strengths, they describe their personal attributes – their analytical ability, energy and determination. With this energy comes what Drath (1990) has called the 'dark side', the inability to share responsibility and control with subordinates and a lack of interpersonal sensitivity. As a significant minority of subordinates reported, there are times when their boss is abrasive, doesn't seek their views, give them feedback about their performance or share information with them.

However, considering empowering capabilities, it is important to note that the group are not homogeneous. They are seen in various ways by observer groups and they differ with regard to their empowering capabilities. Certainly about half were described by at least one person as having unrealistically high expectations of others, of being abrasive, of not engaging in joint decision-making, of failing to share information and of failing to work to build the team. Approximately one quarter were described in this manner by at least two people. Yet, within the same population a significant number of these people were seen as team players, as interpersonally skilled and pleasant and as engaging in joint problem-solving. Over half of the total group were described by at least two people as having team-building capabilities as a strength, and over a quarter as being pleasant and interpersonally skilled.

With regard to the second set of hypotheses, there are clear and significant differences between the way observer groups view the empowering capabilities of the manager. The multiple viewpoints are particularly apparent when one contrasts the view of the boss with subordinates. Nowhere is this contrast greater than within the interpersonal empathy cluster.

Implications for the practitioner community

The results of this study raise a number of issues that are important to the practitioner. These issues include the empowering capabilities of management cadres, the role of this type of qualitative information in the learning process and the role of the boss in appraisal.

It is clear from this study that a significant minority of this high-potential management group are not behaving in a manner which empowers their subordinates. This has implications for those organizations that are attempting to move from a command-control, bureaucratic structure to one based on teamwork and participation. In the short term the implication is that training programmes, coaching and facilitation may be needed to support a transformation of managerial behaviours. In the longer term it may be necessary to realign the management development processes to reinforce and develop team-based behaviours and play down the current emphasis on individualist, competitive behaviours (see Gratton 1992 for a fuller description of the transformation processes).

For this group, the provision of feedback from their bosses, peers and subordinates appeared, for some, to make a significant difference to their self-perception and their understanding of their development needs. It highlighted for us the potential role of this type of feedback data in managing the development process.

The exploration of the second hypothesis showed clearly that views on empowering capabilities differ across the observer groups. This has real implications for the appraisal and rewarding of empowering capabilities. The boss has a view, but an idiosyncratic view, of the empowering capabilities of his subordinates. It may be that they do not have an opportunity to observe their subordinates managing their teams or perhaps they do not evaluate the performance of their team in empowering terms. Whatever the reason, these results clearly demonstrate that a complete appraisal of empowering behaviour can only be gained from a 360-degree feedback process, that is one which involves data collection from the boss, peers and subordinates. This would support the growing trend to use upward feedback in the appraisal and development process. It would also reinforce the importance of upward appraisal in situations where empowering capabilities are particularly important to the success of the company.

REFERENCES

Bakan, D. (1966) *The Duality of Human Existence: an essay on psychology and religion*, Chicago: Rand McNally & Co.

Bennis, W. G. and Nanus, B. (1985) *Leaders: the strategies for taking charge.* Cambridge, Mass.: Harper and Row.

Bennis, W. (1989) *On Becoming a Leader*, Reading, MA: Addison Wesley.

Bowen, D. E. and Lawler, E. E. III (1992) 'The empowerment of service workers: what, why, how and when', *Sloan Management Review, Spring*, 31–9.

Burke, W. (1986) 'Leadership as empowering others', in S. Srivastra (ed.), *Executive Power* (pp. 51–77) San Francisco: Jossey-Bass.

Conger, J. A. and Kanungo, R. N. (1988) 'The empowering process: integrating theory and practice', *Academy of Management Review*, 13(3), 471–82.

Drath, W. H. (1990) 'Managerial strengths and weaknesses as functions of the development of personal meaning', *The Journal of Applied Behavioral Science*, 26(4), 483–99.

Gabarro, J. J. (1979) 'Socialization at the top: how CEO's and subordinates evolve interpersonal contracts', *Organizational Dynamics*, 7(3), 2–23.

Gabarro, J. J. (1987) 'The development of working relationships', in J. W. Lorsch (ed.), *Handbook of Organisational Behaviour*, Englewood Cliffs, NJ: Prentice-Hall.

Gratton, L. C. (1992) 'The development of empowering leaders: the anatomy of a fast-track', paper presented at the Strategic Management Conference, London.

Hall, J. (1976) 'To achieve or not: the manager's choice', *California Management Review*, 18(4), 5–18.

Jaques, E. (1989) *Requisite Organization*, Kingston, NY: Cason Hall.

Kegan, R. (1982) *The Evolving Self: problem and processes in human development*, Cambridge, MA: Harvard University Press.

Kofodimos, J. R. (1989) *Why Executives Lose Their Balance* Report No. 137, Greensboro, NC: The Center for Creative Leadership.

Kofodimos, J. R. (1990) 'Using biographical methods to understand managerial style and character', *Journal of Applied Behavioural Science*. 26(4), 433–56.

Kotter, P. (1982) *The General Managers*, New York: The Free Press.

Kotter, J. P. (1986) 'Why power and influence issues are at the very core of executive work', in S. Srivastra (ed.) *Executive Power* (pp. 20–33), San Francisco: Jossey-Bass.

Lawler, E. E. III, Ledford, G. E. and Mohrman, S. A. (1989) *Employee Involvement in America: a study of contemporary practice*, Houston: American Productivity & Quality Center.

Levitt, T. (1972) 'Production-line approach to service', *Harvard Business Review*, September–October, 41–52.

Luthans, F., Rosenkrantz, S. A. and Hennessy, H. W. (1985) 'What do successful managers really do? An observation study of managerial activities', *Journal of Applied Behavioral Science*, 21(3), 255–70.

Mintzberg, H. (1973) *The Nature of Managerial Work*, New York: Harper and Row.

Mintzberg, H. (1975) 'The manager's job: folklore and fact', *Harvard Business Review*, 53(4), 49–61.

Nielsen, E. (1986) 'Empowering strategies: balancing authority and responsibility', in S. Srivastra (ed.) *Executive Power* (pp. 78–110), San Francisco: Jossey-Bass.

Norburn, D. and Schurz, F. D. (1984) 'The British boardroom: time for a revolution', *Long Range Planning*, 17, 42.

Tichy, N. M. and Devanna, M. A. (1986) *The Transformational Leader*, New York: Wiley.

Torbet, W. (1976) *Creating a Community of Inquiry: conflict, collaboration, transformation*, New York: Wiley.

Part III

Facilitating development
Paul Iles

The six short chapters in this section all look at ways in which line managers can facilitate development, whether of themselves or of their colleagues and direct reports. Chapter 9, by Charles Margerison, usefully summarizes from a British and Australian perspective some of the origins of the action learning approach to management development pioneered in the UK by Reg Revans. After reviewing the key elements of the action learning approach, Margerison contrasts it with other methodologies such as the lecture, the case study and the role play. He speculates on recent shifts in management education and future developments (locating action learning in the context of these movements) to more work-based, output oriented, active formats. It is interesting to note some parallels here with the 'competence' approaches discussed in Part II, often seen as antagonistic to action learning philosophies. Margerison concludes by reviewing the central features of action learning.

Chapter 10, by Clive Fletcher, also from a British perspective, reviews the research evidence on the role of 'feedback' in performance appraisal, especially developmental feedback designed to motivate and facilitate development. He also puts forward 'self-appraisal' as having an important role to play in fostering development.

This interest in the end-user or client perspective is taken further in Chapter 11 by Christopher Mabey and Paul Iles, who examine a range of assessment and career development techniques from the point of view of those on the receiving end of such techniques. Based on a survey of UK managers undertaking an MBA course, they show that procedures which are collaborative, anchored, flexible, catalytic and prospective are regarded most positively. One such technique that meets these criteria is the development centre, and the authors discuss how centres have been used to promote individual and organizational development and manage strategic change in two UK organizations.

Chapter 12, by John Burdett, explores from an American perspective the role of the line manager in coaching staff. Coaching is often prescribed as a follow-up activity to both performance appraisal (perhaps as part of a performance management programme integrating appraisal, coaching, development and pay) and to development centre participation (in the form of follow-up to an action plan). Burdett discusses why coaching is becoming such an important managerial role in the light of the moves towards empowerment and organizational learning discussed in the earlier sections. Burdett also tries to give some guidelines as to what constitutes an effective coaching process, looking at the behaviour which has to change, the need for a coaching model, the role of problem-solving and the need for the manager to involve, probe, share, reflect, summarize, focus on commitment, and show respect. It is striking that many of these features, often at variance with traditional managerial work patterns, are similar to those identified in Parts I and II as promoting organizational and individual learning (see especially Dale, Mumford, and Gratton and Pearson, as well as Fletcher in this section).

Chapter 13, by David Kolb and colleagues, also looks from an American perspective at strategic management development from the point of view of experiential learning theory. Burdett proposes examining individual learning styles in the context of training managers in coaching, and in particular the use of the learning style inventory. This is an instrument devised by David Kolb to assess learning styles and preferences; a British version has been developed by Honey and Mumford. Kolb and his colleagues here try to take an integrative strategic look at management development as a way of responding to the learning and knowledge needs of organizations. In many ways their work seems to pre-figure much of the learning organization literature reviewed in Part I, emphasizing the roles of behavioural, perceptual, affective and symbolic competence in the face of complex environmental and organizational change and the need to link human resource development to the strategic mission of the organization. The starting point is a learning needs assessment process that attempts to identify required competences. These are seen in a similar way to the Schroder model of high-performance competences required in dynamic, turbulent environments and discussed earlier by Cockerill, but the authors map these more specifically on to their experiential learning cycle model.

The authors in particular stress the need for integrative learning and a focus on process and learning to learn, and relate their model to Argyris' work on learning climates mentioned in Part I by Butler and Salaman, as well as to a discussion of action learning. Many of the points made about the factors that facilitate learning are also similar to those made by Margerison.

This focus on active learning as a process, on life-long learning, on self-development, and on learning to learn is also taken up in the final chapter in this section, a report on a British conference on applying self-development in organizations by Mike Pedler. After a brief historical review of the major developments in management training and education in the UK in the 1960s, 1970s and 1980s, including a discussion of action learning and the experiential learning cycle, Pedler discusses the main features of self-development and the role of developers in promoting it, as well as the main themes emerging at the 1986 and 1987 conferences. Many of these themes have been discussed by other writers in this volume. For example, other chapters in this section discuss managing your own learning (e.g. Fletcher) while the then newly emerging theme of the learning company is the central focus of Part I. The theme of differences at work is a major element in Part V, managing diversity. What is particularly interesting in this report of two conferences held in the UK in the mid 1980s is how many of the participants appeared to go beyond an interest in facilitating individual learning to an interest in developing the learning company, as yet seen only dimly. Part I has described many initiatives aimed at helping make this vision a reality.

Chapter 9

Action learning and excellence in management development

Charles J. Margerison

WHAT IS ACTION LEARNING?

It was Reg Revans[1] who developed the notion of action learning. His work, which started in the British coalmines after World War II has been the foundation stone upon which the principles and methods have been built. At that time he recognized that there was a great need for increased coal output from the mines and it would be inappropriate to take managers away from the collieries to train them in the skills of managing. They were too valuable a resource to have sitting in classrooms. They needed to be in the colliery.

Therefore the obvious logic was to help them learn from their day-to-day practice. The problem was, however, that the mine manager could not learn from other managers unless they had some understanding of each others' situation and an opportunity to share and compare what they had learned.

This in itself is the key foundation upon which action learning is based. It is that managers can:

1. learn from experience;
2. share that experience with others;
3. have those colleagues criticize and advise;
4. take that advice and implement it;
5. review with those colleagues the action taken and the lessons that are learned.

Now this is what Revans has called the 'comrades in adversity' approach to learning. He believes that people really begin to learn effectively when they are confronted with difficulties and have the opportunity to share constructively their concerns and experiences with others. This is the basis for assessing how to improve their own individual skills and the tasks which they have to perform.

THE NON-ACTION LEARNING TRADITIONAL APPROACH

The traditional management education sessions are based upon the usual lecture inputs on concepts, ideas, and research. They are followed up by historical standard case studies, together with experiential simulations. These simulations usually involve some role playing and group decision-making. These are all supported by group discussions.

I now look back and consider what I and my colleagues achieved. There is no doubt the managers enjoyed the programmes, for they said so. There is no doubt I developed various skills in the design and delivery of various courses. We also managed on most occasions to pay our way and at least break even financially. However, I wonder if we made a major contribution to managerial development.

However, very rarely did we actually discuss real life managerial practices based upon real life cases brought by real life managers who were present at the time. We tended to concentrate upon the 'there and then' case examples drawn from another time and place, rather than the 'here and now' examples of those who currently have problems and opportunities to tackle.

Our skills development was done outside the context of the normal work environment and the political pressures and exigencies of that situation. Our practice sessions were on simulated problems rather than real action. Therefore I question whether there was a significant transfer of learning from the simulations to real life situations.

On the plus side, I do believe there was a transfer of technology and a transfer of cognitive maps and models. There is a lot of evidence to show that the innovative experiential simulations we devised were taken up and used by managers, particularly those with responsibility for education and training.

HOW TEACHING MISSED THE ACTION

I am surprised, looking back, that I did not spend more time working on real learning opportunities based on the projects and assignments that managers had at the time. My colleagues and I were locked into a skills development and personal growth development mindset rather than a job improvement, profit centred, action-oriented, task results mindset. We had, on reflection, adopted American-based experiential methods, rather than some of the most innovative work which was being developed in Europe.

However, when it came to educational praxis, I opted for a model one stage removed from the action. In the process I learned a lot about educational methods, which I was later able to understand in the context of the various theories ranging from behaviourism, social modelling, experiential theory, humanistic psychology, right through to action learning and action science frameworks. We were still, however, skills and models oriented, working with cases and examples drawn from a place and time distant from the participants.

THE MOVE TO ACTION-BASED MANAGEMENT EDUCATION

It is in this context that I have, over the last few years, developed my thoughts on the way processes are changing in management education and development. I have identified my previous work as experiential and my current approach as more existential. There are, of course, components of both in the way I practise.

From teaching to resourcing

The role of the teacher will decline considerably as the mini computer becomes widely available. There will be little requirement for the mass lecture in an age when everyone will have their own access to interactive self-learning devices. Teachers must, therefore, change their role and become more skilled in personal consulting and counselling. Equally, they must be able to work in the wider sense as resources, providing information, working through current problems, and applying their knowledge on a real-time basis.

From programmes to contracts

Increasingly, we will see more intra-organizational assessments based upon problems and opportunities. This contrasts with the existing product orientation where management educationalists put out a range of holiday-type brochures full of the latest educational offerings.

From individual to group orientation

The traditional emphasis has been on training and developing individuals. People have to work together as a group and increasingly they will want to learn together as a group. Such activities demand flexible educational structures and teachers capable of acting as consultative resources.

From standard cases to real cases

The case method has served us well. However, people will increasingly become less enamoured with the case written ten years ago. They will want to deal with their present case and apply their learning to current issues.

From delegating to developing

Increasingly we shall see line managers taking far more responsibility for the training and educational function. Already there are major signs that managers are prepared to act within their organizations as developers of others. This will be further facilitated by the provision of distance teaching resources.

From top-down appraisal to bottom-up appraisal

We shall also see considerable changes in the way in which people are reviewed. We shall, therefore, see people being asked to take more responsibility for their own appraisals and in addition we shall see innovations such as team appraisal.[2]

From product-centred to marketing-centred orientation

Perhaps the biggest change will be the overall philosophy and attitudial change that will take place. The result is that management educators must be much more output-oriented. Evidence is already emerging on the way in which this will affect our operations.

For example, the degree structures are being radically altered. There are many different ways of gaining an MBA. Increasingly, Masters degrees are being opened up on a part-time basis to people who wish to integrate their organizational work with concurrent research links with management educators.

In addition, there are a number of schemes available for part-time tuition and innovative ways in which industrial organizations are linking with academic organizations to enable managers to further their qualifications as an integral process of their work.

From inputs to outputs

Management education, like all education, has for too long stressed inputs. We have tried to pump into people new knowledge and skills. However, we now need to concentrate more upon outputs rather than inputs. In this context we need to get the managers to learn by producing outputs. This will involve trying to relate knowledge and skills far more to projects and tasks which have a purpose, rather than teaching them as ends in themselves.

From fixed to continuing education

We are moving very fast towards a concept of continuing education. Management education is a vital and integral part of this. The notion of acquiring an education early in life that can fit you for the whole of your career is no longer adequate. The world is changing so fast that we need to structure learning opportunities so that people can join in on a flexible basis and adapt to new requirements.

From experiential to existential management development

So far the emphasis has been on simulations as the basis for learning. We are now moving into real time existential learning.

Applying the principles in practice

I believe there is a future for existential thinking and practice in management development. Indeed, I would go further to say that it is the management education process of the future. Increasingly we have got to get our philosophy, our methods, our structures, close to the managers' life, existence and reality. In this way, we will make an impact on performance and help facilitate improvement in personal and organizational action. See Table 9.1.

How does action learning work?

The important point about action learning is that it is structured and well organized. It is no use just throwing someone a task and asking them to learn by working upon it. There needs to be an integrated and well disciplined approach. Here are some of the issues that need to be considered.

The project

All action learning is centred around some particular project task. Such projects need to be significant. They cannot be 'mickey mouse' tasks, nor can they be tasks that are so complex that they would take a lot of people a long time to do. Typically a good project is something that an individual can do over a period of between one and eighteen months.

Revans has identified four key types of projects. These are summarized in Figure 9.1.

Table 9.1 Differences between traditional learning and action learning

Traditional	Action learning
Classroom based	Work based
Individual orientation	Group orientation
Input orientation	Output orientation
Knowledge orientation	Action orientation
Passive	Active
Historical focus	Concern with the here and now and future
Cost investment	Investment return required
Producer oriented	Market/customer oriented

		Task	
		Familiar	Unfamiliar
Setting	Familiar	1	3
	Unfamiliar	2	4

Figure 9.1 Action learning options

Some examples

1 Quality circles is a good example of Box 1 situation. The Japanese companies such as Honda, Mitsubishi, Toyota and others have used this approach. Although used elsewhere, they have exercised the power of the work group to meet together for a short time each day to consider how to improve performance. This not only develops new ideas but creates better work relationships as people's views are taken into account and acted upon.
2 The early work of Revans illustrates how it is possible to get people to improve performance by exchanging situations. He invited colliery managers who knew a lot about their own mine to meet with and visit the mines run by other managers. In so doing they all learnt a lot.
3 Allied Irish Banks have initiated action learning projects for managers in settings with which they are familiar but on tasks, such as marketing, that they have not done before. This is a Box 3 example.

4 The action learning projects initiated by ACI, a large Australian organization employing over 20,000 people, chose managers to work on assignments where they had no previous experience in order to widen their understanding of the business as well as to solve real problems.

The client

All projects must have clients who identify with the project in the first place and are accountable for receiving the thought that is produced. They are in essence the people who sponsor the project as it is on their territory. Good clients take a genuine interest in helping the person doing the assignment, while at the same time applying normal business pressures to ensure high quality output in a particular period of time. It is important that clients are clear on the brief that they give to participants. It is vital that they provide continuing support and interest throughout the assignment. As Revans has indicated, it is important that the projects are problems rather than puzzles. The difference is that puzzles have a known answer, whereas problems have a number of known answers, each of which has to be assessed and acted upon.

The Set

A powerful element of all action learning is the group of people who come together. This group is known as a Set in action learning terminology.

Rather than people working alone, the action learning approach involves members sharing and comparing their problems. The idea is that by so doing they will learn from each other. It is in this sense that people learn how to tutor each other. Although they may not know a great deal about the issues that other people are working on, they can begin to provide the necessary support and encouragement.

The relationships established between Set members are critical in establishing and developing the right learning atmosphere. Typically a Set will be between six and ten people. It is possible to run programmes with a larger number, but for learning purposes it is wise to have smaller groups working together for project discussions. In these Set discussions, members are asked to outline the work that they are doing and have others comment and critique their thoughts. In this way people both learn and teach as they proceed.

The Set Adviser

The person who acts as the co-ordinator of the Set is known as a Set Adviser. His/her role is to guide and advise on the process rather than the content. In that sense they have a major role in enabling the Set to work effectively. They help build the team. Where problems arise, they encourage the members to develop a process for resolving them rather than imposing an authority pattern.

A successful Set Adviser, therefore, is helping the group to learn how to organize themselves rather than giving specific information. However, a Set Adviser can give direction as to where information can be obtained and enable participants to learn how to learn.

P and Q elements

P stands for programme knowledge and Q stands for questioning. In action learning the balance is more on the Q rather than on the P. It is assumed that if one is asking the right questions, then one can always go out and find the programme knowledge.

This balance is different, therefore, from the traditional model where the programme knowledge tends to come from the tutor who is assumed to be an authority. In action learning, the aim is learnt by doing and therefore the expert is not central to the procedures. Indeed, having too many experts around makes the learners dependent and undermines independent thinking and effort.

The aim is to try and have Q come before P. This means that the expert can only really function when the questions have been adequately formulated by the participants. Some people say this may well slow down the development process, but our experience is that it actually speeds up the real life management development process.

Outputs

It is vital in an action learning group that specific outputs are required. Therefore a timetable has to be set against which people can measure their performance. A key example of this is the identification of what has to be produced in the form of both action and a written assessment to the client by a particular day.

The essence of action learning is that it starts with a statement of what you are trying to change in the future. It then comes back to the present and the past to identify what has to be done and what is known. In short, action learning demands of the participant that you say where you wish to go before you receive any guidance and advice on how to get there. This is in contrast with the traditional model that starts with inputs of past knowledge in the hope they will be relevant to the present and the future.

REFERENCES

1. Revans, R. (1985) *The Origin and Growth of Action Learning*, Chartwell Bratt.
2. Margerison, C. (1976) 'A constructive approach to appraisal', *Personnel Review*, July.

Chapter 10

The effects of performance review in appraisal: evidence and implications

Clive Fletcher

PERFORMANCE FEEDBACK AND APPRAISAL

Giving individuals feedback on how well they are doing in their jobs is held to meet a variety of needs; from the organization's point of view, it assists effective learning so that tasks are completed correctly and helps maintain and stimulate effort towards specified goals; from the individual's viewpoint, feedback can satisfy any personal need for information on progress and facilitate social comparison with others. However, the extent to which this feedback is made available to people varies greatly.[1] One occasion when feedback is generally supposed to be available is in the performance appraisal interview.

The effects of discussing a subordinate's performance in the course of an appraisal interview have been the subject of debate for nearly thirty years, ever since Douglas McGregor[2] took his 'uneasy look' at performance appraisal. He suggested that managers shied away from appraisal because they disliked sitting in judgement on their subordinates. Norman Maier[3] soon followed by asserting that asking managers to give feedback and to help subordinates improve performance in the course of the same interview was putting them in inconsistent roles – those of judge and helper. He said that subordinates would be defensive towards any assessments given and that this would block constructive action aimed at improvement. This analysis was given support by the classic series of studies conducted in the American General Electric Company by Herbert Meyer and his colleagues.[4] They advocated on the basis of their studies that pay should be separated from the appraisal as far as possible – it simply promoted more defensiveness on the appraisee's part – and that a series of work planning and review sessions should be held. These differed from traditional appraisals in that:

1 there were more frequent discussions of performance;
2 no summary judgements or ratings were made;
3 as noted, salary action discussions were held separately;

4 the accent was on participative goal setting and problem solving, in line with the ideas of Maier and McGregor.

Overall, the weight of evidence suggests that criticism does not normally bring about an adverse effect on appraisal, although whether it achieves any beneficial effect depends heavily on a series of other factors, the main ones of which are described below.

Factors determining the effects of feedback

1 The amount of critical feedback conveyed is important. Careful reading of the General Electric studies by Meyer shows that on average the appraisees received no less than thirteen criticisms in each interview! Faced with such a barrage, it is small wonder that they reacted less than positively. A somewhat similar picture emerges from a study by Alban Metcalfe[5] which found that managers in unsuccessful appraisals spent an average of a quarter of their time either disagreeing with, criticizing or personally attacking the subordinate whom they were appraising.
2 A balanced review of performance, covering strengths as well as weaknesses seems desirable. Studies have shown that recognition of good or relatively good performance is associated with useful appraisal outcomes,[6] particularly when the individual has also had some critical feedback;[7] perhaps people feel that the appraiser has been less than frank if the news has been all good.
3 The content of the feedback should be clear, relevant and emphasize the performance of the individual rather than his or her personal characteristics.[8]
4 The availability of other sources of feedback is important. When the individual has ample feedback from the nature of the work, from day-to-day supervision, or from other personnel procedures, the reaction to it in an appraisal interview will probably be somewhat different. There should, in these circumstances, be less need for feedback *per se*, but perhaps a greater need to discuss what is already known.
5 The way the interview is handled and in particular the extent of subordinate participation encouraged, is something which research has repeatedly shown to be crucial.[9]
6 Whatever happens in an appraisal has to be seen against the background of the existing relationship between the manager and the subordinate. In fact, all the evidence is consistent in showing that it is precisely those managers who have the most frequent communication with their subordinates and who give good feedback the rest of the year that have the most productive interviews.[10]

It is not difficult to devise appraisal schemes that embody all the 'right' features, that look good on paper. But in doing so, one is usually making a variety of erroneous assumptions about the circumstances the scheme will operate under; they are generally far from ideal.

SELF-APPRAISAL: A MORE ROBUST APPROACH?

The reluctance to deal with performance issues in appraisal interviews seems to stem from an anxiety over the appraisees' reactions, which in turn is related to the appraising manager's uncertainties as to how to broach the question of weaknesses in the interview. There is the quite justifiable fear that an ill-chosen word may spark off a hostile and defensive response from the subordinate. The situation is exacerbated by the likelihood that the manager's perceptions of his subordinates' performances are going to be based on a limited and possibly biased awareness of their activities. If there has been a lack of communication prior to the appraisal, the subordinates will not only feel that their manager does not have an accurate picture of how they have been doing, but they will also be all too ready to be defensive and difficult in the appraisal.

One way round many of these problems is to implement self-appraisal. The person who has the greatest knowledge of what he or she has actually done is the appraisee. By passing the initiative to the subordinate, with the increase in participation in the process that this makes inevitable, a much higher level of appraisee motivation is engendered.

The obvious objection to such an approach is that an individual's self-appraisal will be subject to self-serving biases; people will give a better picture of their achievements than is justified. Before considering the evidence on this assertion, it is worth pointing out that appraisers' assessments can be biased too, albeit in the opposite direction. There is little doubt that managers' evaluations of their subordinates' performance are subject to a whole series of distortions.[11]

To be sure, leniency effects in self-appraisal are consistently shown, but a number of factors contribute to that and have important implications for the practical use of this approach. First, many of the research studies are just that – research studies. Meyer[12] reports that when subordinates are asked to prepare self-appraisals for real appraisal interviews, they are much more modest, possibly because modesty is a valued attribute in our culture whereas blowing one's own trumpet is frowned upon. The type of ratings make a big difference too, and there is some evidence to suggest that when the individual's self-assessment is anchored on behavioural observation (rather than general ratings of performance qualities) there is much greater objectivity.[13] The context of the appraisal plays a part, because if pay is linked to the ratings given then this will increase leniency effects (as it makes any other aspect of the appraisal more difficult too). So, the final picture is not so bad – people can be encouraged to make realistic self-appraisals when comparing themselves to other people.

There is clearly one type of self-appraisal that holds great promise. This is when individuals are asked to assess different aspects of their job performance relative to one another rather than against the performance of peers. The evidence here shows that subordinates' judgements of this kind are more discriminating (less 'halo' effect) than are those of their supervisors, and that appraisals based on such self-assessments can be extremely effective.[14] Such appraisals become more development-centred, concentrating on the remedying of (relative) weaknesses and capitalizing on strengths. The role that the subordinates have played in identifying these increases their willingness to implement action steps arising out of them. Interestingly, Meyer has found that subordinate-prepared appraisals work very well with poor performers, but less well – unsurprisingly – with authoritarian managers or where there is a dependent relationship between subordinate and manager.

Implications

In organizations that do not see establishing comparability as one of the functions of appraisal, and those where there is less need for overall ratings of performance or potential, the self-appraisal approach seems to have a lot to offer. Where the organization does use appraisal as a means of comparing people and possibly of rewarding them, an element of self-review still seems worthwhile. This can be done by adopting a multiple-source appraisal, such as that operated in one of the companies of the Gulf Oil group where the supervisor, subordinates and peers of the appraisee, along with the appraisee him – or herself, all contribute to the assessment.[15]

CONCLUSION

An appraisal based on an individual's own assessment of his or her performance can overcome many of the problems traditionally associated with performance feedback in the appraisal interview. It is a more flexible and robust approach and one that has ample evidence of effectiveness.[16]

REFERENCES

1 Larson, J. R. (1984) 'The performance feedback process: a preliminary model', *Organizational Behaviour and Human Performance*, 33, pp. 42–76.
2 McGregor, D. (1957) 'An uneasy look at performance appraisal', *Harvard Business Review*, 35, pp. 89–94.
3 Maier, N. R. F. (1985) 'Three types of appraisal interview', *Personnel*, March–April, pp. 27–40.
4 Meyer, H. H., Kay, E. and French, J. P. R. (1985) 'Split roles in performance appraisal', *Harvard Business Review*, 43, pp. 123–9.

Kay, E., Meyer, H. H. and French, J. P. R. (1965) 'Effects of threat in a performance appraisal interview', *Journal of Applied Psychology*, 49, pp. 311–17.

5 Alban Metcalfe, B. (1982) 'Leadership behaviour in the appraisal interview – a critical summary of research findings and a proposal for a new methodology in future research', MRC/SSRC Social and Applied Psychology Unit paper.

6 Brown, K.M., Willis, B. S. and Reid, D. H. (1981) 'Differential effects of supervisor verbal feedback and feedback plus approval institutional staff performance, *Journal of Organizational Behaviour Management* 3, pp. 57–68.

7 Fletcher, C. and Williams, R. S. (1976) 'The influence of performance feedback in appraisal interviews', *Journal of Occupational Psychology*, 49, pp. 75–83.

8 Prue, D. M. and Fairbank, J. A. (1981) 'Performance feedback in organizational behaviour management; a review', *Journal of Organizational Behaviour Management*, 3, (1) pp. 1–16.

9 Wexley, K. N., Singh, J. P. and Yukl, G. A. (1973) 'Subordinate personality as a moderator of the effects of participation in three types of appraisal interviews', *Journal of Applied Psychology*, 58, pp. 54–9.

Hillery, J. M. and Wexley, K. N. (1974) 'Participation effects in appraisal interviews conducted in a training situation, *Journal of Applied Psychology*, 59, pp. 168–71.

Greller, M. M. (1975) 'Subordinate participation and reactions to the appraisal interview', *Journal of Applied Psychology*, 60, pp. 544–9.

10 Fletcher, C. A. (1978) 'Manager/subordinate communication and leadership style: a field study of their relationship to perceived outcomes of appraisal interviews', *Personnel Review*, 7, 1981, pp. 59–62.

Ilgen, D. R., Peterson, R. B., Martin, B. A. and Boeschen, D. A. (1981) 'Supervisor and subordinate reactions to performance appraisal sessions', *Organizational Behaviour and Human Performance*, 28, pp. 311–30.

11 Fletcher, C. (1984) 'What's new in performance appraisal', *Personnel Management*, February pp. 20–2.

12 Meyer, H. H. (1982) 'The use of self-assessments in performance appraisal', paper presented at the 20th International Congress of Applied Psychology, Edinburgh.

Bassett, G. A. and Meyer, H. H. (1968) 'Performance appraisal based on self-review,' *Personnel Psychology*, 21, pp. 421–30.

13 Downs, S., Farr, R. M. and Colbeck, L. (1978) 'Self-appraisal: a convergence of selection and guidance', *Journal of Occupational Psychology*, 51, pp. 271–8.

Latham, G. P. and Wexley, K. N. (1981) *Increasing Productivity through Performance Appraisal*, Addison-Wesley, Reading, Mass.

14 Meyer, H. H. (1980) 'Self-appraisal of job performance,' *Personnel Psychology*, 33, pp. 291–95.

Thornton, G. C. (1980) 'Psychometric properties of self-appraisals of job performance,' *Personnel Psychology*, 33, pp. 263–71.

15 Stinson, J. and Stokes, J. (1980) 'How to multi-appraise', *Management Today*, June, pp. 43, 45, 48, 53.

16 Some elements of this article appear in Fletcher, C. and Williams, R. (1985) *Performance Appraisal and Career Development*, Hutchinson, London.

Chapter 11

Career development practices in the UK: a participant perspective[1]

Christopher Mabey and Paul Iles

Despite the fact that more organizations are taking career development seriously and adopting a wider range of practices and techniques in order to facilitate this, relatively little is known about how managers and other employees react to the career development they receive and how they compare the effectiveness and value of such programmes as developmental experiences. Those participating in career development activities are, in an important sense, the end-users or internal customers of career development yet their perspective is often ignored or underplayed. Perhaps organizational leaders misguidedly believe that any help they provide employees in this area will be received positively because it is better than none at all.

CAREER DEVELOPMENT PRACTICES: USE AND EFFECTIVENESS

To find out how widely various career development techniques are used and the reactions of managers towards them, we report here on the findings of a survey of Master of Business Administration (MBA) students at the Open Business School. The participants at two residential schools were presented with a list of nine career development techniques, each briefly defined (see Table 11.1). They were asked to indicate their personal experience and their organizations' usage of each technique and then to record their reaction to each technique in terms of fairness and usefulness. Completion of the survey was voluntary and 120 out of a possible 164 returned questionnaires, a response rate of 73 per cent. While we recognize that findings from such a small sample can hardly be generalized to middle managers in the UK, we have reason to believe that they are more representative than might at first be imagined. Respondents were typically managers in their mid-thirties (60 per cent were aged between 30 and 39 years) and 17 per cent of the sample group were female. Almost two thirds were employed by private sector companies, 29 per cent came from the public sector and 3 per cent came from voluntary or non-profit organizations. There was a reasonable spread across organizations according to their size:

17 per cent from those employing under 100 people, 17 per cent from those employing between 10 and 500, 7 per cent from those employing between 500 and 1000 people, and the remainder (53 per cent) worked for companies of 1000 staff or more. They were not asked to identify their employer, but we know from course registration data that the sample of 120 represent almost as many different organizations. In general, the sample also seemed demographically very similar in age, experience, background, gender and organizational affiliation to the wider popular of Open Business School MBA students.

Perhaps the greatest source of potential distortion is the fact that the sample group are studying for an MBA, which despite the growing numbers of managers pursuing such a qualification sets them apart as more ambitious and career minded than their peers. This, together with employer sponsorship of the MBA, would suggest that the incidence and experience of other career development techniques would be more prevalent in this sample than in the wider population of middle management. Having said this, a recent survey of 827 fellows and members of the British Institute of Management reported that 60.2 per cent of respondents undertook management training at their own initiative, with the employer bearing the cost, and a further 12.7 per cent were not only responsible for initiating the training but also bore the cost themselves (Mansfield and Poole 1991). These figures are not inconsistent with our MBA sample: 60.5 per cent were being sponsored or part-sponsored on the programme by their employer, while 30.2 per cent initiated the training and were paying their own way. Our findings also cast light on the relative availability of different career development procedures to our admittedly select sample, as well as the relative acceptability of such techniques. With these caveats about representativeness in mind, we can now describe the findings.

Table 11.1 shows how extensively such techniques were experienced by

Table 11.1 Assessment and career development techniques: extent of use (120 MBA managers in the UK)

Technique	Used in present organization (%)	Personally experienced in present or previous organization (%)
Career reviews	77	70
Informal mentors	43	30
Career-path information	35	27
Fast-track programmes	34	12
Assigned mentors	26	11
Psychometrics with feedback	22	20
Self-assessment materials	19	18
Development centres	18	6
Career planning workshops	14	6

this sample. The most frequently encountered career development procedures were career reviews with superiors, followed by informal mentoring and the provision of career path information. This finding is similar to the results of a US study of 266 professional and managerial students attending business courses by Portwood and Granrose (1987) who found career reviews, job posting and monitoring to be the most frequently used techniques. These appear to be procedures that can be conducted as part of day-to-day organizational life, not requiring particular investment in some kind of 'special programme'.

Assigned mentors, development centres, psychometrics with feedback, career planning workshops, self-assessment materials and fast-track programmes were less likely to have been experienced by our sample. These are programmes that require some kind of specific investment of resources, as well as internally generated or 'bought-in' expertise.

Table 11.2 shows that there is little difference between the public and private sectors in the use of career review, psychometrics with feedback, career planning workshops, career path information, or informal mentors. However, public sector organizations seem to make less use of development centres, fast-track programmes, and self-assessment materials, though more use of assigned mentor programmes. Table 11.2 also shows that larger organizations in general made more use of career assessment procedures, especially development centres and fast-track programmes, though self-assessment materials were favoured by smaller organizations.

Table 11.3 shows that women reported having more experience of a

Table 11.2 Use (%) of assessment/career development techniques by sector and size of organization (120 MBA managers in the UK)

| | Sector | | Size (no. of employees) | | | |
	Public	Private	1–99	100–499	500–999	1000+
Career reviews	73	79	64	70	50	87
Psychometrics/ feedback	24	22	11	15	37	25
Career planning workshops	12	16	5	5	0	23
Self-assessment materials	12	20	16	35	13	14
Career path information	33	32	11	40	38	38
Fast-track programmes	21	34	6	20	0	45
Development centres	9	16	0	10	0	21
Assigned mentors	27	20	11	15	38	27
Informal mentors	43	37	28	30	28	48

Table 11.3 Personal experience (%) of assessment/career development
techniques by gender and age (120 MBA managers in the UK)

| | Gender | | Age (years) | | |
	Male	*Female*	*Under 35*	*35–39*	*40+*
Career reviews	65	78	67	73	63
Psychometrics/ feedback	18	35	22	31	7
Career planning workshops	5	24	6	10	7
Self-assessment materials	16	24	16	17	19
Career path information	24	28	26	17	33
Fast-track programmes	10	18	14	17	0
Development centres	6	6	12	0	0
Assigned mentors	11	12	12	10	9
Informal mentors	23	41	22	28	31

wide range of procedures, informal mentors, fast-track programmes, self-assessment materials, psychometrics with feedback, and career planning workshops in particular. It is unclear whether many of these programmes (especially psychometrics with feedback, career planning workshops, and self-assessment materials) have been specifically targeted at women as part of positive action efforts to identify and overcome career blocks, or whether the relatively few women in this sample (17 per cent) are a very highly selected group of women who have experienced many management/ career development efforts in their careers. Alternatively, this finding could be related to their younger age. Table 11.3 also shows that younger respondents were more likely to have encountered development centres, fast-track programmes and psychometric tests with feedback. This is possibly because the introduction of procedures is relatively recent and/or because such procedures are usually used only at initial career stages.

REACTIONS TO CAREER DEVELOPMENT PROCEDURES

Earlier work on assessment centres (Robertson *et al.* 1991; Fletcher 1991) has demonstrated the significance of procedural acceptability and adequacy, so it is of interest to determine how our sample reacted to the techniques they have experienced.

The MBA sample of 120 managers representing private, public and voluntary organizations were also asked to evaluate a range of career development techniques that they had personally experienced, either with their existing or previous employers (see Table 11.4). Though absolute

Table 11.4 Reactions (%) to career development techniques (120 MBA managers in the UK)

	Fair	Useful	Helped personal develop- ment	Helped career develop- ment	Increases organization effective- ness	Makes me more positive
1 Assigned mentors (n = 10)	90	78	67	50	60	50
2 Psychometric tests with feedback (n = 19)	84	84	84	78	80	56
3 Career review with superiors (n = 67)	79	82	76	76	82	73
4 Career path information (n = 10)	77	71	64	67	58	63
5 Self assessment materials (n = 17)	77	77	50	65	75	69
6 Informal mentors (n = 28)	68	75	76	74	74	70
7 Developmental assessment centres (n = 6)	67	100	100	67	75	75
8 Career planning workshops (n = 6)	67	67	72	50	50	43
9 Fast-track programmes (n = 12)	50	60	60	67	64	64

numbers were small for some techniques, some interesting findings have emerged. Having mentors assigned to them was seen as the fairest process of those listed, but with a relatively low impact on career development. In contrast, informal mentors were not only more widespread but also seen as more useful and influential in career terms. However, probably because of its hit-and-miss, 'who you know' nature these were perceived as considerably less fair than assigned mentoring. Fast-track programmes appear to suffer from a similar concern about fairness, even by those on them!

Career reviews with superiors were highly rated across all dimensions. Tapping into the power nexus of the enterprise may be the crucial factor here: not only is the technique seen to be just and useful but it is also anchored in organizational reality. It is perhaps for this reason that the more passive techniques of career path information and self-assessment materials meet with a more muted, though still favourable response.

Psychometric tests with feedback were also highly rated by participants. They were perceived as assisting personal and career development, as well as enhancing the organization's effectiveness. This represents a remarkable difference from the relatively low ratings of psychometric tests when used in a selection context (Mabey and Iles 1991), and the opportunity for feedback appears to account for this favourable reaction to similar techniques. Only a small sample had experienced developmental assessment centres, all of whom saw them as useful and helping personal development. While not all felt it a fair process, of all techniques it engendered the most positive feelings about the organization, as against career planning workshops, which engendered the least, and surprisingly were rated as helping least in career development. This could well be the result of the individual focus of development centres and the collaborative nature of ensuing feedback sessions. By contrast, career planning workshops may be viewed as providing useful tools for personal development, but not organizational specific enough to assist career planning.

Overall, there seems to be a disparity between the low usage of some techniques and their favourable reception as career development tools. This applies particularly to psychometric tests with feedback and development centres, which on the basis of these data represent unexploited potential in terms of human resource management. See Table 11.4.

It would appear that career reviews, together with the provision of informal mentors and development centres are the career development techniques that generate the most positive feelings among managers.

How can we explain these results and what lessons do they contain for implementing more user-friendly career development? Before we go on to give some tentative answers to these questions, let us take a closer look at particular career development programmes run in some UK organizations.

Some company specific examples of career development

One major financial services organization we shall call NATCO had instituted a managerial assessment and development programme for internal staff designed to identify and develop employees with executive potential. Managers selected for the programme were assessed at various parts in their career, and if successful, maintained a place on the organization's 'fast-track' development programme. In their late teens, successful performance on a biodata questionnaire gave participants access to a situational interview, where they were presented with a series of job-related situations. High scorers in this interview then entered a management development programme, with an initial assessment in a one-day centre in their early twenties. If successful in this centre, they gained access to a self-development programme, which included a five-day development centre in their mid-twenties. Passing another assessment centre at around age 30 led

Table 11.5 Financial services organization management development
          programme

Average Age	Procedure	Main empirical findings
c. 18–20	Biodata	Negative reactions to technique.
c. 18–20	Situational Interview	Negative reactions to technique, especially for 'fail' group. Perceived career impact linked to post-assessment commitment.
c. 24	Assessment Centre A	Positive reactions to technique by both pass and fail groups. Perceived career impact linked to post-assessment commitment.
c. 26	Self Development Centre	Fairly positive reaction.
c. 28–30	Assessment Centre B	Generally positive reactions: stronger for 'pass' group. Adequacy of assessment procedure linked to post-assessment commitment.
	Executive Interview	

to an executive interview, and final career tiering at the executive level. Table 11.5 shows the structure of the programme, and summarizes the key results obtained from a survey of participant attitudes and reactions after assessment at the various career stages.

In terms of our interest in end-user reaction to career development, one important finding is that assessment and development centres were the most well regarded procedures. They are seen as fairer, more valid, and more accurate than other procedures, and participants also welcomed their motivational impact, the value of the feedback they received and the worthwhileness of the development recommendations made.

In fact, these findings accord with the results of other studies evaluating the effectiveness of assessment and development practices in UK companies. For instance, in research with another financial services organization, Fletcher (1991) confirmed the positive impact of assessment centres for career development purposes on participants' work commitment and psychological well being. Finally, an empirical evaluation was conducted of the career development process for first level managers in Rank Xerox UK (Mabey and Iles 1993). This included a diagnostic development centre, personal development plans (incorporating a range of off-the-job skills modules, self development via distance learning and on-the-job projects, culminating in an assessment centre to determine readiness for management appointment. Among the aspects of this 12–18 month programme regarded most favourably by participants were: the relatively vigorous and objective assessment of managerial skills resulting in 'hard-hitting' but fair feedback, the fact that the job dimensions against which they were developed and assessed were important to the company generally (as expressed in other HR policies and processes) and didn't shift during the course of the programme, and the occasions where individual development was taken seriously by the candidate's line manager who would supervise and coach their development over time.

What can be learnt about effective career development practices?

What these empirical studies show is that some procedures are much better regarded than others by recipients, in terms of their perceived accuracy, validity, fairness, usefulness and value. In particular, development centres, psychometric tests with feedback and career reviews with superiors seem particularly well regarded. Why should this be? What features do such procedures have in common that differentiate them from other procedures much less well regarded, such as biodata, situational interviews, career planning workshops and self-assessment materials? What such procedures seem to share is that they are:

- *Prospective, not just retrospective* – they focus on future actions and plans as much as past or present activities. The feedback received and the action plans generated can be useful in developing new insights, skills and attitudes.
- *Catalytic, not just analytic* – such procedures do not just present a measurement of personal qualities or skills at a certain point in time, they can also promote personal reflection, greater self-insight, and a stimulus for personal growth.
- *Collaborative, not just controlling* – such procedures do not solely produce a one-way assessment of the person by the organization, with the organization making all the decisions about what happens next. If used appropriately, the participant can also have significant input into what judgements are made and what actions should be undertaken.
- *Overt, not opaque* – such procedures can enable participants to see clearly the connections between the criteria they are being assessed against, the way the various activities undertaken relate to their job, organization and career, and the ways feedback and action planning can be useful to their own personal and career development.
- *Anchored, not abstract* – such procedures can be firmly anchored in organizational reality, including the realities of power and influence, by involving line managers as assessors or reviewers, by employing criteria and activities clearly relevant to career progression and organizational

effectiveness and by demonstrably tying feedback and action planning to organizational objectives and strategies.

Development centres in particular seem to perform well when assessed against such standards, in contrast to some other procedures which might be seen negatively – as retrospective (e.g. psychometric tests), controlling (e.g. psychometric tests), opaque (e.g. some personality tests, biodata), or abstract (e.g. biodata, some psychometric tests, career planning workshops, self assessment materials). In addition, development centres seem to be a useful vehicle for career development when they:

- use skilled, trained assessors. This establishes a climate which encourages participation, involvement, dialogue and mutual decision making, and which create an ethos which is facilitative and supportive rather than judgmental and evaluative. In this way participants can feel that they have experienced something of value. Not all centres will be so well designed or use such skilled assessors, but it is likely that the centre experience can be positive if such design features are built in.
- enable feedback and development plans to be tailored personally to individual need in ways that are beyond the reach of more standardized, mass-produced training courses and packages.
- when they facilitate diagnosis, action planning and decision making. If the focus is less on the means or particular techniques than on ends or goals, a variety of development options can be constructed and tailored to individual needs, wants and preferences. In a very real sense, line managers, assessors, designers and delegates are all co-producers of the experience, and the development centre framework is flexible enough to include the perspectives of all parties as they evolve over time.

CONCLUSIONS

We started out by saying that not a lot is known about the extent of usage of different career development techniques. Our cross-section of MBA managers has helped to fill this knowledge gap, but has also demonstrated an area of unexploited potential. Development centres are not widely used, but they can combine the objectivity of psychometric tests, the organizational salience of well-designed assessment centres, together with the collaborative benefits of a good career review conducted with your boss. Furthermore, a closer observation of career development practices in other UK companies has shown that in many cases participants' commitment to the organization and career intentions are related to their attitudes towards the assessment/development procedures used. Using 'user-friendly' procedures will not only result in more satisfied employees, but probably more committed ones as well.

NOTE

1 This chapter was developed from an earlier article in the *British Journal of Management* (1993, 4, 3, 103–111).

REFERENCES

Fletcher, C. (1991) 'Candidates' reactions to assessment centres and their outcomes: a longitudinal study', *Journal of Occupational Psychology*, 64, pp. 117–27.

Mabey, C. and Iles, P. A. (1993) 'The strategic integration of assessment and development practices: succession planning and new manager development', *Human Resource Management Journal*, 3 (4), 1–19.

Mabey, C. and Iles, P. A. (1991) 'HRM from the other side of the fence', *Personnel Management*, February, pp. 50–3.

Mansfield, R. and Poole, M. (1991) 'Advancing the horizons: the central role of the manager', paper presented at the British Academy of Management, Annual Conference, Bath, September.

Portwood, J. D. and Granrose, C. S. (1987) 'Organisational career management programs: what's available? what's effective?', *Human Resource Planning*, 9 (3), pp. 107–19.

Robertson, I. T., Iles, P. A., Gratton, L. and Sharpley, D. (1991) 'The impact of personnel selection and assessment methods on candidates', *Human Relations*, 44 (9), pp. 963–82.

Chapter 12

To coach, or not to coach – that is the question!

John O. Burdett

INTRODUCTION

In a business world marked by complexity, long-established paradigms of management marked by manager-centred control must give way to employee-centred self-management. Making the transition, however, is for many managers, both difficult, and at times painful. At the heart of empowerment lies an entirely different role for the manager, a role that in many instances owes little to traditional assumptions regarding the manager/subordinate relationship.

The organizations that will thrive are those which build sustainable competitiveness, stimulate learning, and provide meaning for all of those involved in the enterprise, and not just those who are at the apex of the corporate triangle.

At the eye of this competitive hurricane lies the basic relationship between a manager and those who report to him or her – a relationship dependent in large measure on the manager's ability to facilitate growth. A role that reframes the management of resources to one perhaps best described as the 'management of context'. A role where the pivotal competency becomes, above all else, the manager's ability to coach.

Few managers are natural coaches. Few have an inherent flair for bringing out the best from those around them. The majority of managers find that coaching is an acquired skill – a skill that must be honed over a lifetime. Even for those who appear to have highly developed natural skills much can be learned, from the experience of others, and by focusing on personal growth as a critical dimension.

The challenge for managers is further extended in that effectiveness and growth represent complementary paradigms of management that paradoxically necessitate that managers engage in learning while concurrently creating a context of learning for others.

The coaching discussion, which is a critical element in the coaching process, is poorly understood and poorly carried through. Performance appraisal, coaching, tutoring and mentoring processes if not linked to coaching actions represent additional parts of the problem rather than integral and linked parts of the solution.

All of these issues represent barriers to coaching – barriers that are in some instances difficult to overcome, barriers that if not addressed add to and generate a multiplier effect on the overall degree of complexity.

At the same time it is worth pointing out that there are a number of factors that are strongly in favour of effective coaching. Managers invariably recognize that coaching is of paramount importance and are very enthusiastic when offered development in 'how to coach'.

One way to view the factors for and against coaching is to do so by means of a force-field analysis (see Figure 12.1). The challenge is to encourage and reinforce the positive forces while at the same time working hard to remove the negative.

IDENTIFYING THE BEHAVIOUR THAT HAS TO CHANGE

In his work on change Michael Beer identifies the fact that organizations must build on or create a sense of dissatisfaction for change to flourish.[1] This dissatisfaction sometimes fuelled by crisis must, in normal times, be generated by building dissatisfaction among employees as to their ongoing performance or behaviour.

Central to the issue of building this dissatisfaction is feedback. Top management can do its part by focusing on the company's competitiveness, costs, level of service and quality. Dissatisfaction can be further engendered by moving issues of competitiveness from an abstract to a specific level of understanding – visits to customers, bringing customers in-house, and even having employees examine competitors' products are ways of doing this.

At the micro level with individual employees, however, the feedback must focus on easily identifiable issues and encompass specific elements of behaviour.[2]

Unfortunately, this is often where coaching breaks down, for where the manager has difficulty identifying specifically what behaviour has to change it is unlikely that effective coaching can be carried out. The net result is a strong tendency to criticize the employee when results have not been achieved, and a managerial lack of ability to use critical incidents as a means of reinforcing and crafting self-fulfilling employee behaviour.

A further dimension lies with the task orientation of many managers. While action is a critical dimension of successful managerial performance, a lack of ability to step back and focus, not only on what is being achieved but on how subordinates are going about it, results in going activity which gives little time for reflection and little time for understanding the context in which manager and subordinate operate. Obviously, managers need some help.

The form of help with most impact was training managers to work with

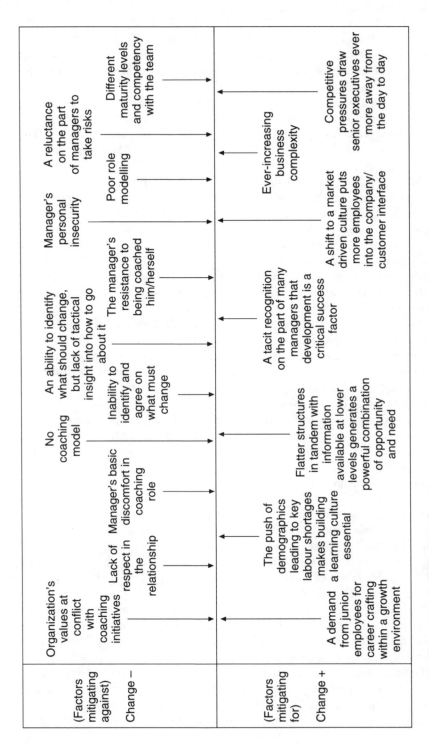

Figure 12.1 The factors impacting on coaching

subordinates to develop an outline of the behaviour characteristics for the role in question (see Figure 12.2). Essential characteristics were developed twice, once as the job existed in real time, and a further set based on the way the job was perceived to be in three to five years.

Getting managers to develop the essential characteristics is not as difficult as some might think. In fact the value from both a coaching and recruitment standpoint was grasped at the beginning. Equally important, like any good process, it soon had a life of its own and ownership passed quickly to line managers.

Managers had a remarkable facility to think through the answer to questions such as 'What is the worst thing that can go wrong?', and 'Describe the qualities of the current job incumbent'. Managers were also able to go over, in detail, critical incidents related to a wide range of positions in their businesses. Similarly, in going through possible future scenarios the focal issues were never far from their grasp. Moving the critical job success factors from those based on responsibilities to those based on behaviour was, in the early stages, basically a matter of coaching managers to make the mental shift.

From the organization's point of view, although tempting in that it would have simplified things, it was believed important not to develop a shopping list of generic essential characteristics. Line management's ownership of the process came about because the essential characteristics captured the nature of the position in what, for the manager concerned, was literally the unique role of their business.

Apart from the issue of ownership, the belief was that producing a series of generic essential characteristics was inadequate in capturing issues such as the stage of growth of the individual business, the maturity of the management team, the turbulence of the marketplace and the degree of teamwork demanded.

A second level of help for managers was to identify the terms used in defining the essential characteristics that were common. To achieve this, definitions were written for each of the common behavioural terms in question. This process not only extended the manager's behavioural vocabulary, an important point in itself, but also an in-depth understanding of a broader range of behaviours became an important building block in starting to improve the quality of coaching.

The ability to identify behaviour that has to change is an essential element of a successful coach. Without such a shared understanding, development plans lack meaning and the time and energy spent on coaching starts to be seen as time wasted.

Defining the behaviour that has to change is only one of the critical issues for managers who wish to be effective coaches. A focus on essential characteristics helps define what must change but, without appropriate structure to the coaching discussion commitment to the new direction

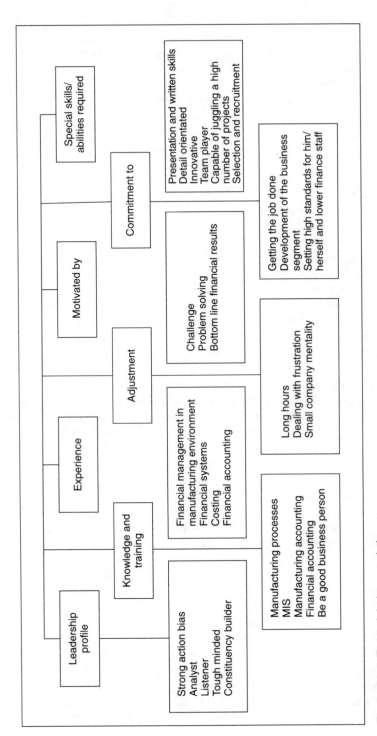

Figure 12.2 Essential characteristics

from the coachee is highly unlikely. Similarly, unless the manager fully understands the nature of respect as the basic building block in behaviour change, little of meaning is likely to occur.

Most important of all the environment must be supportive of coaching initiatives, otherwise the initial energy and enthusiasm from those creating the learning culture dissipates into feelings of frustration and even anger.

THE NEED FOR A COACHING MODEL

It is not sufficient for the employee to be given or have access to data regarding his/her contribution. There must also be discussion to provide meaning. The dialogue must also provide an opportunity for underlying assumptions to be explored. Commitment is a quality not easily generated in a non-interpersonal context.

The dialogue implicit in the coaching discussion may be a structured time-consuming activity or, alternatively, a few minutes exploring the employee's response to a problem or opportunity.

Our own model (Figure 12.3) emphasizes the problem solving central to the coaching discussion as well as the need for the manager to involve, probe, share, reflect and summarize, as dimensions of active listening. The desired output of the discussion being a mutual commitment/contract to focus on one or more critical behaviours.

We perceive the model not as a straight-jacket but as a flexible tool establishing key steps in the discussion itself and outlining the interpersonal skills implicit in the discussion. Our experience has been that comfort with the model facilitates a higher level of comfort when a coaching discussion is carried out. This in turn not only increases the number of coaching contacts but results in contacts being more specific by way of content.

Our approach to training managers in how to coach encompasses a comprehensive review of learning styles as well as an analysis of the participant's own style using: the learning style inventory; an in-depth review of why managers derail, utilizing research from the Centre for Creative Leadership; as well as extended use of case studies drawn from inside the organization.

In a two-day workshop, managers move from artificial case studies to situations they face in the work situation. Learning, around the latter, and especially the skills involved in problem sharing and reflecting, are supported by using teams of five – two carrying out the discussion and three observing, using a predeveloped checklist.

From our own viewpoint, we found difficulty in separating tutoring, mentoring, counselling and performance improvement, in that we had numerous examples of where all four processes were being used concurrently to address one key problem. In giving managers insight into the difference of emphasis we developed a simple outline of both the syner-

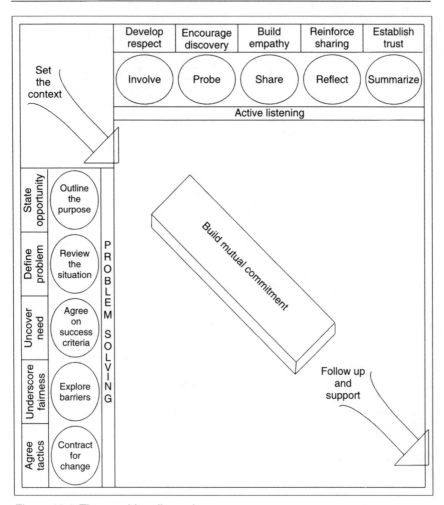

Figure 12.3 The coaching discussion

gistic relationship between the four processes and the power base of each (see Figure 12.4). We considered all four processes to be coaching in that all were focused on extending or improving the employee's contribution.

An understanding of the difference between tutoring, mentoring, counselling and performance improvement was important in that it was our perception that only the employee's immediate boss could undertake performance improvement planning. Our rationale was based on the premise that only the manager had a power base consistent with all of the issues. Debate regarding the role of the manager as a mentor was, however, less conclusive. We perceived that there were occasions, especially when a seasoned executive was working with a younger manager, where the boss

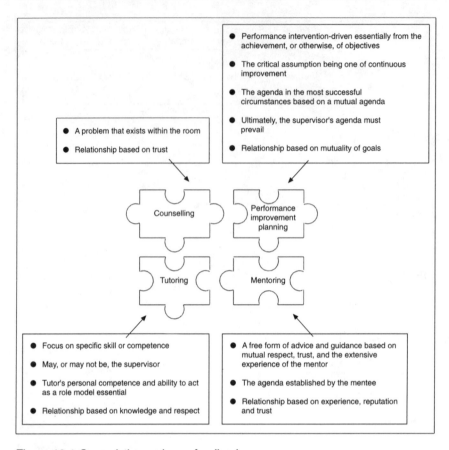

Performance intervention-driven essentially from the achievement, or otherwise, of objectives

The critical assumption being one of continuous improvement

The agenda in the most successful circumstances based on a mutual agenda

Ultimately, the supervisor's agenda must prevail

Relationship based on mutuality of goals

A problem that exists within the room

Relationship based on trust

Counselling

Performance improvement planning

Tutoring

Mentoring

Focus on specific skill or competence

May, or may not be, the supervisor

Tutor's personal competence and ability to act as a role model essential

Relationship based on knowledge and respect

A free form of advice and guidance based on mutual respect, trust, and the extensive experience of the mentor

The agenda established by the mentee

Relationship based on experience, reputation and trust

Figure 12.4 Synergistic employee feedback

could act as mentor. Alternatively, where manager and employee were at similar stages of career growth, the mentoring role was often impractical.

RESPECT AS A CRITICAL FACTOR

In the coaching interaction the manager must actively participate by guiding the discussion over ground that is relevant. Equally important, the employee's learning is dependent to a great extent on the ability of the coach to set the context for the coachee to draw out meaning from such a discussion.

The role of the coach is that of active listener, questioner and a partner in the act of reflection. As Mumford points out in his work on coaching, these are characteristics often at variance with the pattern of work displayed by successful managers whose focus is invariably on action and decisive decision making.[3]

This does not mean that managers who focus aggressively on making things happen are not, in a real sense, coaching. Mutual exploration of a problem, exchange of ideas, and synergistically building on the ideas represents a significant learning opportunity for both.

In reality, effective managers coach in two ways: a directive coaching approach, drawn out of shared problem solving; and a reflective approach where the manager becomes a collaborator with the employee attempting to draw meaning out of experience.

Managers who want to foster empowerment in their team have to learn how to do both. Directive coaching is rooted in a power base linked directly to formal authority flowing from the job. Reflective coaching not only engenders empowerment, but is significantly helped where the arena or dimension in which the coaching discussion takes place is based on collaboration and consensus.

What then of criticism and advice, unsolicited or otherwise, in the coaching process? This presents something of a dilemma in that some of the most irascible, hard-driving managers continuously turn out first-class subordinates. In examining this question we started with the premise that even taking into account the impact of some directive coaching, the greater the degree to which the boss/subordinate relationship was employee centred, the higher the probability of coaching success. An empowered environment gives an opportunity for the employees to practise and even experiment with new ideas. Evidence that a number of more traditional managers use criticism and advice to good effect, however, was undeniable.

The important element in the equation is respect (see Figure 12.5). For while there is organizationally, we believe, a strong correlation between coaching success and the degree of participation in the work environment, some managers, even those somewhat autocratic in their approach, are able to influence positively the behaviour of their subordinates, or indeed, others in the organization if they are highly respected. On the other hand, the corollary is also true in that lack of respect is damaging even where other elements of the coaching process appear to be in place.

A further issue is what can perhaps best be described as 'situational respect'. Managers faced with a major turnaround tend not to welcome input into aspects of the business that fail to address the immediate issue in hand. Staff specialists, in particular, when introducing new processes or when fulfilling tutoring and even counselling roles, often fail to recognize the need to operate in a role that equates to the strategic driving force of the business. A need to understand the risk/quality of the management equation in conjunction with an ensuing focus on the critical issues is an essential ingredient of the coaching process in general, and critical for those in influence roles specifically.

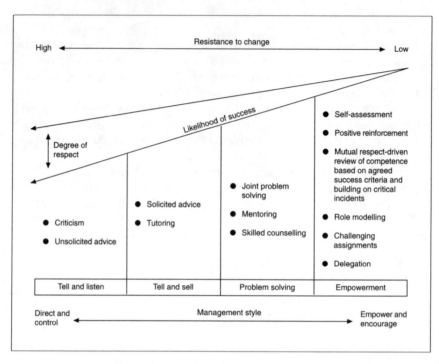

Figure 12.5 Building a learning environment

A great deal of what we might call coaching is implicit, an integral aspect of day-to-day problem-solving discussions. Directive coaching, however, must be balanced with a reflective approach to coaching. The latter is especially important in an environment encouraging empowerment. Respect lies behind both approaches, a respect inevitably based on four things: consistency, personal competence, personal commitment and values congruency. A consistency not derived from tackling every problem the same way, but drawn from an understanding of the values that drive the business; a competence based on pride in striving to achieve results at the highest possible standard in conjunction with a propensity to learn, and a commitment to get the job done by looking at ways to satisfy customer needs both in the marketplace and, where appropriate, within the organization. The importance of shared values speaks for itself.

SETTING THE CONTEXT FOR COACHING TO SUCCEED

The basic conditions that must be present if coaching initiatives are to have impact are: what has to change must be identified as specifically as possible; the employee must be committed to change; there must be an opportunity for the new behaviour to be practised; and the overall environment must support and encourage the ongoing enactment of the new behaviour. From our experience, failure to set the right context frustrates coaching even where the other components of the coaching process are well handled. Of the many issues involved in setting the context, we believe the following four are especially significant.

The first issue central to setting the context is an understanding on the manager's part of how those reporting to him/her learn. Learning starts with a question,[4] a problem, or a challenge. The lesson for the manager is that an employee does not change because the manager wants him/her to change but because the rationale for change is overwhelming. Learning is a highly practical activity and most powerful when derived from direct experience.

Most often missing from the learning process, and a critical dimension of learning as endorsed by both Mumford[5] and Handy,[4] is an opportunity to review what happened and draw meaning from it. Supporting the 'reflective' phase of learning is an essential dimension of coaching. At its simplest, the sales representative might want to discuss with his/her boss how a new approach to a key customer sales call was handled. Insightful questioning by the manager is a critical element of drawing out meaning.

Managers, however, tend to be poor in such situations mainly because they lack the analytical framework from which to structure the questions. The problem lies not with the manager's motivation, but how he or she acquired selling skills. In all likelihood the manager learned to sell by a form of osmosis, intuitively learning what worked and what did not, but not really understanding how he/she succeeded. A high-performance manager needs both analytical and intuitive skills,[6] in conjunction with a facility to know how and when to draw on each. To complement his/her intuitive understanding managers must be trained in how to ask questions, and perhaps more important – trained in how to listen to the answers.

The second important component in structuring an environment for coaching lies with the other dimensions of the human resource planning process in general, and the performance appraisal process in particular. The latter is especially important to the overall effectiveness of coaching because when managed effectively the performance appraisal process should move to a point where performance improvement actions are part of an explicit contract between manager and employee.[7]

Performance appraisal systems have a number of inherent challenges including managerial guilt, the contradiction between honesty and negativity impacting on the employee's self-esteem, and the ever-present problem of linkage to the compensation system.[8] From our experience performance appraisals are especially poor complements to coaching where:

- The approach fails to recognize the difference between results and performance (the environment in which the results took place).

- The performance rating reinforces mediocrity (e.g. the majority of employees are given feedback along the lines of competent, average, rather than, in a self-fulfilling way, given feedback that reinforces success.[9]
- The performance improvement actions are not linked to critical incidents.
- More than one or two performance improvement actions are focused on at a time.

The third issue in setting the context for coaching lies with the team. The implication from a coaching standpoint is that without team support new behaviours fail to become institutionalized. Examples of this dilemma abound, but are typically expressed in the frustration of an employee sent on a training programme only to return to his/her home team to find that there is little or no receptivity to the employee's new ideas, language, or way to approach problems.

Lack of team receptivity is often symptomatic of a greater problem, however: the company's values, as reflected in the team's behaviour not emphasizing learning. Peter Senge[10] points out that unless teams can learn, the organization cannot learn. It is our belief that the corollary is equally true, that unless the organization supports and encourages learning, teams inhibit the adoption of new forms of behaviour by team members. Thus, team receptivity to act is enhanced not so much by a focus on coaching through teams, although this almost certainly helps, but by emphasizing learning as a driving value in the organization.

The fourth critical element of building a coaching context is that managers, in addition to identifying what must change and as an extension to the coaching model, must have an understanding of the tactics of change. The following list of tactics, for example, represents only a small number of the alternatives available:

- Job enlargement
- Job environment
- Job rotation
- Expanded customer contact
- Planned reading
- Keeping a diary
- Developing an understudy
- Troubleshooting
- Consultancy
- Task team involvement
- Sitting in on meetings
- Exchange of information
- Planned and structured networking.

Unfortunately managers all too often fail to recognize the breadth of tactics available and either look for simple solutions to complex coaching situations or pass the problem along to the training department.

CONCLUSION

Much has been made of the concept of a learning culture. A learning culture is not an end in itself but the medium in which initiatives such as coaching flourish. This medium is in some sense an intangible, but in a business environment of rapid change may well be the primary dimension of competitive advantage.

Global competitiveness and increased access to information necessitate that employees at every level move outside of what have been traditional job boundaries. Supervisors and managers faced with increasing complexity must marshal and gain optimum leverage out of all their resources, and especially their human resources.

Coaching becomes not just a desirable component of managerial competence, but an imperative. Coaching, when an aspect of the way the company does business, equates to sustainable competitive advantage.

Coaching is not a function that the majority of managers perform well. Coaching is not well understood or easy to develop in others. Our experience is that the place to start is by understanding the changes taking place in the business environment and the coaching implications. Awareness then must be followed by meaningful action.

REFERENCES

1 Beer, M. (1986) 'Managing change beyond quick programs', Harvard Business School Working Paper 9–786–016, Ref. 1/86, January.
2 Early, C. P., Northcraft, G. B., Lee, C. and Lituchy, T. R. (1990) 'Impact of process and outcome feedback on the relation of goal setting to task performance', *Academy of Management Journal*, 33 (1), pp. 87–105.
3 Mumford, A. (1989) *Management Development Strategies for Action*, Institute of Personnel Management, p. 128.
4 Handy, C. (1989) *The Age of Unreason*, Harvard Business School Press, pp. 58–9.
5 Mumford, A. (1980) *Making Experience Pay*, McGraw-Hill, p. 67.
6 Simon, H. A. (1987) *Making Management Decisions: the role of intuition and emotion*, Academy of Management Executive, February, pp. 58–9.
7 Kirkpatrick, D. L. (1982) *How to Improve Performance through Appraisal and Coaching*, Amacom, pp. 61–72.
8 Kay, E., French, J. P. Jr and Mayer, H. (1965) 'Split roles in performance appraisal', *HBR*, January/February.
9 Burdett, J. (1988) 'Results driven performance', *The Human Resource*, February/March.
10 Senge, P. (1990) *The Fifth Discipline*, Doubleday, p. 10.

Chapter 13

Strategic management development: using experiential learning theory to assess and develop managerial competencies

David Kolb, Stuart Lublin, Juliann Spoth and Richard Baker

This chapter is addressed to an educational agenda that is of critical importance for the effective functioning of modern organizations, an agenda that
has been given scant attention until recently. The educational agenda is the
development of the specialized competencies and integrative knowledge
(sometimes referred to as wisdom) necessary to prepare managers for the
complex dynamic leadership roles they occupy. Management of change and
uncertainty requires that increasingly sophisticated and highly differen-
tiated specialized knowledge be brought to bear on organizational problems
and that these specialized viewpoints be integrated into effective solutions
to these problems.

The way that corporate training and development functions respond to
the learning and knowledge needs of their organizations is of particular
interest. There is in many of these functions a recognition of the need for
learning to cope with change and complexity, a relative openness to innovation, and the availability of resources to develop educational technologies
that respond to the organization's learning/knowledge needs. At the same
time it is in their organizations that the race between learning and survival
is most heated. From the perspective of management development we see
increasingly that the organization's ability to survive and thrive in a complex dynamic environment is constrained by the capabilities of managers
who must learn to manage both this greater environmental complexity and
the complex organizational forms developed to cope with the environment.
With the clarity of hindsight we see how the complacency, limited vision,
'me-too' business strategies, and short-term perspective of top management
have nearly destroyed companies in the automotive, aircraft, steel and other
major industries. What is most disturbing is that these failures to revitalize
and innovate are not the result of isolated cases of mismanagement. Rather
there is a general pattern of limited vision and lack of knowledge that is a
result of a systematic failure to provide managers with opportunities to
learn and prepare for the complex realities they face.

TOWARD A STRATEGIC VIEW OF MANAGEMENT DEVELOPMENT

Should not education have a role to play in helping managers at all levels to prepare in advance to cope with these challenges? Historically this has not been the case as training and development functions have focused primarily on lower management level, high certainty, specific skill training. But as organizations have become more complex in their attempts to master dynamic, uncertain environments, this new educational agenda is catching the attention of those concerned with management development. A major stimulus for this attention is the fact that the complex organizational structures and management systems required to deal effectively with environmental complexity and change are not working; primarily because managers are not prepared to use them effectively. Matrix management, for example, is currently out of favour because of the confusion and conflict it has caused in many organizations. This is in spite of the increasing need for such integrative mechanisms.

Much more is required of managers in these circumstances than was the case in the classical organization structure with a limited span of control, non-overlapping job definitions, a single chain of command, and formal authority that matched responsibility. Greater behavioural competence in taking initiative and responsibility under conditions of risk and uncertainty, greater perceptual competence in gathering and organizing information and taking the perspective of different organizational sub-units, greater affective competence in empathizing with others and in resolving conflicts among managers with different viewpoints and greater symbolic competence in one's ability to conceptualize the organization as a system are all required to make modern organizational forms work effectively. The same is true of modern management processes such as participative management or sophisticated operations management systems such as just-in-time inventory system.

A strategic approach to management development recognizes these critical linkages among complex environmental circumstances, the sophisticated organizational structure and processes necessary to cope with these circumstances, and the ability of managers to make the organization work effectively. Such a perspective suggests an expanded role for the human resource development function by linking management development programmes to the strategic mission of the organization. This perspective anticipates emerging management development requirements by analysing strategic projections for the organization's future environment, and develops educational programmes to help managers prepare in advance for these complex responsibilities. It suggests the development of systematic long-range career development programmes designed to grow the skilled human resources necessary to manage the organization's future challenges.

ASSESSING MANAGERIAL LEARNING NEEDS

The focal point of strategic management development is a learning needs assessment process that identifies the managerial competencies required effectively to manage complex organizations in complex environments. Such a system needs to identify not only highly specialized, specific knowledge requirements, but also the more integrative learning and problem-solving competencies needed to cope with uncertainty and complexity.

Experiential learning theory[1] provides one such approach for mapping the terrain of managerial competence based on what is called the 'competency circle'. This two-dimensional map arranges the specialized adaptive competencies of managerial knowledge around the experiential learning cycle based on their association with the four basic modes of the experiential learning process – affective competencies (e.g. being sensitive to people's feelings) are related to the concrete experience mode; perceptual competencies (e.g. gathering information) are related to the reflective observation mode; symbolic competencies (e.g. building conceptual models) are related to the abstract conceptualization mode; and behavioural competencies (e.g. making decisions) are related to the active experimentation learning mode.

The focus on adaptive (learning) competence accomplishes two things. First, since adaptation and learning are the central characteristics of all person/situation transactions, the competency circle technique is holistic, making it possible to compare and contrast the essential learning needs in different jobs, in different organizations, career paths and professions. Second, the focus on competence emphasizes the importance of congruence or 'fit' between managerial knowledge and job demands. Competence is not a judgement about an individual alone, but about the effective match between individual knowledge and skill and work environment demands. The competency circle approach defines individual knowledge and job demands in commensurate terms such that this effective match can be determined. Mismatches between current and future job demands and current managerial knowledge identify the educational objectives for management development programmes.

Figure 13.1 shows the difference in competency circle profiles among the major job roles in the engineering profession – 'bench' engineer, technical manager, and general manager. These data were collected in a cross-sectional study of engineering alumni from a major engineering school and represent individuals at different career stages from many different organizations. Generally these results show that managerial jobs require more affective (e.g. dealing with people) and behavioural competence (e.g. making decisions and setting goals), while direct engineering work requires greater symbolic (e.g. testing theories and ideas) and perceptual competence (e.g. gathering information). Among other things, these results suggest

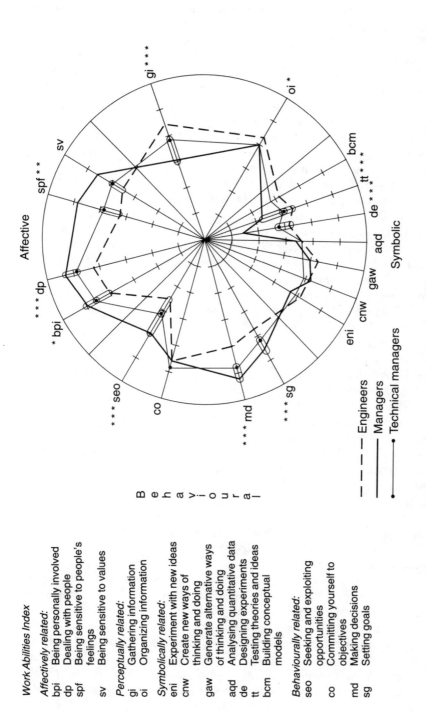

Work Abilities Index

Affectively related:
bpi Being personally involved
dp Dealing with people
spf Being sensitive to people's feelings
sv Being sensitive to values

Perceptually related:
gi Gathering information
oi Organizing information

Symbolically related:
eni Experiment with new ideas
cnw Create new ways of thinking and doing
gaw Generate alternative ways of thinking and doing
aqd Analysing quantitative data
de Designing experiments
tt Testing theories and ideas
bcm Building conceptual models

Behaviourally related:
seo Seeking and exploiting opportunities
co Committing yourself to objectives
md Making decisions
sg Setting goals

Behavioural

Perceptual

– – – Engineers
———— Managers
●—— Technical managers

Key: F Probabilities * = p<.05
                        *** = p<.001

Figure 13.1 Competency circle profiles of job demands for three job rules in the engineering profession

specific management development implications for professional engineers who are making transitions into management roles.

While this two-dimensional map of managerial competence has proven useful in identifying specialized managerial competencies, it became clear as we began using the technique in organizational settings that a third dimension needed to be added to describe the increasing complexity of managerial jobs as one moves up the organizational hierarchy and as organizations seek to relate to more complex environments. Elliott Jaques'[2] work on the time span of discretion, for example, shows that the work environment that managers must adapt to and master increase in their extension in time and space as one moves to higher levels of management. The first line supervisor works within a time span of days or weeks in a single location with highly certain information, whereas at the highest levels of the organization, managers operate within time spans of decades in a worldwide environment, characterized by high uncertainty and rapid change. Managerial competencies differ, therefore, not only in their specialized focus but also in the degree of sophistication and flexibility of application – in integrative complexity.

As a result the competency circle has been extended into a hierarchical map of managerial competence (see Figure 13.2). The competency circle shown in Figure 13.1 has been refined and elaborated into a competence clock that defines twelve generic performance competencies whose hourly position on the clock is determined by their association with the higher level learning competencies of experiential learning. Affective competencies are located at the 11, 12 and 1 o'clock positions, perceptual competencies at 2, 3 and 4 o'clock, symbolic competencies at 5, 6 and 7 o'clock and behavioural competencies at the 8, 9 and 10 o'clock positions. These twelve generic performance competencies are then extended downward one or two levels to analyse managerial competencies in a specific organizational setting and to identify the specific learning needs and management development activities required. The 12:00 competence dealing with people, for example, can be further divided into 'working in groups', 'being sensitive to feelings' and 'communicating with others'. In a specific work setting further specifications of working in groups might be made to identify learning needs associated with a particular type of group such as cross-functional product teams.

This specialized learning needs analysis is complemented by an integrative needs analysis focused on the integrative competence required to cope with the complexity and uncertainty inherent in higher level jobs and complex organization/environment relationships. While the specialized performance competencies become increasingly simple, behavioural and content focused as one moves down the hierarchy, the integrative learning and development competencies are more complex, internalized and process focused. Affective learning competence, for example, represents a set of

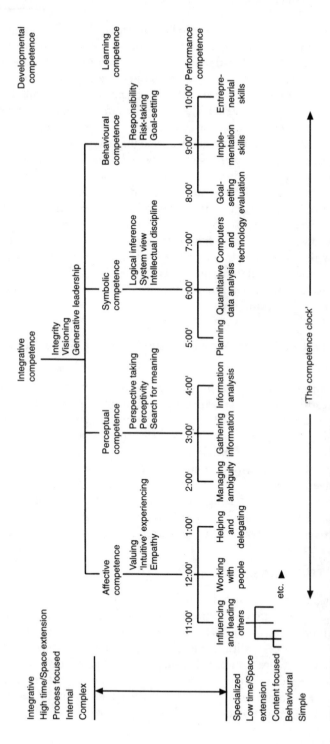

Figure 13.2 A hierarchical map of managerial competence

higher level, process centred 'learning how to learn' skills – valuing, 'intuit-ive' experiencing, and empathy – that facilitate the acquisition of lower level specialized skills in the affective area and direct the flexible and timely applications of these skills. Integrative competence represents the highest level of development wherein affective, perceptual, symbolic and behavioural learning competencies are integrated into a highly sophisticated and flexible adaptive process that can organize and focus highly differen-tiated knowledge and skills on rapidly changing environmental demands.

One measure of these integrative learning and development competencies that has shown great promise in our research to date is the Adaptive Style Inventory.[1] This self-report inventory is an advanced form of the Learning Style Inventory that assesses an individual's learning style in eight different specific situations in that person's life. The inventory measures integrative learning by determining the person's level of adaptive flexibility (i.e. the degree to which one changes his or her learning style to meet the varying learning demands of different situations in their life). The assumption is that flexibility of response in learning orientations reflects a more integrated and sophisticated learning style.

EDUCATION FOR THE MANAGEMENT OF COMPLEXITY AND CHANGE

One result of our work with the strategic management development con-cept and learning needs assessments based on the hierarchical map of managerial competence has been the recognition that training and develop-ment functions in organizations focus their efforts largely on training for specialized competencies. This is and will continue to be an important function for management development. But the unmet need for education in integrative competence will continue to grow and must somehow be addressed. By taking leadership in meeting this need, corporate training and development functions can contribute to their organization's ability to respond actively and creatively to the strategic challenges they face.

INTEGRATIVE LEARNING

How is this to be accomplished? Integrative learning requires learning conditions that are different, at times in opposition, to the approaches that have proven effective for specialized learning. Integrative learning is more concerned with process, with learning how to learn rather than simple skill acquisition. It is more concerned with executive problem solving about which competence to apply in which circumstance, rather than the execution of the competence. As such, it is more internalized and specifi-cally tailored to each unique individual. There are no simple 'right' or 'wrong' answers, or more specifically, there is only one correct answer for each unique individual in each unique circumstance.

Integrative learning is holistic and as such addresses the whole person physically and mentally; not only in a specialized skill or job role but in the context of his or her total life situation. Indeed, the fundamental challenge of integrative learning is to integrate oneself, to become a whole publicly and privately and to operate from the 'centred' judgement that such wholeness produces.

From the holistic perspective, disagreement, conflict, and differences among people are the fuel that energizes the integrative learning process. The constructive use of differences to explore the parts of the whole and the contribution each makes defines a cooperative approach to differences and disagreements that stands in contrast to the competitive view underlying analytic approaches to learning. Integrative learning programmes, therefore, need to focus on learning from differences in content, point of view, and learning style by creating a climate where these differences can be examined constructively. Argyris and Schon,[3] for example, have found that the learning climate in most organizations discourages learning from differences by norms that reinforce winning over understanding and suppression of conflict by unilateral protection of self and others. They have identified the elements of organization learning climate that stimulate what they call double-loop learning – norms supporting valid information, free and informed choice and internal commitment.

Experiential learning theory and the associated methods of experiential education provide a framework for the conduct of integrative education. The use of experiential exercises, games, and simulations in training programmes actively engage learners in situations where they must act and observe the consequences of their actions. Since everyone shares the same experiences, learning occurs through dialogue among participants who share observations, feelings, and thoughts and arrive together at conclusions about what has been learned. The facilitator or manager of this learning process is an expert with his or her own ideas, but so are the other participants who bring their own expertise and point of view for understanding the experiences. Most importantly, participants are not only learning specialized content, but are at the same time learning how to learn the specialized material which is under study.

Integrative learning occurs best when the learning process is integrated with work in real time. While off-site sessions and training programmes have some role to play in developing integrative competence, a greater payoff lies in the creation of organization climates that allow learning from experience during work itself. Other approaches to experiential learning emphasize these 'real-life', on-the-job learning experiences such as Revans' action learning programmes[4] and systematic career development processes that use careful assignment and rotation of job functions to develop the integrative general management perspective.

SUMMARY

Integrative learning requires a reexamination of our role as teachers or trainers. Rather than being dispensers of knowledge and wisdom, our role in integrative learning is to manage the process of learning; to facilitate adult learners in the process of learning from their own experiences in life. In all its forms, experiential learning emphasizes the integration of the abstract concepts of social knowledge with the concrete, subjective experiences of personal knowledge. One means to this integration is dialogue – a special form of communication where both abstract ideas and personal feelings about them are shared in a spirit of provisionalism, mutuality, and co-inquiry. Adult learners learn best in situations where they are acknowledged as experts and equals. As adults they have a need to teach as well as to learn.

Finally, integrative learning suggests an open system, networking approach to the management of knowledge and learning resource acquisition. A key function of strategic management development at the integrative level is to provide managers with access to knowledge and relationship networks that can help them become life-long learners and cope with the issues on their continually changing agendas. Of particular value here is the establishment of alliances between business and higher education that promise to increase the effectiveness of both.

REFERENCES

1 Kolb, D. A. (1984) *Experiential Learning: experiences as the source of learning and development*, Prentice-Hall, Englewood Cliffs, N.J.
2 Jaques, E. (1979) 'Taking time seriously in evaluating jobs', *Harvard Business Review*, September–October, pp. 124–32.
3 Argyris, C. and Schon, D. (1978) *Organizational Learning: a theory of action perspective*, Addison-Wesley, Reading, Mass.
4 Revans, R. W. (1981) 'Action Learning and Development of Self' in Boydell, T. and Pedler, M. (eds), *Management Self-Development*, Gower Press, 1981.

Chapter 14

Applying self-development in organizations

Mike Pedler

This chapter is a short report on two conferences concerned with 'Applying Self-development in Organizations' and summarizes the current position of the self-development idea in management education and training. It concludes that many management development practitioners have accepted the practical value of self-development and are now concerned with attempting to apply the concept within organizations.

WHAT IS SELF-DEVELOPMENT?

In the context of management education self-development is a term for a growing family of approaches, which give the learner control over the processes and tasks of his or her own development. Self-development methods stress that it is the learner (and not the trainer or any other) who takes primary responsibility for diagnosing need and choosing the goals for learning and development, for choosing the methods, means, times and places for learning and for evaluating the results. First and foremost it is about learner power to act autonomously rather than trainer power to direct and prescribe. It is this aspect of self-development that makes it problematic within the organization where direction from above is usual. However, the attraction of self-development stems from the observation that, like horses and water, learners cannot be made to learn. Where work organizations rely increasingly upon self-motivated, self-starting, entrepreneurial, resourceful, responsible members it is clear that the means of equipping people with the necessary skills and abilities must also reflect these self-directing values.

The short history of organized management development in the UK accelerated rapidly in the 1960s even as the economy entered increased comparative decline. Retrospectively those were years of hope, of never-ending growth and prosperity for all and in sharp contrast to the situation that faced managers in the 1980s beset by problems of low growth, high unemployment, fiercening overseas competition, rapid technological change, increasing social divisions at home and abroad and so on. Management self-development, as an idea, has gained momentum in these straitened times, not always for honourable reasons, but in contrast to two earlier ideas which dominated the 1960s and 1970s.

The 1960s was the era of systematic training, fuelled by skills shortages in a full employment economy and encouraged by the Industrial Training Act. Training is outer-directed; training needs stem from 'organizational goals'; skilled training officers diagnose individual needs, set measurable objectives, devise programmes and so on. 'Individuals' are trained in squads; cohorts whose training needs are all the same. Systematic training was effective (and still is) for much training, especially in manual skills, but when the approach was applied to management development, a critical problem known as the 'transfer of training' problem emerged.

Programmes were excellent and trainees learned a lot – according to post-course evaluation instruments – but their actions and behaviour back at work did not change.

Learning

This problem led to a focus upon learning. Instead of concentrating upon what the trainer does, let's see what happens when people learn. The 1970s and late 1960s saw the discovery of the learning cycle of Revans, Kolb *et al.*, and others, and the pursuit of the art of 'learning how to learn' became the new Holy Grail. Carl Rogers provided an inspiration for the learning movement with his 'non-directive' or 'learner-centred' views in remarks like 'that which can be taught directly to another is relatively trivial, whereas things of significance can only be learned'. Learning was very inner-directed, concerned with the feelings and thoughts of the individual, was relatively unrelated to 'organizational goals' and was successful when the learner said that he or she had learned.

Development

Development as an idea embraces both the outer reality of environment and 'organizational goals' and the inner reality of the emerging self. Each of us is a unique being in the process of becoming a person – as Rogers and Maslow taught – but we can only make progress by interacting with other people, and by exercising our ability to make personal choices as constructively as possible. It is making the most that we can out of opportunities in both these respects, which provides the impetus for self-development. See Figure 14.1.

Methods such as action learning and self-managed learning stress the interaction of inner and outer where the acquisition of managerial skills requires both an inner choosing and transformation and a changed outer performance. Self-development as an idea is then a synthesis of earlier ideas

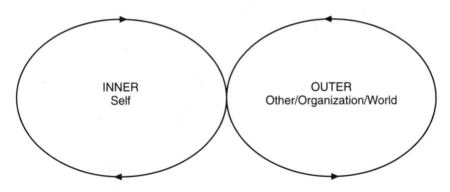

Figure 14.1 Interaction of the inner and outer world

being neither this or that but both . . . and, where development involves a continuous passing from outer actions (experience) to inner processes (reflection) back to action and so on.

Other important dimensions of the self-development idea are:

• that we must create order first in ourselves before we can do this with others – the principles of 'managing ME first' and 'managing from the inside out' (in contradistinction to much conventional teaching which extols the virtues and seeks to pass on the homilies of 'great men').

• that development is a 'whole person' transformation and not just the training of the 'worker' and therefore that there are many points for taking the next step in one's development – from one's home life, from important relationships, from life 'crises', health, age and so on, as well as from issues of managerial skills, style and competence. Work and life within the organization, while an important and critical part of the life of the manager, is by no means the whole.

• that the 'self' in self-development means at least two things – first that this is a BY-SELF process where the manager takes the prime responsibility for initiating and managing her own development. Second, that this is an OF-SELF process in which the manager as a person grows in her ability and willingness to take control over and responsibility for events and particularly for herself and her own development.

• that the role of management development and training people becomes less that of 'providers', directors and initiators and more that of 'facilitators', resource creators, counsellors and supporters.

Before leaving the topic 'What is self-development?', it is important to point out and realize some of the limitations which are now appearing. First amongst these is the looseness and width of the idea which may make it all things to all people. Self-development currently holds a very wide church, from mystics and religious prophets on the one hand to Victorian values merchants on the other. This width helped the establishment of the idea but now threatens its integrity as, increasingly, different exponents fail to recognize each other's wares – are self-development groups and 'distance learning' really part of the same idea? Second, development within organizations is inextricably linked with careers. Does this mean that successful self-developers are those who rise to the top and that those at the top are there because they are the best developed? Self-development is all too attractive an idea to those wishing to justify an elitist position in terms of the allocation of resources and indeed that some are more capable of development than others. Third, there is a very real danger in these straitened times for the idea of self-development to be seized upon by those seeking to make savings via training budgets. There are some good precedents for banning all course-going and the dismantling of expensive training centres while making statements about it being every manager's duty to be a self-developer. Such actions can stem from a serious concern to improve and enhance provision for education, training and development. They can also stem from a short-term and cynical standpoint, which seeks all the best tunes – to save money and be right up to date in terms of management development philosophy!

CURRENT THEMES IN APPLYING SELF-DEVELOPMENT WITHIN ORGANIZATIONS

Four main themes can be discerned from the formal and informal offerings at the conferences.

Managing your own learning

The first main theme – managing your own learning – formed a foundation stone for many of the other applications in that contributors were often concerned with developing new methodology. Examples included: Learning to Learn; Open and Distance Learning; The Learning Community and Self-managed Learning. The main emphasis lay in designing programmes – including those leading to academic qualifications – with a view to maximizing and supporting the self-management of learning and development. Contributions to this theme sometimes contained material of a conceptual as well as a practical nature.

Differences at work

Differences at work formed a second theme and pointed up the relevance of self-development designs for equal opportunities work in organizations. Sessions on this theme turned out to be more or less exclusively concerned with gender difference, for example: Women Managers' Self-development;

Women and Men as Working Colleagues, and Transformations for Men. The importance of this theme indicated just how much work is being done in this area and how powerful the recognition of difference can be as a spur to development. Such work stands as an important corrective to the elitist tendency noted earlier in some organizations where self-development is described as being suitable for top managers or for those who have proved themselves capable of taking the initiative in terms of their own development. Self-development designs were shown as helpful in releasing the energies of 'oppressed' minorities stuck in limited and disadvantaged positions, including women, black and redundant managers, supervisors, and even, in one example, short-stay prisoners. My own work with self-development groups suggests that such a milieu may be just what is required for the 'plateaued' or stuck person, of whatever age and whatever the cause of the stuckness, be it externally or internally imposed (Pedler 1986).[1]

Career development

The third theme – career development – is in some ways, a mirror image of the second and is perhaps the most obvious locus for the application of self-development in many organizations. This is likely to be true wherever the need to link individual with organizational development has become an issue for managerial action. For many large organizations such a link is a major preoccupation. Sessions included: Self-appraisal; Integrated Career Planning; Using a Career Planning Workbook; Working with Biography, and Transforming Your Career.

The learning company

It is more difficult to name the fourth theme, which was distinguished by attempts to apply the notion of self-development more holistically to organizations as compared with focusing on specific aspects. One title – the learning company – was a phrase and a concept which took up a good deal of discussion and debate, particularly in the second conference. Contributions in this theme included: Evaluating the Organizational Effects of Self-development groups; Developing Small Businesses via Self-development; Quality in the Organization, and The Learning Company.

Clearly, there is some fitting of self-development activities within organizations into this neat fourfold division. The overall impression was that activities on themes two and three could be most easily identified. These tend to be discrete and, as noted above, perhaps self-development marries most easily with efforts concerning career development or the lack of it. There were quite a number of examples of organization-wide systems of resources and resource centres being set up backed by a self-development philosophy. These and the open and distance learning approaches in general are clearly an important part of the basic equipment of the 'Learning Company'. However, it is equally clear that, unless they are linked to other processes, such as appraisal, support groups or qualification courses, then they are only likely to be taken up by a small minority of members. Companies reporting more than, say, a 10 per cent involvement are rare. Those which do, like Jaguar, have extensive links with outside educational establishments that can grant qualifications. The appeal here is not only that of personal development but of increasing personal 'marketability' – always an important aspect of self-development perhaps, and one which tends to place such efforts in the career development theme.

Particularly at the second conference, it was clear that some people's visions went beyond individual or organizational efforts at career development, and centred on the concept of Learning Organization or Learning Company, a notion which has been about in the literature for some time but which has not yet received much attention at the applied level (see, for example, Argyris and Schon 1978).[2]

It is apparent from the evidence of the two conferences that self-development is easily applied to certain aspects of organization. In particular, the link with appraisal, career planning and development is well advanced with a number of self-review and self-appraisal schemes in use. Another area in which great strides have been taken is in the provision of organization-wide resources centres together with the guidance systems to make them accessible to managers. The simplicity and cheapness of these schemes, such as the ASSET scheme in Texaco, are not the least of their charms. Such approaches are increasingly being linked with qualification programmes validated by educational institutions. Self-development groups and support groups are now a well established means of providing a stimulating and mutually helpful milieu within which individuals can pursue their self-development goals, before they are concerned with acquiring qualifications, skills, knowledge or in taking the next step. In the light of all this it seems fair to conclude that some of the social technology and, indeed, some of the educational technology for applying self-development within the organization is already in place.

There is a recognition that the familiar hierarchical structures do not easily lend themselves to members taking responsibility for their own development together with an understanding that self-development opportunities are only taken up by more than a minority if they are partially structured. Furthermore that 'culture' feels like a better word than 'structure' for what we are striving for at the organizational level and, finally, a welcome corrective lest we should get too enthusiastic that a continuing purpose which has to be balanced with that of learning is the production of bread and motor cars.

On the first of these points, the need for a freeing from hierarchic structure together with the provision of a certain supporting structure, there is here a vital insight for those interested in applying self-development in organizations. Some people have used the term 'facilitating structure' as a response to this dilemma (Torbert 1978)[3] and a useful further explanation of this may be found in the cybernetic concept of 'minimum critical specification'. This recognizes that hierarchic organization results in the 'over-engineering' of learning opportunities and attempts to preserve maximum capacity for self-organization by suggesting that one should specify no more than is absolutely necessary for a particular activity to occur. In theory this creates a capacity for a system to be self-forming and in terms of facilitating self-development might consist, say, of giving members the right to a number of 'development days', making rooms, equipment and other resources, including skilled trainers, available and leaving it at that.

It is the search for appropriate facilitating structure to support a culture of self-development that led to participants interest in the notion of 'Learning Company'. The Learning Company is a vision for an organizational strategy to promote self-development amongst the membership and to harness this development corporately by continuously transforming itself as part of the same process.

REFERENCES

1 Pedler, M. J. (1986) 'Developing within the organization: experiences with management self-development groups', *Management Education & Development*, 17 (1), Spring, pp. 5–21.
2 Argyris, C. and Schon, D. A. (1978) *Organisational Learning: a theory of action perspective*, Addison Wesley, Reading, MA.
3 Torbert, W. R. (1978) 'Educating towards shared purpose, self-direction and quality work', *Journal of Higher Education*, Ohio State University Press, 49 (2).

Developing team effectiveness

Christopher Mabey

Much of the literature on organizational learning is couched in the language of teams and teamworking. Chapter 15 by Richard Wellins, which opens Part IV, is just one example of many we could have chosen which extols the virtues of self-directed teams (SDTs). Working under minimal direct supervision, such teams appear to usher in a host of benefits for the organization prepared to 'relinquish' control in this way. Individuals feel empowered and take more responsibility, innovation and continuous improvement becomes the norm, the workforce becomes more flexible and the company less stratified. Wellins rightly emphasizes the need for human resource policies (recruitment, training and reward systems) to reinforce what amounts to a radical change of culture for most organizations.

In contrast to this upbeat and 'powerful empowerment strategy', Chapters 16 and 17 present a somewhat more sober view of developing team effectiveness. In an extract from her book *The Change Masters: corporate entrepreneurs at work*, Rosabeth Moss Kanter highlights some of the dilemmas of teamworking. Despite an appearance of equality, team members can be frustrated by others who use their seniority to dominate, by lack of access to information or resources and by group dynamics or covert political conflicts, which inhibit contribution. However, Kanter argues, the surfacing of differing interests and the recognition of diversity in a team (rather than pretending that differences do not exist) can lead to more informed decision-making and effective teamworking.

Elliott Jaques is altogether more sceptical about the currently fashionable use of participatory forms of organization such as self-managed teams, which – it is claimed – spell the end of managerial hierarchy as we know it. In Chapter 17 Jaques debunks such 'democratic' systems as counterproductive and undermining of competitiveness and efficiency. In a controversial yet compelling manner Jaques calls for a right use of hierarchy where the number of layers is appropriate, where roles within that structure are filled with people of the right calibre and where such individuals (rather than a diffused team) are held accountable for the right kind of clearly defined outputs.

Finally, in this part, we turn to two more specialist applications of teamworking. Chapter 18 by Mick Marchington describes the growing practice of teamworking in the broader context of work redesign. In fact, autonomous work groups have a long history and Marchington assembles some of the evidence for effective teamworking – primarily in the manufacturing sector – in the USA and Europe. Once again, the evident advantages of allocating work in this self-regulated way have to be offset against some of the less apparent implications, notably upon supervisors, trade union organizations and employees themselves.

In Chapter 19 Neil Anderson and his colleagues Gillian Hardy and Michael West switch focus to the public sector. Their pioneering work in the UK Health Service concerns what makes teams innovative. Once again, any assumptions that putting a collection of individuals together will automatically result in a synergistic and creative team are confounded by their research. A number of conditioning factors are necessary, and the authors describe with reference to two NHS teams how strategies for facilitating innovation and creativity within workgroups and management teams can be fostered.

Chapter 15

Building a self-directed work team

Richard S. Wellins

Today's organizations face unprecedented challenges. Fierce competition, globalization, deregulation, technological change, and shorter product life cycles can create new opportunities for them – or economic disasters. To survive, companies will have to focus on total equality, speed to market, and cost containment; mastering only one or two of these three key areas will not be enough. In addition, the values and attitudes of today's workforce have changed. Today's workers demand greater participation, flexibility, and autonomy; they want opportunities to work with their heads as well as their hands. The organizations that have positioned themselves for success are those that focus on empowering their workforces. Business leaders have come to realize – albeit slowly – that innovations to reduce defects will not come solely from the minds of a few 'super leaders' but will be the products of cultures that foster continuous improvement – small, incremental changes made by every worker, every day.

One successful strategy for creating an empowered work culture is the use of self-directed teams. SDTs are small groups of employees who have day-to-day responsibility for managing themselves and their work. Members of SDTs typically handle job assignments, plan and schedule work, make production-related decisions, and take action on problems. SDTs require minimal direct supervision. They differ in design from quality circles and cross-functional task groups in that SDTs are formal, permanent organizational structures. SDTs operate with fewer layers of management than do traditional organizational structures. They require team members to learn multiple jobs or tasks and to take on many tasks that were once reserved for supervisors or managers – including hiring, firing, conducting appraisals, and setting schedules.

A recent survey conducted by Development Dimensions International (DDI), in conjunction with *Industry Week* magazine and the Association for Quality and Participation (AQP), estimates that about 25 per cent of US companies are implementing SDTs somewhere in their organizations. Companies that already use SDTs include Corning, Toyota Automotive,

Texas Instruments, Digital Equipment Corporation, Procter & Gamble Co., and Colgate-Palmolive.

The results have been impressive: Organizations that use SDTs have maintained or reduced labor costs while improving productivity by 50 per cent or more.

Instituting a culture that places a premium on empowerment is no small feat. Establishing SDTs requires major organizational and cultural changes. Without such changes, implementation can turn into a management-directed nightmare. And because SDTs require extensive employee involvement and trust, failed implementations can set back an organization's employee-involvement effort for years.

An organization must focus on five major issues in order to make self-directed teams work:

1 Designing teams for success.
2 Selecting team players.
3 Training for success.
4 Initiating leadership transitions.
5 Rewarding team performance.

What follows are some suggestions for addressing each of those five important issues.

Designing teams for success

The most important suggestion for creating a successful team implementation is a simple one: Make planning a priority. In moving toward self-direction, the organization and its employees need to consider such questions as these:

- Where do we start?
- What training do we need?
- How will SDTs affect our work and our jobs?
- What role will support departments play?
- What responsibilities will be transferred from leaders to teams?

The following six-step process can help companies get started in creating a successful SDT implementation.

Step 1

Learn about SDTs. The odds of success are better if upper management is properly schooled in the concept of SDTs. Resources about work teams are abundant. Dozens of articles and books have been written on the subject. Several companies sponsor conferences about the team concept. And visits to team-based organizations can serve as valuable learning tools.

Step 2

Conduct a 'readiness' assessment to determine if teams are right for your culture. Off-the-shelf instruments and interview guides can help you decide if teams or alternative forms of empowerment strategies are bound for success or doomed to failure in your organization.

Step 3

Communicate to your employees the organization's vision and values as they relate to empowerment and teams. Management must have a clear picture of where the company should go and how the concepts of self-direction ties in with the existing mission and cultural values.

Step 4

Take your organization through a process known as "work-place redesign." This process, also known as "sociotechnical design," requires an organization to take a hard look at the nature of its work (work flow, job design, and layout) and its systems (compensation, training, hierarchy, and appraisal), and to blend them for maximum productivity and employee satisfaction.

In most cases, workplace redesign involves the formation of a committee that takes the organization through the design process. The committee should include managers, line workers, and support staff, because all three groups have a stake in the success of the team implementation.

Step 5

Implement. The actual implementation should include the positive features found in any sound change process: open communication, leadership support, and training.

Step 6

Continually evaluate the progress of SDTs. Most organizations convert either on a trial basis or in start-up locations, so constant evaluation is critical. Team implementations can always benefit from critical and continual adjustment and improvement.

Selecting team players

Companies that are moving to self-directed teams must select workforces that are equipped with – or capable of acquiring – the competencies, skills, and values necessary for successful performance in high-involvement organizations.

Of course, employee selection is not a key concern in a conversion at an existing organization, where a workforce is already in place. But many self-directed teams have the advantage of being implemented in start-up operations. In these companies, selection becomes a key issue. Any good selection system should have four major features:

1 The selection system must be accurate in identifying candidates who are most likely to succeed in the new organization.
2 It must be legally defensible.
3 It must be perceived as fair; candidates should believe that they are treated in a just manner and that the system has accurately assessed their potential for performing the jobs in question.
4 The selection system must be efficient.

The first step in setting up a team-oriented selection system is to identify the targets – called "dimensions" or "job competencies" – against which a team member's or team leader's performance will be assessed. Many organizations accomplish this through the process of job analysis. A job analysis generates a list of behaviors, technical knowledge, skills, and motivational areas that differentiate successful performers from unsuccessful ones.

A study of more than 100 job analyses conducted for team-oriented organizations identified typical team-member dimensions. The dimensions included teamwork, problem identification and solution, the ability to learn, communication, initiative, work standards, coaching and training, job motivation, technical ability, and work tempo (the ability to work at a relatively fast and constant speed).

Team-leader jobs usually involve additional dimensions, including individual leadership, group leadership, judgement, delegation, and encouragement and support of initiative.

Once the dimensions have been identified, the company can design its selection system. Many system designers find it difficult to select instruments and tools that accurately reflect the dimensions to be assessed. The best selection systems tend to include a combination of techniques, including interviews, paper-and-pencil cognitive-ability tests, technical tests, reference checks, simulations, and "realistic job previews."

Those last two assessment tools – simulations and realistic job previews – are particularly interesting.

Simulations provide a unique and highly accurate method of measuring job potential. Candidates encounter a series of structured activities that closely resemble procedures used on the job. For example, a large automobile manufacturer required a team of people to work together to assemble parts according to a set of job instructions. This single, three-hour work simulation assessed each candidate's ability to learn, work tempo, attention to detail, and teamwork and cooperation skills.

A realistic job preview is another feature of many selection systems. It may take the form of a video that depicts the working environment and culture of a team-oriented facility. A realistic job preview is not meant to be a marketing video. It is a "down-to-earth" preview of what work will be like in the new facility and what will be expected of workers in the team-oriented environment.

The realistic job preview serves as a mechanism for discouraging applicants who decide that a team environment is not the place for them, and for encouraging applicants who see it as an exciting new workplace opportunity.

A final note regarding selection: it is important when implementing a selection system of this sort to make sure that the people involved in the selection process are well trained in the use of the various, powerful selection techniques that will be used. Without such training, the whole selection system may be worthless. Data show that this kind of investment made up front eventually tends to pay off in terms of increased productivity and reduced turnover and absenteeism.

Training for success

When moving toward team-oriented environments, companies tend to underestimate the need for new types of training. SDTs encourage multi-skilling and job rotation, which require a heavy investment in technical training. Workers must learn to work together as a team – workers who have been rewarded in the past for individual performance.

Successful self-directed organizations commonly find that 20 per cent of a team member or team leader's time during the first year of team operation is spent in various training activities.

Three categories of training are essential for effective team performance.

1 *Job Skills* are the technical skills required for job performance.
2 *Team/interaction skills* are the interpersonal and communication skills needed by team members – including giving and receiving feedback, handling conflict, valuing diversity, working in teams, and training and coaching.
3 *Quality/action skills* involve identifying problems and implementing improvements. These skills include statistical process control, the use of various quality tools, continuous improvement techniques, and trouble-shooting.

Workers who are in leadership positions will probably need additional training in such topics as coaching for success, reinforcing effective performance, encouraging and supporting initiatives, and leading work teams.

The success of self-directed teams is dependent on training for management and for staff- or support-department employees. For example, engineers, accountants, and training professionals might not be part of the self-directed teams in a manufacturing firm, but they should be as well-versed in team and interpersonal skills as the team members themselves are.

Training works best when it is provided over time rather than in one "lump sum." Some organizations that have implemented SDTs offered all of their training in four- to six-week "training colleges." Such a schedule turned out to be difficult for everyone, especially for production workers, who were used to roaming the floors, not sitting in class.

Initiating leadership transitions

In reality, few organizations have totally converted to SDTs. In most cases, managers and supervisors still serve the teams as valuable resources after SDT implementation, but their roles change radically.

In a traditional organization, managers control and schedule work, appraise and discipline employees, and hire and fire. In many cases, they are solely responsible for the quality of the product or service.

The reverse is true in SDT organizations. The team assumes those functions, freeing managers and leaders to take on entirely new sets of responsibilities:

- Coaching and training the team members.
- Serving as the contact points for suppliers.
- Helping teams gain access to the resources and training that are needed for success.
- Filling in when team members are absent or during peak-demand periods.
- Helping teams coordinate efforts with other teams and other units within the organization.

It is important that organizations help their supervisors and managers make successful transitions. Companies should ensure that these people have clear expectations about their new roles, as well as the necessary training in different types of leadership skills. Change should occur slowly, to allow team leaders and managers the time they need to learn their new roles. And the smoothest transitions involve leaders and managers in the change process.

Unfortunately, first- and middle-level managers often get in the way of a company's successful transition to a team-oriented environment.

Many managers find that the adjustment from old managerial responsibilities to new ones is not easy. At the heart of the concept of SDTs is the fact that teams take on many of the responsibilities that were previously reserved for supervisors and managers. As a result, some supervisors and managers find themselves in a catch-22: Bosses must serve as coaches to help SDTs work effectively, but successful SDT implementation could threaten the security of the bosses' jobs.

In the survey conducted by DDI, *Industry Week*, and AQP, 68 per cent of organizations using self-directed teams said they were able to operate with fewer managers. Ninety-five per cent of the responsibilities found this change to be beneficial.

Typical questions that supervisors and managers might ask themselves at this point:

- How will I be involved in the SDT design effort?
- Will I lose my job?
- Do I have the right skills to make the transition?
- Will I lose my power and authority?
- Will I be blamed if things don't work out?

Reducing the number of managers and supervisors is not the only option that an organization can exercise when making the transition to self-directed teams.

Some organizations ask supervisors to take on responsibilities as team members, but allow them to remain at their former levels of compensation. Unfortunately, some employees may have been promoted to supervisory positions in the past based on their technical competencies, not on their motivation to lead and manage others. Such managers may even prefer to move to team-member positions.

In other cases, organizations have asked managers to assume technical-expert roles in particular production processes, making them process managers. A manager or supervisor who is moved to such a position is not responsible for leading other people but is perceived as a resource expert in his or her particular technical skill or process area.

Other managers fill new roles as team facilitators and coaches, helping their organizations and the new teams make the transition to self-direction.

Rewarding team performance

For years, American industry has focused on rewarding the lone hero. Pay increases have been based on either individual performance or seniority.

The move toward self-directed teams is changing US companies' view of compensation and reward systems. Many organizations that use self-directed teams implement various types of "gain-sharing" or team-bonus schemes, along with skill-based compensation plans.

Skill-based plans hold a unique advantage with SDTs because they focus on rewarding the number of skills a team leader has mastered and applied, thus increasing production flexibility. Such compensation schemes reward team members in three areas:

Job depth

Team members are paid increasing amounts for learning a specific process in greater depth. For example, first they might learn how to operate a piece of equipment, and then they might learn to do basic preventive maintenance on that machine. Finally, they progress to performing advanced maintenance on the same piece of equipment.

Job breadth

Every team member learns all the jobs or tasks required of the entire team. For example, in an automobile company, the seat-assembly team might have six or seven different production tasks, each performed by one team member. All team members would be required to learn all of the tasks.

Vertical skills

With this third and least common method, team members learn leadership skills that are used in all jobs. Examples include troubleshooting techniques, training other employees, safety procedures, and meeting leadership – skills that are required for successful team performance.

Performance of teams also can be rewarded via gain-sharing or team-bonus programs. These programs reward teams for increases in productivity that exceed some measure of baseline performance. In many cases, management divides the bonus equally among team members; occasionally, team members decide how to distribute the bonus among themselves.

A powerful empowerment strategy

SDTs are one of the most powerful empowerment strategies available to today's companies. Hundreds of organizations are using them to some extent, with great success.

Organizing into self-directed work teams requires a combination of planning, selecting the right team members and leaders, designing teams for success, training continuously, and carefully managing the shift of power and responsibilities from leaders to team members.

The conversion to teams can fortify organizational structures to withstand the storm of pressure that batters today's marketplace. SDTs can also prove to be an exciting innovation for the improvement of employees' workplace participation, productivity, and quality of life.

Chapter 16

Dilemmas of teamwork

Rosabeth Moss Kanter

One of the things that helps a team to work well is the feeling on the part of members that they are an integral, connected part of the group. In a task-oriented team, this means that their contributions are welcome and valued, that they are as important as any other member of the team to the final product. After all, why waste scarce organizational time to feel irrelevant? "Participation" must mean much more than observation and tacit approval of others as they do all the important work.

But four kinds of "inequalities" can drive a wedge between individuals and the team.

The seductiveness of the hierarchy

Segmentation cannot be overcome just by sudden definition of "teams." Teams that are pulled together from different external statuses, with the awareness that they will be returning to them, may slip into deference patterns which give those with higher status more air time, give their opinions more weight, and generally provide them with a privileged position in the group. There is a great deal of experimental social-psychological evidence that external status strongly influences the reactions of others in a group discussion. Similarly, stories from marooned military units indicate that people fall into positions determined by their place in the military hierarchy even though external constraints are removed, and the survivors constitute a "community" more than a hierarchy.

So teams, especially in segmentalist environments unaccustomed to the mixing and matching of an integrative culture, may end up duplicating the organizational hierarchy in miniature inside themselves: higher-status people dominating, lower-status people dropping out. Members of one task force in the Petrocorp Marketing Services Department felt that the most important factor inhibiting their participation was the presence of the boss. At two different high-technology companies where I observed cross-hierarchical task forces in operation, the same pattern was repeated: I could guess the relative levels of participants in meetings just by noting who "took over" and whose comments were treated most attentively – regardless of who was officially in the chair. In another sense, the chair was the highest-status member of the group, and meetings were run as though the rest of the participants were staff that had been assigned to him, instead of partners in a joint task.

The seductiveness of the hierarchy has emotional roots. The emotions that make it easier to reproduce the hierarchy than to operate as partners are principally fear and comfort. The basis for fear is obvious: "crossing" a powerful figure in a group, even if the purpose of the group is to get diversity of opinions, can make people afraid of external retribution later. So the lower-status people hold back, or feel very daring if they contribute. But there is also a comfort factor: it is easier to maintain familiar patterns of relationships and interaction than to experiment with the unfamiliar. Over time, with appropriate support from the higher-status figures, people are more likely to try to act in ways that place them outside the hierarchy. This is what we mean when we say that a group "loosens up."

"Participators are made, not born": the knowledge gap

There are also task-related reasons that hierarchies magically reproduce themselves inside teams designed to "level" status and improve cross-hierarchical communication and cooperation to solve a problem, or that other forms of "inequality" develop. Effective participators are, to an extent, "made, not born." It takes knowledge and information to contribute effectively to task teams, and this has to come from somewhere. Those people with more information about the matters at hand have an advantage over the others, and those in communication-rich integrative companies are all more likely to have the tools for effective participation than those in companies when segmentation significantly reduces information flow.

Often organizational position, with resulting differentials in information access, can create this difference in the team. Wherever there is a knowledge gap that is not closed with information before the team meets, inequalities develop that are often frustrating to the less well-informed group members, who respond by dropping out or failing to appear at meetings.

Participation *per se* does not always equalize power and may even increase discrepancies. If more poorly informed members sit with the more knowledgeable and skilled in meetings where all of them are theoretically making joint decisions, the less knowledgeable not only may be "shown up" for their lack of knowledge, thus losing power, but may also be forced to endorse, *de facto*, the decisions they supposedly helped to make. Their right to complain later is lost. This is one reason that worker participation on boards of directors was found to have mixed, rather than positive, benefits in Europe. People of managerial or equivalent status had an automatic information advantage. (Of course, the same thing is true of inside versus outside directors, leading to the common observation that manage-ment's viewpoint dominates board discussions.)

The secretaries in the commercial section of the Petrocorp Marketing Services Department eventually decided not to continue their rotating participation in section meetings because of the knowledge gap, which in turn stemmed from the segmentalist culture. Far from making them feel included and giving them a voice, sitting in on section meetings made one of them feel "dumb," since she could not follow the content of all the discussions. A few others felt they had to keep quiet, since they clearly knew less than anyone else. Some were bored and felt it was a waste of time. Special briefings by one of the managers before the meetings were a help, but not enough to compensate for the inequality caused by differential organizational status. This is not a "woman's" problem, either; I have observed the same hesitation and frustration on the part of male production workers in non-innovating companies suddenly thrust into management meetings unprepared.

Differential personal resources

There are also related problems from unequal distribution of skill and personal resources. People bring to groups different levels of personal attractiveness, verbal skill, access to information-bearing networks, and interest in the task. Victor Vroom and other psychologists have argued that there are personality differences among people that make some "fit" better than others in participatory groups requiring responsibility and active involvement, although the evidence for these differences is mixed. It is easy to see, however, that personal characteristics and mutual attraction can play a role in helping people become connected to social networks outside the team that give them an advantage inside it: more informal status, better reputation, earlier gossip. Furthermore, interpersonal attrac-tions among team members can lead to subgroups engaged in 'natural' patterns of friendly communication, which give people an advantage in team discussions. It is not simply that people may support one another on the basis of friendship, but also that the opportunity for people to discuss issues in smaller units outside the group may mean that they come to the meetings with their thoughts better formulated and their arguments rehearsed.

There are also specific skills involved in articulating opinions, developing arguments, and reaching decisions that are differentially distributed across organizational populations – and not just because individuals are intrinsi-cally different. Hierarchy, or at least the structure of the line organization, intrudes on the participative team again. Development of the kind of skills necessary for effective participation – ability to push a point of view, ability to see issues in context, and so on – is closely associated with job characteristics. The effectiveness of participation in local department committees at British Rail, for example, was a function of the job; jobs with high autonomy (which required working alone and unchecked, as well as initiating action) predisposed people to learn the requirements of decision making. Then, on top of that, actual involvement in a decision-making process on the job (obtaining and processing information, evaluating outcomes, defining action strategies) tends to teach people to articulate corporate goals. Finally, jobs with more information passing through about local and corporate issues also give their occupants an advantage in effective participation.

The seniority/activity gap

A final source of inequality comes from relative seniority or activity in the team itself. Outsiders or newcomers or those not attending meetings regularly often feel uncomfortable about speaking up, especially if the group has developed its own language, abbreviations, or understandings. Sometimes the group will deliberately close ranks in the presence of a newcomer as an occasion to reinforce its own solidarity. And in what has been termed a "competence multiplier," the most active members may gain a monopoly on the skills required for effective decision making and therefore become even more active, beginning an exclusionary cycle.

Thus, in general, the "best" participators who come to dominate team discussions may again turn out to be those already best placed in the hierarchy and in the networks spawned by it. "What kinds of things inhibit your participation?" members of a functional area were asked in an anonymous survey, in reference to their quality-circle-like problem-solving meetings. Among the replies: "Know-it-all centers"; "Owl and Pussy-Cat group glances" – meaning sidelong looks exchanged by just a few members; "lack of information on subject under discussion"; "things outside my responsibility and interest"; "fear of being attacked by group"; "older members who make newer members feel insecure."

Overwhelmingly, the element of the meetings that everyone liked best was the presentations by the group's boss – relying on the familiar hierarchy and reducing any feelings of peer competition, because during his presentation no one had to feel unequal to a peer. There were also feelings that individual participation would be improved if people did not feel they had to perform and if they all got the same information in advance.

The internal politics of teams

Of course, declaring people a "team" does not automatically make them one, nor does seeking decisions in which many people have a voice ensure that democratic procedures will prevail. A philosophy of participation in no way eliminates jockeying for status or internal competition if people bring self-serving interests into a group, or if they have differential stakes in the outcome, or if they come from segmented organizations whose structure and culture encourages divisiveness and non-cooperation across areas. There may be differential advantages to individual members to be gained by pushing particular decisions over others; there may be differential benefits to be reaped outside the group by appearing to be a dominant force in it – like the ambitious young manager who wants to impress his boss with his "leadership" skills. People bring different needs and interests into any kind of group from their location outside it, and these can serve as the origins of team politics.

How much differential needs and interests politicize a team is in large measure a function of how the team is set up in the first place. Group dynamics becomes more competition-centered when rewards or recognition outside the team are scarce, and members are direct competitors for them. There is also more internal politicking when some functions, represented by team members, think they stand to lose by certain decisions of the team, and the representing member is under pressure from colleagues as well as personally concerned. It is a simple psychic-economic calculation: do the gains from dropping certain interest/goals in the name of cooperation outweigh the losses? Cooperation and reduced politicking are more likely to occur when team members are participating in the group as individuals rather than as representatives, because they can make individual deals free of the pressure of a "shadow group" symbolically looking over their shoulders. (Indeed, when teams begin to jell as cooperative entities, even representatives sometimes forget their external group affiliation in favor of team identification – sometimes to the detriment of the constituency supposedly being served by the participation of its representative.)

Beyond the politics of interest maximization, teams are also arenas for the flexing of power muscles in and of themselves. There is often nothing inherently more "democratic" about certain decisions because they were made by teams rather than individual managers. Teams can turn into oligarchies, with a few dominant people taking over and forcing the others to fall into line. There are many examples in history of supposedly representative mechanisms' sliding into oligarchies – (e.g. the reputed takeover of some unions by small groups with shady ties). The benign "tyranny" of peers can substitute for the benign "tyranny" of managers, with conformity pressures as strong and sanctions for deviance as impelling. In one highly participative factory, workers complained that they felt too dependent on their teams for evaluation and job security and feared being ostracized by a clique. Members of autonomous work teams in a Cummins Engine plant were likely to be harder on absent members, according to a former plant manager, than management would have dared to be; they would often appear at the doorstep to drag a person in to work if the claimed illness did not satisfy team members. (Of course, they relied on each other's contributions more than in a conventional work situation.) Indeed, management often counts on this peer pressure to stay in line as a side benefit of participation.

Finally, teams become politicized when there are historic tensions between members that have not been resolved before the "team" is formed, tensions that are more likely in category-conscious, segmentalist cultures than in integrative ones, where ties cut across levels, functions, and social categories.

These tensions can rise to greater importance when hostile parties are thrown together and forced to interact, especially if they have to rely on each other for reasonable outcomes. This statement challenges a classic social-psychological cliché, based on a famous experiment by Muzafer and Carolyn Sherif, that groups in conflict who suddenly find themselves dependent on each other for survival develop "superordinate goals", which relieve the tensions; they discovered this by fostering group rivalry and then imposing a crisis at a summer camp. But that was summer camp, not a corporation. Experience from joint labor-management participation in problem solving suggests that there are circumstances in which hostility may increase, rather than decrease. If no attempt has been made to create a more integrative system, to resolve tensions and improve communication before the meeting, and if the situation is frustrating – as meetings can easily be – the emotions may rise to the surface, and members of the opposing camps may start blaming each other for team problems. At British Rail, participation by worker representatives in management meetings resulted in increased tension between managers and workers, especially because worker representatives tended to include those more critical of management.

Successful labor-management committees that seem to belie this do so not because participation automatically created a "team" out of adversaries but because careful groundwork was laid before the parties ever came together to begin joint problem solving. The Sherifs' hypothesis seems to be borne out by the cooperative relationship of the automobile manufacturers and the United Auto Workers, making mutual concessions in a time of crisis, where the "superordinate goal" is survival of the US auto industry. But the two groups got to the point at which joint participation was possible only because of preceding efforts to improve communication, demonstrate good faith, and remove irritants.

Thus, "power" and "community" can run at cross-purposes. The more forces there are that fan the political flames within a participative "team" the more likely it is that members will feel uncommitted to the team and unwilling to invest scarce organizational time to make it work. "Political" conflicts and tensions need not be conscious or overt to be disruptive;

there may simply be subtle discomforts that members can barely articulate which tell them that this is a place to withhold commitment.

The myth of "team"

"Inequality" and "politics" in team discussions are not generically so bad. After all, the people we are talking about have learned to live with both in the rest of their service in the corporate hierarchy. Dominance of the "best" – most skilled, most informed – participators seems likely to produce better decisions. "Political" discussions may mean that a variety of interests are more accurately reflected in ultimate decisions. So the solution to the problems of lowered commitment that these phenomena create should not lie in expecting the skilled and informed to stay out of discussions or those with special needs or interests to forget them. But that "solution" – holding back – is in fact what is fostered by the next dilemma of participation: "team" mythology.

The mythology that surrounds the idea of "team" in many organizations holds that differences among members do not exit – because they are now a "team" – and therefore it is not legitimate to acknowledge them or talk about them. Everyone has to act as if they were all sharing equally in the operations of the group. While inside the team, they have to pretend that they do not see that some are more able than others, or that the highest-level people are dominating, or that the chair is railroading another decision through. Where "team" mythology is strong, only an outsider – a consultant or facilitator or naive visitor – can open it for examination.

In some organizations (or perhaps it is an American phenomenon), the idea of participation is imbued with a mystique that makes legitimate differentiation among participants difficult. Falling back on the external hierarchy is easier for a group than developing internal rankings, because the hierarchy was created by someone else and does not force the group members to confront their own differences or inadequacies. Even though implicit "rankings" are manifest in practice, as the group carries out its deliberations, it is threatening to the fragile solidarity of a newborn team to acknowledge them. This is a good example of "pluralistic ignorance": everyone knows individually but assumes that no one else does. And as long as no one says it aloud, it might not even be true.

Thus, the members who feel out of the group cannot bring up their concerns because of the myth that everyone is in. People with less to contribute because they are less informed do not feel comfortable seeking help in getting more information to contribute more because of the myth that everyone has an equal chance to contribute. At the same time, the dominant participants might feel slightly guilty or uneasy about their absorption of a major share of the air time, so they decide to keep quiet for a meeting or two, thereby depriving the group of speedier motion toward solutions.

I have heard variants of all of these feelings expressed by members of participative groups. The more task-driven the group, the more they are muted in the urgency of the task, but they still exist where "participation" is assumed to mean rote equality, non-differentiation. The task may get accomplished, but people harbor secret feelings that participation is not worth the emotional drain, or they may decide that involvement makes them feel worse rather than better. Or they simply stop coming to meetings.

Differentiation within a participative team is difficult, of course, in seg-mentalist corporate cultures that have not found a way to make people feel important or valued for their contributions unless they are in charge. Teams of peers, for examples, might thus prefer to pretend that no one is any different from anyone else rather than have it appear that some are admitting to being less important on some issue. But again, where groups are task-driven they may manage to create some kinds of differentiation without too much trouble: individual assignments, choice of a leader or chair, nods to specialized competencies.

However, there are some kinds of distinctions among members that it is difficult for any team to make – some decisions that might be better handled by a hierarchy rather than by participation, as we see in the next dilemma.

"It is hard to fire your friend"

If a team works, it often develops close bonds, which mean that people cannot always be open and honest with one another for fear of hurting or because of norms developed in the group. Groups develop a variety of social and emotional pressures resulting from friendship that make it diffi-cult sometimes for people to confront one another, rate one another accu-rately, or discipline one another. Thus, there are some issues for which managers need to stop in and take responsibility. For example, if teams are asked to evaluate the performance of their members, they often resist singling out individuals either positively or negatively and want to give everybody the same rating. There are some issues on which it is a relief to have a higher-status authority figure who simply takes over and decides; it would be too difficult, or too emotionally pressuring, for the group itself.

Chapter 17

Managerial leadership: the key to good organization

Elliott Jaques

There is a seriously disruptive movement afoot in American management. It bids fair to undermine our business competitiveness steadily and relentlessly. This movement is centered around the general idea of workplace democracy and worker involvement. These aspirations towards a better and more humane workplace are admirable; they cannot be gainsaid. The difficulty is that the steps proposed for fulfilling these aspirations are unrealistic and self-defeating. They demoralize the managerial system and take the heart out of the innovativeness of individual contributors.

These current ideas center upon replacing the managerial hierarchy, which is considered undemocratic, with so-called democratic group practices of various kinds. But the issue is not one of democracy versus hierarchy. What is required is to leave democracy and democratic voting to the political field where they belong and to find ways of transforming the managerial hierarchy into systems of accountable, human, value-adding managerial leadership.

To try to eliminate the managerial hierarchy in order to eliminate managerial autocracy is to throw out the baby with the bathwater. For the exercise of authority tied properly to accountability is one of the most constructive of all human activities. The real task – and the difficult one – is to replace autocratic management with accountable authoritative[1] management. It can be done. I propose here to show how.

BACKGROUND

For some years now there has been a constant stream of publications by human resource experts and academics forseeing the end of the managerial hierarchy and its replacement by some vague and unspecified new form or forms of organization. Peter Drucker, Tom Peters, Rosabeth Moss Kanter, Ed Lawler, Warren Bennis, Quinn Mills, Michael Hammer, Shoshana Zuboff, Barker and Ghoshal, Stan Davis, and countless others have forecast the end of the industrial age and the entrepreneurial age, and the coming of what has been called variously the information age, the services age, or the post-modern age.

This new age will supposedly require a transformation of the managerial hierarchy into an extraordinary array of "new" organizations – all of them democratic in tone. Thus we see arguments in favor of: workplace democracy, the company without boundaries or walls, cluster organizations, self-managing teams, corporate hubs, global matrix networks, symphony-orchestra-type systems, groups that grow spontaneously around information flows and just as spontaneously dissolve, quality circles, continuous improvement councils, substitution of leaders for managers at higher levels, and even the replacement of organization altogether by the inculcation of everyone into "a matrix frame of mind." But, ominously, nowhere is there any indication of where accountability and authority can be placed for work or competitive effectiveness in any of these arrangements.

These ideas have influenced the outlook of many senior executives. Thus, for example, James Houghton, chairman of Corning Inc., endorses the idea of Ralph Kilmann that we need organizational networks with a corporate hub that acts as negotiator, facilitator, broker, or think tank to a "global network of people and information, each exerting an influence on the other." Gone are accountable chief executive officers, and accountable presidents of subsidiary companies spread throughout the world connected to the corporate CEO and to their own subordinates through an accountable management hierarchy.

Similarly, experienced and successful CEOs such as Robert Haas, chairman and CEO of Levi Strauss has picked up the idea that managers are no longer to direct and "control" their subordinates, but rather to function as facilitators to help them arrive at effective group decisions. And Jack Welch extols the GE workout program of corporatewide town meeting discussion groups led by academics to identify unnecessary practices, letting managers off the hook for inefficiencies.

The trouble with these ideas is that they are based upon unrealistic fantasies about what the managerial hierarchy should be. None of them gets rid of the managerial hierarchy, nor can they do so, despite Tom Peters' unfounded notion that the managerial hierarchy at Citicorp, Federal Express, and other corporations has begun to disappear. For the reality of the ubiquitous employment systems by which modern societies mainly get their work done today is that people are employed as individuals in hierarchies in which some individuals – managers – are held accountable for the work of other individuals – their subordinates. This individual managerial accountability does not, and cannot, disappear merely by the introduction of groupthink. Boards of directors are in gross dereliction of duty if they allow their corporate CEO's to abandon their individual accountability and thereby abdicate. Nor can any other appointed manager be allowed to do, whatever his or her level in the organization.

Organizations need to be able to employ individual people who are accountable, and clearly accountable, for getting work done. I challenge any protagonist of these "new" organizational styles to identify where accountability lies in their systems: in fact, they are organizational monstrosities tailor-made for buck passing. And by accountability, I am referring to accountability for new designs, for bringing new products rapidly to market, for establishing new world markets, for maintaining quality, for reducing costs, for developing the executive talent pool, for acquisitions and new ventures – in short, accountability for all the work at all levels and in all functions that make an organization competitively effective.

Can so many human resource practitioners, academics and consultants be wrong? Unfortunately, yes. This has happened because they have bought three misleading notions.

1 First is the impression that managers are coercive autocrats who lord it over subordinates and that more democratic group decision making is needed. This is incorrect. Autocratic managers are symptoms not of the managerial system *per se* but of badly organized managerial systems – for example, with too many layers and with people breathing down each other's necks – that are almost universal.
2 Second is the supposition that the Japanese competitive miracle was achieved by quality circles, continuous improvement councils, and other kinds of democratic teams and groupthink. Those procedures were peripheral. The Deming miracle in Japan was achieved by building quality, just-in-time working, and continuous improvement into the process, that is, instituting accountability in the managerial system, where these ideas flourish to this day.
3 Third is the naive assumption that the new information technology will make managers redundant. None of the proponents of this idea has so far given any indication even of having considered where accountability would lie for ensuring that action was taken and for the quality of that action.

Along with this disruptive attempt to put "democratic teams" in place of good management is the idea of "participative management," as though ordinary good management were not necessarily based upon effective two-way working relationships between effective managerial leaders and their subordinates. Indeed, the very phrase "participative management" suggests the possibility of something called "non-participative management"! But surely "non-participative" management is not management at all. It is coercion and should not be associated with the concept of management.

In the same vein is the currently popular idea of empowerment. This is a direct reflection of the failure to establish a satisfactory hierarchical organization in which the right amount of accountability and the accompanying authority are allocated to each layer in the hierarchy. We do not need "less layers and power down," we need the correct number of layers, and the correct authority at each level, as I shall describe below.

We also go wrong with vague ideas like "networking" – an aspiration with no indication of how to get it. And we go equally wrong with the fallacious and damaging idea of employees dealing with each other like suppliers and customers. It is the duty of effective value-adding managers to mediate between subordinates in a constructive, human way. Letting subordinates fight it out like suppliers and customers is an abdication from this duty, and, in fact, can be shown to dehumanize working relationships, as false propositions always do.

BAD PSYCHOLOGICAL IDEAS

Reinforcing the overriding falseness of these ideas of democratic teams and processes within the managerial hierarchy, two other equally misleading and disruptive ideas have been promoted by the experts.

The first is that personality conflicts have a large part to play in the problems that beset hierarchy. Personality inventories like the Myers-Briggs test are said to match personalities so as to get groups that have just the right amount of aggressiveness, sociability, proactive initiative, risk taking, reflectiveness, and so on distributed among the members. The members of such groups theoretically take into account their knowledge of each other's personality makeup and so avoid conflict.

This emphasis upon personality actually focuses upon serious psychopathology. For if members are not disturbed to the point where they are unable to control their behavior, if they are able to leave their psychopathology at home, then they should be left to express their personalities freely. If the organization is requisitely established and the working relationships clearly specified, then nothing but good comes from leaving their "personalities" alone.

Finally we have the unfortunate contribution of wage and salary economics and motivation theory. Economists tell us that human labor is a commodity and its value should be determined by the marketplace like any other commodities. Wrong! Real human beings have an inherent relative value determined by their level of capability. They seek levels of work in which they can exercise their capability to the full – and feel justly and fairly treated as human beings when they are paid on a scale that pays differentially for varying levels of work.

Given an equitable differential pay system and opportunities for work at levels consistent with one's capability, people do not need to be motivated by bonus incentives. We are humans, not pigeons. Whereas political equality is basic to political democracy, people do not really seek equality at work, nor do they seek to be judged either as groups or by groups. In our work, we seek accountable, value-adding managers with the right degree of higher capability to judge our effectiveness, assess our capabilities, and recognize our merit. That is what good management ought to be about – and can be about.

One of the hallmarks of a truly democratic free enterprise society is to ensure that each and every citizen really does have the opportunity for work in which he or she can utilize his or her full potential capability as that potential unfolds and matures throughout life to levels higher in capability. Our employment organizations should have the bounden duty to contribute to that process, not by hollow fads and practices and denial of authoritative management, but by the hard work of establishing requisite organization structure and requisite managerial leadership practices.

MANAGERIAL LEADERSHIP: THE HEART OF COMPETITIVENESS

What, then, is needed to reverse these destructive fads and to get on with the task of strengthening America's business competitiveness? The answer is to improve our managerial systems to produce humane, decisive, value-adding managerial leadership, at all levels right across the board and to establish worker roles at the correct level for the work to be done. Note that I have not said to get back to traditional management, for here, also, the pundits are wrong when they say that traditional management is satisfactory for the industrial age but not the new age. Managerial organization has never been used at anything like its true potential. But some companies in some countries, such as the few outstanding Japanese companies, have begun to get closer to getting full value out of their managerial systems and workers. Fortunately (for us), there is plenty of room to outpace them because they too are far from understanding how to realize the full potential of the managerial organization.

Here is an outline of the main steps by which organization and managerial development can contribute to the winning of a global competitive edge.[2]

Accountability

First, it is necessary to recognize that our corporate work organizations are built upon contracts with individuals to work for the company. Thus a board of directors cannot shift accountability for corporate effectiveness from its appointed CEO to a corporate hub, any more than it can allow the CEO to shift accountability from his or her immediate subordinates to networks, councils or teams. In the final analysis, accountability for successful work rests on the shoulders of individuals. To spread vaguely specified authority over non-accountable groups is to create non-responsible buck-passing organizations. This is costly!

Organizational structure

Second, in order to promote value-adding decisive managerial leadership, the organizational structure has to be right. Too many organizational layers means having so-called managers breathing down their subordinates' necks, without that sufficiently large difference in capability between them necessary for effective management. Business tends to suffer from grossly excessive managerial layering. My studies have shown that our large multibillion-dollar corporations may have from ten to twenty layers from corporate CEO down to the shop and office floor, whereas they need only seven. (Supercorporations need eight and smaller companies proportionately less.) Excessive layering is serious, for example, at the shop floor level, where there is a glut of middlemen and straw bosses variously called lead hands, charge hands, team leaders, supervisors, or junior foremen, who clog up the organization. They make it impossible to achieve the kind of first-line managerial roles in which, as a permanent fact of ordinary everyday working life, true first-line managers are in a position to be able to be held accountable for quality, just-in-time working and continuous improvement *à la* Deming.

Lateral working relationships

Third, lateral working relationships need to be spelled out far more clearly in terms of accountability; for example, the relationship between departments engaged in corporate technical and business development work with a global thrust and departments in product development and improvement work within strategic business units with emphasis upon local diversity. Failures in these working relationships cannot be overcome by passing the vague magical wand of "networking" or "facilitator," or "negotiator" over everyone. Hard, painstaking and detailed specifications of mutual accountability and authority need to be worked out for every pair of roles between corporate center and the business units, as well as within the center and within each business unit.

Individual calibre

Fourth, once organizational structure has been more clearly analyzed and requisitely established, we need to do a far better job than we are doing at present of filling both management and worker roles with people of the right calibre to do the work. It is now possible to evaluate individual calibre not only more precisely, but also directly in relation to the level of complexity of the work to be done – from CEO to shop floor, sharpening up career development and talent pool development (starting with graduate interns) to the great advantage of each and every individual.[3]

Managerial leadership

Finally, it is essential to revise our managerial leadership practices in the following ways;[4] require managers to explain things and engage in two-way discussions with subordinates; pay workers in relation to level of work; and hold everyone accountable for achieving work of the right quantity, within quality standards, on time and within allocated resources, unless the manager is warned beforehand of possible deviations.

Also we must hold managers accountable for ongoing continuous improvement work based upon the best statistical or other procedures for identifying process variances; and hold managers-once-removed account-able for the evaluation of potential capability of subordinates-once-removed, and for mentoring. Our current procedures unfortunately reflect the unsound principles and woefully inadequate ideas upon which our HR, training, compensation, and organization professional work is currently based.

Conclusion

Here, then, is the true road to global competitiveness. Let us not attempt to replace our managers and managerial systems with pie-in-the-sky groups, but rather work to establish new and higher standards of mana-gerial leadership and development. It is the companies who can rely upon decisive value-adding managerial leadership right down to the shop and office floor, supported by effective lateral working relationships and by well-positioned workers who will win the competitive day and make the genuine contribution to competitive, free enterprise democracy.

REFERENCES

1 Authority, from the Latin *augere*, to grow or create (also the root of author) is one of the most creative words in the language. It is not to be confused with autocracy, which comes from the Greek *auto-kratein*, to rule by myself. They really are different ideas!
2 See Jaques, Elliott (1989) *Requisite Organization* and Jaques and Clement (1991) *Executive Leadership*, both published by Cason Hall & Co. Arlington, VA.
3 Study by Jaques and Cason, Cason Hall and Co., 1992.
4 Jaques and Clement (1991) *Executive Leadership*, Cason Hall and Co., Arlington, VA.

Chapter 18

Job redesign

Mick Marchington

INTRODUCTION

This chapter is concerned with a variety of forms of job redesign. Some of these are rather older in origin, for example based upon the research of Herzberg (1972) on job enlargement and enrichment, or Walker and Guest (1952) on job rotation. Conversely, others – such as teamworking and attempts to reduce demarcation – have become more widespread since the mid-1980s as employers have sought to gain both greater flexibility and the commitment of employees to organizational goals. Many of the better-known experiments in job redesign have taken place in the USA or Sweden, although there are a growing number of publicized examples from the UK.

Teamworking

Teamworking represents the most extensive form of job redesign. It combines both horizontal and vertical additions to existing jobs so that individual employees not only move between different tasks on a particular operation, but also take over some or all the responsibilities for managing the team as well. The tag 'autonomous' has typically been dropped from the concept of this kind of group, and teamworking provides a more accurate description of their activity. In 'flexible' work groups, as Kelly terms them, 'work is assigned to the group rather than to particular individuals or roles' (1982: 119). Buchanan prefers the term 'high performance work design', but the description of activity is much the same: 'a work group is allocated an overall task and given discretion over how the work is to be done. The groups are 'self-regulating and work without direct supervision' (1987: 40). Grayson uses the terminology of 'self-regulating work group'; he defines this as:

> a democratic form of work organization which ascribes to the group of workers responsibility for the regulation, organization and control of their jobs, and the conditions immediately surrounding them. It involves the establishment of specific group responsibilities and bound-

aries of autonomy to undertake defined tasks in a way to be decided within the group . . . Within (these) boundaries, the group is free to make decisions about its day-to-day work.

(Grayson 1990: 1)

Ignoring the fact that Grayson tends to underestimate the constraints on these kinds of group, especially with regard to autonomy, the key features of teams – cooperation, task variety, responsibility for a complete operation, and diagnosis – are central to all three definitions.

Examples of teamworking can be found in a number of different industries and countries, but analyses of those in chemicals and vehicle production are predominant. One of the first examples used by Walton to illustrate the nature of a 'commitment' strategy is from chemicals, in which he notes that 'jobs are designed to be broader than before, to combine planning and implementation, and to include efforts to upgrade operations, not just maintain them . . . Teams, not individuals, are often the organisational units accountable for performance' (1985: 79). Research by Buchanan and myself has examined the nature of teamworking in different plants in the chemical industry. Buchanan (1986: 71–2) reports on the operation of a new pigments factory at Ciba Geigy in Scotland, on which plant operators were not supervised and rotated jobs on a daily basis. All the operators had been trained for at least one year prior to working on the plant, and they were given responsibility and discretion for how the plant should operate to meet production targets. They had to understand the process, the product and the equipment, and their experience, judgement and initiative were critical to ensure that the plant maintained its output. In addition, they needed to use their tacit skills to override computer messages as appropriate; to keep production going if they 'knew' nothing was wrong, or to close down operations if they recognized a serious fault.

My own studies in the chemical industry paint a similar picture; at Ichem for example (1990: 107–8), process operators on the more automated plants typically worked as teams undertaking a whole range of tasks from the most technologically advanced through to the heaviest and most mundane. Again, as with Buchanan's study, operators underwent long training periods, often achieved externally recognized qualifications, and operated without much direct supervision; indeed, the supervisor operated more as a facilitator for the teams, and a technical officer was also available to assist with more difficult problems. All the operators were qualified to do every task on the plants, and they rotated between manual operations (checking the plant, bagging products, mending minor leaks) through to work in the control room, where they had responsibility for overseeing the process in line with production requirements. The process operators seemed to value the opportunity to undertake a wide range of jobs, especially the 'simple' tasks because this 'makes a nice change'. Increasingly, they are expected by management to take responsibility for the production of a particular batch or process, and they have been well rewarded financially for so doing.

At another plant, which is renowned for being at the forefront of teamworking in the chemical industry, there is even greater flexibility between process operators and craft workers, and indeed the two jobs have now been merged into a common enhanced grade. Maintenance and repair work, which was previously centralized for the site as a whole, has now become a part of each team's tasks, and craft workers have been assigned to each plant and shift. Again, a key feature of the change process has been a massive investment in new plant and equipment, which is bolstered by a high commitment to training. Ultimately, all process workers will gain the capability to undertake any job across the plant, but there is still a tendency for employees to rely upon their specialist area of expertise, especially amongst the ex-craft workers and at times when the speedy resolution of a problem is seen as crucial to maintain production. The 'old' role of supervisor has now been removed and instead operations are coordinated by a team leader who works in conjunction with plant managers who are themselves part of a much reduced hierarchy. Interviews conducted at both of these plants suggest that employees appear to be satisfied with the new arrangements and are particularly keen about the variety which is now contained within their jobs.

Teamworking is not just restricted to the chemical industry, of course, although a whole range of factors (technological, product and labour market) make it especially appropriate for this sector. Recent studies have shown how teamworking has been developed in computer manufacture and food processing. At the former (Digital Equipment VLSI, in Scotland), small groups (10–12) were set up with full 'front-to-back' responsibility for product assembly and test, fault finding and problem-solving, and some equipment maintenance. Management had to adapt a supportive style, and team leaders were present initially, but were expected to withdraw once they had developed a greater sense of autonomy in the groups (Buchanan 1987: 40–3). A subsequent assessment of the scheme regarded it as successful because of improvements in quality, reductions in work-in-progress, and smaller batch sizes, and employees generally reported satisfaction with the new methods of working. The best features appeared to be greater job interest, variety, and freedom to make their own decisions, and there was overall support for the cell-based approach to work organization. Although attitudes to other colleagues and the complay were generally positive, areas of dissatisfaction were also identified, particularly in relation to pay, a lack of adequate training, and management style (IRRR, No 475, 1990). Teamworking was also introduced into RHM Ingredients when a new site was opened in 1989, and most of the features are similar to those already discussed; again, it is interesting to note that team members are expected to exercise responsibility for planning and organization, including quality assurance and the coordination of maintenance work (IRRR, No 477, 1990).

The motor vehicles industry has also seen a number of attempts to bring in teamworking, especially in Sweden and the USA. In the case of the former, the second and third waves of development at Volvo have extended task-based EI beyond the simple job rotation (horizontal job redesign) experiments of the early 1970s. The second wave of the early 1980s comprised a number of features of both horizontal and vertical job redesign; among the former was job rotation between workers on the assembly lines, whereas the latter included a new mix of tasks – for example, allocating responsibilities for administrative work within the team, such as scheduling vacation times, hiring and training new workers, and rotating the position of team leader on a regular basis (Pontusson 1990: 322–3).

A similar process of teamworking has been introduced at one of Volvo's truck assembly plants, and evaluations by employees four years after the system had been implemented yielded highly positive results. For example, 'jobs at LB (the plant) are considered to be more varied, to involve more responsibility and challenge, and to foster more helpful attitudes'. However, the survey evidence also found many employees still regarded the work as degrading and exhausting (much lower than at a sister plant though) and a large minority suffered from back pains (nearly 40 per cent) and felt there was a strong time pressure (20 per cent) connected with their work. While the new truck plant was consistently seen as better than the others, one of the interviewees commented:

> It is good here if you have something to compare it with ... It is definitely better than a line ... but I do not feel any pride about what I do, the work is so monotonous and boring that anyone can do it.
>
> (Berggren 1989: 194–9)

In the USA the teamwork concept has been introduced in a number of organizations, often as part of a QWL (Quality of Work Life) Programme and sometimes referred to as the 'new industrial relations'. As we shall see below, its implementation has been greeted with differing sets of reactions by different people. On the one hand, it is seen as the key to a more successful future, while on the other, it is viewed with alarm as the latest management move to intensify and control labour – 'management by stress' as Parker and Slaughter (1988) term it. One of the first examples of a 'team-concept' plant, according to Kochan et al. (1986: 96) was at TRW Inc, a diversified manufacturing firm located in a small community in the mid-west of the USA. Most teams had between eight and fifteen members, and some operated as autonomous work groups, with a team manager – generally appointed from within the team – to oversee its work. The manager was expected to act as a facilitator, and many tasks which would traditionally be undertaken by management were given over (at least partly) to the team members – training or production scheduling, for example. Employees did not work solely on one job, but rotated as appropriate, often after they had acquired the skills to make this effective. Compared with other similar plants in the company, wage rates were low, although they were in the upper half of wage distribution in the local area. Incidentally, this represents a somewhat different picture from the British examples from chemicals quoted earlier, where wages were well above average.

The team concept came to the US car industry in newly opened non-union plants in the south during the mid-1970s, and it was negotiated into the large northern plants in the early 1980s. The stimulus for change was a combination of economic problems in the American car industry and the growth in international competition, especially from the Japanese, which together led the key negotiators to reach agreements about introducing new methods of working as a way to 'save the industry'. The teamworking systems that were initiated look remarkably similar to those which have been discussed above. However, as Kochan *et al.* note, compared with traditional methods of job design,

> The operating-team system entails a fundamental reorganization of shop floor labour relations because it integrates changes in work organization with increases in worker decision making. The operating team provides both a reduction in job classification and a broadening of (individual) jobs.

> (Kochan *et al.* 1986: 160)

In addition, there is provision for semi-skilled employees to take on maintenance tasks, allocation of work, and inspection, as well as regular team meetings. By the spring of 1988 the team concept was in use or planned for 17 GM assembly plants, in 6 Chrysler plants, in addition to 2 Ford plants and all the wholly- or partly-owned Japanese factories (Parker and Slaughter 1988: 4). As an example, Black and Ackers (1990: 3) analyse the operation of the 'joint process' at a GM components plant which has a cell-based manufacturing unit known as Team Syracuse. All employees on the team are fully flexible, but in addition members have responsibility for production start-up, shift scheduling, inspection, statistical process control, machine loading, and tool change. The team area has also been established as a separate accounting base so as to track the efficiency of the unit. Local union representatives were involved in the design of the system, which led one shop committee chair to note that for the first time, local hourly workers had managed to provide an input prior to the assignment of employees to the area (Black and Ackers 1990: 5).

Perceptions of work and involvement had changed due to the introduction of the team concept; some were pleased to have more control over their immediate work environment, whereas others felt that the new system did introduce extra stress by having to work faster to cover for absent colleagues and due to peer pressure (Black and Ackers 1990: 11). Even the most stringent critics of teamworking in US car factories acknowledge that at NUMMI (one of the plants where the team concept has made most impact) there have been substantial gains in productivity (Parker and Slaughter 1988: 10). Furthermore, this improvement was achieved at an old plant, with an existing workforce, and without any advanced technology or an overt confrontation with the union.

What are the implications of teamworking, however, for employees, supervisors, and workplace trade union organization? Although there are several reports that suggest that employees find the new methods of working more attractive than traditional techniques (especially in Sweden where teamworking has been introduced jointly with the unions), there are also indications that it produces a more stressful factory environment. Many of the independent studies agree that teamworking, especially on car assembly lines, does induce higher levels of stress among employees. For example, Berggren indicates that workers perceive greater time pressures in the most technologically advanced Volvo plants than in the others (1989: 197), and Black and Ackers report a similar finding from studies at GM in the USA (1990: 11). Others, and in particular Parker and Slaughter (1988: 16–30), view the whole concept of teamworking as little more than a managerial technique to intensify work yet further, to 'stretch' the production system as far as it will go, and 'manage by stress' (MBS). They illustrate the principle of MBS with reference to an andon board, located over the assembly line, which has red, yellow and green lights. A red light indicates there is a problem and the line needs to be stopped, yellow indicates that an operator is falling behind and needs assistance, while a green means that production levels are acceptable and there is no problem. In the traditional US operation, they state, management wants nothing but green lights and would design the system accordingly. However, in the team concept plants (MBS, as they term it) green is not a desirable state because presumably the line could run even faster. Instead, management speeds up the line until the light is mostly on yellow, with the odd red light to pinpoint areas where further improvements can be made. Perhaps Parker and Slaughter's conspiratorial notions of management strategy go rather too far, but this account is a useful corrective to the view that job redesign represents a panacea whereby both managements and employees automatically gain substantial benefits. It also helps us to remember that management's primary interest in new production techniques is not – with the possible exception of some of the Swedish experiments – specifically aimed at increasing industrial democracy and worker participation (Wood 1986: 442).

Vertical role integration and teamworking both have an impact on the traditional supervisory role, and all the studies point to potential problems for this group of staff. In theory, the more that subordinates take over responsibility for running operations (scheduling the line, controlling the process, prioritizing the paperwork) the more that supervisors are released to concentrate their energies on higher level activities. This should then reverberate all the way up the hierarchy. In practice, however, supervisors seem to have seen the situation in a rather different way. The introduction of teamworking is often associated with other organizational changes, especially those to reduce the number of levels in the management hierarchy, and there have been fears amongst supervisors that their jobs will be lost. Even if they do not actually lose their jobs, it has proved difficult for many supervisors to adapt their roles to that of facilitators, people who assist the team to complete their work and act as troubleshooters. Given the fact that most supervisors are promoted from the shop floor or office, they understandably lack confidence in their abilities to cope with new expectations (see Daniel and McIntosh 1972: 49); Marchington 1982; Dawson and Webb 1989: 236). Other supervisors are dubious about the advantages of greater operator control and teamworking in any event, viewing this – as part of a drive to develop a strategy of 'responsible autonomy' – as pandering to the workforce, as a misguided approach propagated by 'the long-haired idealists at corporate HQ' (Marchington et al. 1992: 112).

The impact of teamworking on workplace union organization is rather more difficult to determine, especially because many of the deals in the US car industry have been the subject of joint union–management agreements and those in Sweden were at least partially instigated by the union movement. On one level, given the number of unionized workplaces in which teamworking has been introduced alongside a desire to maintain the role of the union (at least in formal terms with the continuation of existing agreements), it could be argued that the two can co-exist quite satisfactorily. On the other hand, however, the longer-term implications of teamworking, with its unitary undertones, can spell problems for employee commitment to workplace union organization. This appeared to be happening at the Ichem plant studied by Marchington and Parker (1990: 224) as employees identified more with the production processes on which they worked and saw problems increasingly within the context of organizational goals. The situation in the US car industry, which is summed up by Wood in the following way, appears to have a wider relevance:

> The aim, at least from management's point of view, is to change the rules of the game, or to substitute one game for another. That is, one in which the union plays a less active role in defining the terrain of contest on the shop floor, the expectation being that it will be the inevitable contingencies of production, as well as the continual search for improvement, which define shop floor controversy.
>
> (Wood 1986: 439)

In addition, teams may be encouraged to compete with one another, with the inevitable consequence that notions of plant-wide solidarity are not achieved or maintained.

REFERENCES

Berggren, C. (1989), 'New production concepts in final assembly – the Swedish experience', in Wood S. (ed.), *The Transformation of Work?* Unwin Hyman, London, pp. 171–203.

Black J. and Ackers P. (1988), 'The Japanisation of British industry; a case study of quality circles in the carpet industry', *Employee Relations*, 10(6), pp. 9–16.

Black J. and Ackers P. (1990), *Voting For Employee Involvement at General Motors*, paper presented to the 8th Labour Process Conference, University of Aston, March.

Buchanan D. (1979), *The Development of Job Design Theories and Techniques* Saxon House, Farnborough.

Buchanan D. (1986), 'Management objectives in technical change', in Knights D. and Willmott H. (eds), *Managing the Labour Process*, Gower, Aldershot, pp. 67–84.

Buchanan D. (1987), 'Job enrichment is dead: long live high-performance works design', *Personnel Management*, May.

Daniel W. and McIntosh N. (1972), *The Right to Manage?* Macdonald, London.

Dawson P. and Webb J. (1989), 'New production arrangements: the totally flexible cage?', *Work, Employment and Society*, 3(2), pp. 221–38.

Grayson D. (1990), *Self-Regulating Work Groups – an aspect of organisational change*, ACAS Work Research Unit Occasional Paper No 46, July.

Herzberg F. (1972), 'One more time; how do you motivate employees?', in Davis, L. and Taylor, J. (eds) *Design of Jobs*, Penguin, London.

Industrial Relations Review and Report (1990), 'Change to cell-based working, multiskilling and teamworking at Digital Equipment VLSI', *IRRR, IRS Employment Trends*, 2 November.

Industrial Relations Review and Report (1990), 'Moving to autonomous work groups at RHM Ingredients', *IRRR, IRS Employment Trends*, 7 December.

Kelly J. (1982), *Scientific Management, Job Redesign and Work Performance*. Academic Press, London.

Kochan T., Katz H. and McKersie R. (1986), *The Transformation of American Industrial Relations*, Basic Books, New York.

Marchington M. (1980), *Responses to Participation at Work*, Gower, Farnborough.

Marchington M. (1982), *Managing Industrial Relations*, McGraw Hill, Maidenhead.

Marchington M. (1987), 'Employee participation', in Towers B. (ed.) *A Handbook of Industrial Relations Practice*, Kogan Page, London, pp. 162–82.

Marchington M. (1989), 'Joint consultation in practice', in Sisson K. (ed.), *Personnel Management in Britain*, op. cit., pp. 378–402.

Marchington M. and Armstrong R. (1981), 'A case for consultation', *Employee Relations*, 3(1), pp. 10–16.

Marchington M. and Armstrong R. (1985), 'Involving employees through the recession', *Employee Relations*, 7(5), pp. 17–21.

Marchington M., Goodman J., Wilkinson A. and Ackers P. (1992), *New Developments In Employee Involvement*, Employment Department, Research Series Number 2.

Marchington M. and Harrison E. (1991), 'Customers, competitors and choice:

employ relations in good retailing', *Industrial Relations Journal*, 22(4), pp. 286–300.

Marchington M. and Parker P. (1990), *Changing Patterns of Employee Relations*, Wheatsheaf, Hemel Hempstead.

Marchington M., Parker P. and Prestwich A. (1989), 'Problems with team briefing in practice', *Employee Relations*, 11(4), pp. 21–30.

Parker M. and Slaughter J. (1988), *Choosing Sides: Unions and the Team Concept*, South End Press, Boston.

Pontusson J. (1990), 'The politics of new technology and job redesign: a comparison of Volvo and British Leyland', *Economic and Industrial Democracy*, 11, pp. 311–36.

Walker C. and Guest R. (1952), *Man on the Assembly Line*, Harvard University Press, Cambridge.

Walton R. (1985), 'From control to commitment in the workplace,' *Harvard Business Review*, 63(2), pp. 77–85.

Wood S. (1986), 'The co-operative labour strategy in the US auto industry', *Economic and Industrial Democracy*, 7, pp. 415–47.

Chapter 19

Innovative teams at work

Neil Anderson, Gillian Hardy and Michael West

Many organizations have survived throughout the 1970s and 1980s by responding to the demands of external change in an *ad hoc* and unplanned manner, but the 1990s look set to impose an increased burden, which will necessitate more proactive and strategic human resource management approaches towards coping with change.

One central technique in the repertoire of coping mechanisms is that of self-generated innovation and creativity from within the organization. The process of conceptualization, development and implementation of new and improved work practices and products constitutes an essential means of responding proactively to external change. Yet capacities for innovation within organizations at both individual and work group levels are too often underdeveloped and undervalued. Good ideas and proposals are frequently stifled in a morass of bureaucracy and complacency or, even worse, never come to the attention of those in power for fear of failure through rejection. The likelihood, then, is that many are failing to capitalize on their full propensity for innovation.

How can HRM specialists facilitate and foster the innovation process? In the past the typical personnel department has had little input to this process, except perhaps for conducting training aimed at general teambuilding and development. Our programme of research at Sheffield University is revealing key elements in innovation processes, which have important implications for the role of HRM specialists in developing creativity and innovation.

The Sheffield innovation research programme was established in 1985 with the objective of answering four major questions abut innovation at work:

1 What factors act as helps and hindrances to innovation?
2 What distinguishes between highly innovative and less innovative work groups?
3 How does the innovation process develop and progress over time?

4 What practical measures can be recommended to facilitate innovation and match the demands of the work to team innovativeness?

Over the last five years a diverse range of organizations, work groups, and individual job roles have been studied. The results highlight the importance of work groups or teams as the crucial medium through which new ideas are proposed, shaped and re-shaped through interpersonal negotiation and pursued towards implementation. Four factors have consistently surfaced in both private and public sectors as key determinants of group innovativeness:

1 Vision;
2 Participative safety;
3 Climate for excellence;
4 Support for innovation.

Vision

Vision is a shared idea of a valued outcome within a group. For a marketing team it might be to stimulate sales growth in the long term; for a human resource manager it might be to influence the strategic business plans of the organization to maximize personnel productivity; and for a researcher it might be to advance understanding of factors promoting the effectiveness and psychological well-being of people at work. If it is to facilitate innovation in a group, it is important for vision to be negotiated and shared; visions imposed by those in power are less likely to generate innovation. Since groups are constantly in flux, with some members leaving and joining and others gradually changing their values and attitudes, shared visions are likely to be constantly evolving. Another component of vision is its relative clarity. To the extent that a vision is clearly stated, it will facilitate innovation, since it will provide a distinguishable target encouraging focused development of new and improved ways of working.

Much evidence has been amassed to support the claim that a clearly understandable, shared and negotiated vision is a fundamental determinant of innovation.[1] The implication for HRM specialists is clear: if they are to foster innovation in groups at work, close attention needs to be given to the group's shared vision. Crucially, the question should be posed: 'has the group negotiated a clear, shared vision, and to what extent is it motivating and attainable?'

Participative safety

Much research has shown that high levels of participation are associated with less resistance to change and a greater likelihood of innovation. The more people are involved in decision-making through having influence, through interacting and through sharing information, the more likely they are to support the decision and also to offer ideas for new and improved ways of working.

However, the notion of participation should not be misinterpreted as necessarily implying cohesion and democracy. Organizations are often highly political in their internal processes, and inter-group conflicts are played out in situations of both low and high levels of participation. People may participate very fully in the decision-making process solely in order to achieve their own political ends. For instance, two departments may constantly be at loggerheads over the distribution of resources, and so attempt to be involved as much as possible in decision-making processes so that their own views are well represented. But such a situation is unlikely to lead to high levels of innovation, since people tend not to take risks in situations which they perceive as 'unsafe'.

In order for innovation to occur, therefore, safety is an important element in a participative environment. Team members are more likely to take the risk of proposing new ad improved ways of working in a climate which they perceive as personally non-threatening and supportive. Where an individual feels that proposing a new idea will lead to censorship or ridicule, the person is less likely to take the risk of proposing that idea.

Climate for excellence

Climate for excellence means a real commitment to achieving first-rate performance through modifying procedures and implementing improved methods of work or work practices. Discussions within the team of standards of work, methods for achieving objectives, and critical reviews of performance levels are indicators of a climate for excellence within the group.

The result of a climate for excellence is that new ideas are born into a demanding group environment in which proposals are appraised and challenged in a constructive manner. Such a climate for constructive controversy will militate against the falsely coherent and unjustifiably compliant group atmosphere which tends to stifle the emergence of radical innovation.[2]

Support for innovation

As many managers have emphasized to us during the progress of our research, it is often the case that support for innovation within organizations is articulated but not enacted. That is, senior executives often profess support for innovation, but actually do little to nurture it by providing encouragement, sufficient resources, and personnel or finance to develop good ideas and proposals. The notion of support for innovation also

Table 19.1 Team innovation checklist

Vision	**Climate for excellence**
Does the team have a clearly articulated vision, mission or set of objectives?	Is excellent task performance of central importance to the team?
Is this vision (set of objectives) shared by all team members?	What procedures and methods are used to monitor and improve performance levels?
Is the vision or set of objectives clearly stated?	Are all team members committed to excellent standards?
Was the vision (set of objectives) originally developed and negotiated by the whole team?	Are team members prepared to discuss opposing ideas fully?
Is this vision (set of objectives) attainable?	**Support for innovation** Do team members support new ideas?
Participative safety	Do team members give time, co-operation and resources to help each other implement new ideas?
Do team members share information fully with each other?	
Do all team members participate in decision-making?	Does the team leader support and encourage new ideas?
Are team members ready to propose new ideas which challenge existing ways of doing things?	Does the team leader offer practical help and resources for the developing of new ideas?
Do team members discuss each other's work-related anxieties and successes?	
Is there a climate of trust and warmth within the group?	

implies that, proposals which prove not to be effective do not result in the innovator being penalized.[3]

To summarize, the four factors of vision, participative safety, climate for excellence and support for innovation have emerged from our research as key determinants of team innovativeness. The checklist in Table 19.1 can be used by any team to assess areas of potential strength and weakness.

Of course, innovation is rarely experienced as a smooth and non-conflictual process. Virtually all innovations can be seen as a challenge to the status quo likely to provoke reactions of both support and resistance from other members of the group. Innovation is therefore a political activity and demands political behaviour to persuade other key individuals to support proposals.

But how can personnel specialists facilitate innovation within their own organizations? As the function has developed from its historical industrial administration and welfare role towards a more strategic HRM role, personnel specialists are providing strategic input to work group innovation and effectiveness.

An outcome of our research has been the development of practical techniques and strategies for facilitating innovation and creativity within work groups and management teams. We have developed a programme of organizational interventions grounded on the four factors described above. A typical intervention might proceed as follows.

Generation of a vision statement

In working with teams to help them develop a team vision, we first encourage individuals to work in pairs and to come up with what they see as the group's objectives or vision. Then the pairs work in small groups, negotiating over the ideas produced, before the whole group meets and the accumulated 'visions' are presented. Then begins a process of negotiating and wordsmithing to produce the final statement of vision/mission or objectives – what we call 'sculpting'. This is the shared, negotiated and attainable vision the team has determined for itself.

Encouragement of participation

In order to encourage participation, the group is asked to focus on three areas: interaction, information-sharing and influence over decision-making. First, the frequency of formal and informal contacts is examined, along with checking that all group members are involved in these. If necessary, new mechanisms for encouraging interactions are put in place, and these could range from formal meetings to shared coffee breaks, weekly lunch meetings or telephone conferencing. Efforts are made to ensure all group members are involved, especially those who have previously been isolated.

Participation, however, is encouraged only after a climate of safety and trust has been suggested. Each group member is asked to discover each other's job-related anxieties and job satisfactions and successes through discussion and through sharing their own experiences in this area. This is accomplished in a climate of support, trust and openness with the group.

The information audit

Each group member asks 'what information do I get from (each other group member)'; 'what information do I want from ...'; 'what information do I want more of from ...'; and, in relation to each question, 'in what form do I get/want information from ...' (i.e. written, verbal, computerized). This information is then discussed in appropriate pairs within the group and new deals about information-sharing are struck, with the emphasis on the free flow of necessary, desired and helpful information.

In order to encourage influence over decision-making, formal rules and hierarchies are challenged, and mechanisms and procedures for tapping views and incorporating these in decisions are worked out by the group. Group leaders are encouraged to develop new roles as facilitators and co-ordinators, with a remit to encourage involvement of all in the group as decision-makers and decision-shapers.

Enhancing the climate for excellence

This appeals to the drives for excellence, mastery and achievement within each of us, often above and beyond the 'routine calls of duty', and we use specific techniques to encourage group excellence. For example, many groups benefit from the use of negative brainstorming. This involves brainstorming on all the possible deficiencies of an existing practice or new idea and then, on the basis of the most salient problems, refining the practice or idea to take account of them – or abandoning it. This institutionalizes and depersonalizes the criticism process and has a constructive orientation too. Another technique is to have a period of disagreement during meetings when decisions already taken are disagreed with by all in the group, to ensure that major weaknesses have been considered. Above all, we encourage constructive controversy within the group, which we describe as task-centred, rather than person-centred.

Supporting innovation attempts

Finally, in relation to support for innovation, each group member is asked to indicate to each other member (working in pairs) what practical co-operation, time and resources they have given/could give to him or her. Groups are recommended to use this technique particularly when new ideas are being proposed. The whole group also assesses the extent to which the leader enacts rather than merely articulates such support. A meeting technique that many groups find useful is the mandatory use of 'yes, and . . .' responses to suggestions from others rather than the convention 'no' or 'yes, but . . .' reactions. Overall, the whole approach is placed in the context of raising group members' awareness of what constitutes a supportive climate for innovation.

Conclusion

To conclude, we would argue that HRM specialists should be placing the issue of work group innovation high on their agenda for the 1990s. Given the rapid pace of change being experienced by many organizations, fostering team propensity to innovate may not only be an important determinant of business success, but an area within which HRM professionals can have a fundamental strategic impact. Whether or not the majority of personnel specialists grasp these opportunities to contribute to the strategic management of human resources within their own organizations remains to be seen.

CASE STUDY: TEAMWORK IN THE NHS

With the introduction of the Resource Management Initiative, new challenges have faced management and staff in many hospital sites in the NHS. Resource management, itself an innovation, involves a new way of organizing and managing resources by increasing the involvement of clinical staff in management and of providing more accurate and useful information about costs and clinical practice. The resulting changes in management structure have led to the development of new management teams in one form or another. Of interest here is how some of these were assisted in their development process. These teams were newly formed and often lacked clarity about their terms of reference, and some members were not used to working in teams and dealing with management issues, particularly those related to human resource management.

Following discussions with hospital general managers and personnel managers at a number of hospital sites, team development workshops were offered to several teams. The aims of these workshops were to improve the team's effectiveness, to develop a more innovative style of working and to specify goals and objectives for the coming year. Before the workshops started, team members were asked to complete a questionnaire designed to measure the team's innovative style based on the four factors. This data was then summarized and used by the teams during their workshop. Profiles were used to highlight strengths and weaknesses and to focus the content of the workshop.

Below we illustrate the profiles of two hospital management teams, Team A and B (names are not used in order to maintain confidentiality), and describe the course of interventions based on the questionnaire responses. The teams' profiles are summarized in Figure 19.1.

Team A's profile showed them to be a group that had much preparatory work to do, especially in establishing a climate of 'participative safety' and from this moving on to articulate the overall aims or 'vision' of the group. It is important to stress that, for all of the teams involved, the personnel manager asked for the workshops to be practically based to allow teams to reach a consensus on immediate task objectives.

Team A

So for Team A we began by looking at how they met, their communication and information flows, and how decisions were made (i.e. 'participation'.

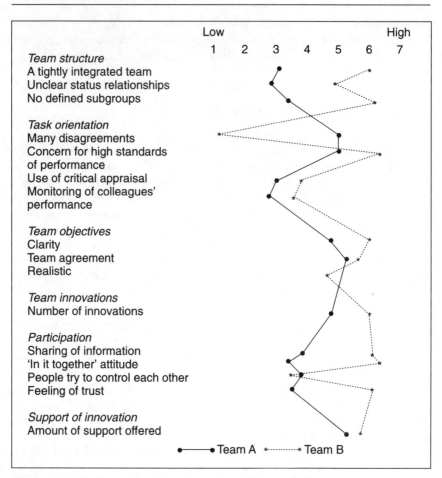

Figure 19.1 Profiles of the innovation style of Teams A and B

These areas were discussed in small groups; then in plenary sessions. When all the information was laid out, the group was then asked to brainstorm ways of improving their meetings and informal get-togethers. Additional ideas and prompts were given through the use of handouts and feedback comments were made on group processes, group environment, and the way ideas and comments were dealt with (i.e. 'safety').

Through looking at communication patterns, weaknesses and inadequate links were highlighted and simpler structures suggested. The workshops also focused on the team themselves: what information did they share/withhold? Why did this happen, and what was the result? How could information-sharing be improved within the team? Finally, the group looked at how it made decisions. Feedback was offered in terms of our own observations of group processes. The team was asked to agree methods of decision-making.

As a result of this work a number of underlying issues arose. First, it was clear that the size of the team itself (15 members) led to difficulties and time wasting. Although team members felt they could not reduce their numbers at present, they agreed to tighten up the structure of their meetings and use small groups to do much of the preparatory work. That they felt confident in delegating such work was a sign of increased trust and a sense of 'safety' within the group. Second, the team identified and improved information flows within the team and how it related to other hospital teams. Third, a decision-making strategy was developed with agenda items to be marked for discussion or decision. The team decided to try to ensure an open, participative and non-judgmental style and, during decision-making, to adopt a more formal structure.

The team then moved on to define its mission statement through the exercises described in this chapter. This work, which strengthened the team's decision to use small groups, required it to identify and negotiate core values and aims which in itself was new and often difficult. It also helped to make explicit underlying assumptions. Probably the greatest value of this work was in providing guidelines or the boundaries to the objective and action planning work. It also helped members to consider problems in new ways and with a different focus.

Team B

Team B's profile (see Figure 19.1) shows this team to be better-established; members were cohesive and supportive. When their data were fed back to them in one sense they were pleased with the results, but expressed reservations about the quality of their decision-making and about the resistance they were meeting within the hospital when trying to implement changes.

It was agreed with this team, therefore, to look at how they managed criticism and disagreement within the team ('climate for excellence'), and resistances outside the team ('participation'). Information-sharing practices were also considered. Initially this team was asked to consider the ways they had established to monitor their performance and check their decision-making. The team members were surprised at the former request: as the questionnaire had shown, they worked well as a team and worked hard at maintaining this. It became clearer during the workshop that this aim of team loyalty and cohesiveness sometimes overrode finding the best solution to the problem. This also accounted for their surprise at negative reactions from other staff in the hospital when implementing their decisions. The team members then agreed to ensure they became more visible on the 'shopfloor' and to use feedback from staff to appraise decisions made within the team.

One formal method they used successfully during the workshop was stakeholder analysis. This exercise requires participants to view an issue from the position of each of the main stakeholder groups. This enabled them to step out of their roles as team members and to think more creatively about problems. This method also enabled the team to anticipate and therefore work on reducing resistance from other staff groups.

REFERENCES

1 Kanter, Rosabeth Moss (1983) *The Change Masters: corporate entrepreneurs at work*, Allen and Unwin.
2 See King, N. and Anderson, Neil, 'Work group innovation', in West, M.A. and Farr, J. L. (eds), *Innovation and Creativity at Work: psychological and organisational approaches*, John Wiley.
3 See Nicholson, Nigel and West, Michael A. (1988) *Managerial Job Change: men and women in transition*, Cambridge University Press.

Part V

Managing diversity
Paul Iles

Many of the earlier sections have emphasized the constructive role that managing differences can play in promoting individual and organizational learning. For example, Kolb and colleagues (Part III, Chapter 13) argued that differences can energize integrative learning; organizations need to foster learning climates where conflict is not suppressed but learning from differences is encouraged; and Pedler (Chapter 14) has described an emergent theme of differences at work as important for managing self-development.

Several of the chapters in Part IV also touched on the need to value differences if creativity is to be fostered in teams. This theme of valuing differences is taken up in more detail in Part V. Barbara Walker (Chapter 20) leads off from a North American perspective, discussing the concept of valuing differences and relating this to more traditional conceptions of equal opportunity and affirmative action. She points out that it is wider in focus, embracing all kinds of differences, with race and sex acting as metaphors for other differences. She describes a five-step model where people in safe core groups learn to strip away stereotypes, listen and probe for differences in assumptions, build authentic relationships with people regarded as different, enhance personal empowerment, and explore and identify group differences. The chapter concludes with an exploration of the growth of the 'valuing differences' model at DEC in promoting equal opportunity and affirmative action and in achieving a range of other goals where difference and diversity are critical to success.

This chapter briefly mentions the benefits of the 'valuing differences' model in international management. Indeed, the processes Walker describes in the context of domestic diversity seem even more relevant to international diversity, which is increasing due to the globalization of business and the growth in international enterprise. Eliminating stereotypes, learning to listen, exploring individual and group differences and building empowering relationships are all crucial elements of effective cross-cultural management and of successfully managing multi-cultural teams. Chapter 23 by Berger and Watts describes a more traditional course-based training programme focusing on presentation, communication and negotiation skills and aiming to build greater intercultural awareness among managers from France and Britain. Identifying four major elements of language, tolerance (a more neutral term than the more positive valuing used by Walker!), teamwork and cultural collaboration issues, it also offers a number of practical guidelines on how styles and values affect negotiating strategies and on the skills required for intercultural effectiveness.

Despite Walker's positive emphasis on valuing differences and her description of the ways in which adopting such a model can help organizations move beyond traditional equal opportunity concerns, it remains the case that in Britain and other European countries women, black and minority ethnic groups and people with disabilities remain discriminated against and under-represented in many areas of organizational life. Focusing on gender in particular, Beverly Alimo-Metcalfe (Chapter 21) discusses ways in which women's career advancement is blocked by organizational socialization practices and by the kinds of assessment and appraisal practices described in Parts II and III. Much of her analysis is clearly applicable to other under-represented groups. Of particular interest here is recent work associating more transformational leadership styles with women, and their greater relevance to the new organizations discussed in Part I. Of equal interest is her assertion that assessment criteria such as the competencies discussed extensively in Part II may reflect male assumptions of what constitutes good management, based as they are on research with male-dominated samples. Alimo-Metcalfe does not discuss here organizational responses to such a situation. Useful training and development responses might include positive action training for women and minority managers and would-be managers to equip them with the knowledge, skills, and other attributes necessary to compete successfully in white male-dominated organizational cultures (e.g. career planning, assertiveness) and the training of white male managers in awareness of blocks and barriers and the skills and strategies necessary to remove them. Walker's 'valuing differences' model or similar models may help gain acceptance and validation for different kinds of leadership and managerial styles.

Chapter 22 takes a somewhat different perspective on diversity, though it does relate to differences in management style. Based on intensive work with a small number of American male senior managers, Joan Kofodimos argues that too often promotion, pay and status are won at the cost of damage to personal and family lives. She argues that a more balanced approach to work would mitigate some of the 'downside' symptoms to success, like stress, burn-out, workaholism and family breakdown. Stress management and similar projects often address this issue, but only in terms of modifications the individual can make. Perhaps of greater importance are modifications organizations can make to policy, practice, and culture. Employers often demand great commitment in time and energy, and reward such manifest displays of commitment. Kofodimos defines such a dominant striving for management positions and mastery as expansiveness. Organizations seek out such people for senior management positions and reward them accordingly. The avoidance of intimacy, vulnerability and emotion are also often rewarded, and these dynamics may have their origins in childhood experiences. Though Kofodimos confines herself to male executives, the compromises and dilemmas she describes may apply even more strongly to successful women managers, as alluded to by Alimo-Metcalfe. The chapter discusses some organizational and individual strategies for addressing these imbalances, including flexitime, day-care, and parental leave policies. The 'valuing differences' approach developed by Walker may also help in this regard, as many imbalances seem to result from organizational cultures, which assume there is one best way to manage and lead – a style perhaps more associated with traditional, male, hierarchical organization, than the learning organizations described in Part I. The demands for commitment, long hours and relocation seem more characteristic of Anglo-Saxon, and perhaps Japanese organizations than Nordic and North European organizations. Here balance between work and personal life seems more acceptable, and working long hours is more likely to be seen as a symptom of inefficiency than commitment and dedication.

Chapter 20

Valuing differences: the concept and a model

Barbara A. Walker

VALUING DIFFERENCES: THE CONCEPT

"Valuing differences" is a cluster of concepts that shapes an approach to helping people deal with issues created by their differences. This approach focuses people on the value of differences to help them become open to learning from people they regard as different and to help them build empowered relationships in which they work together interdependently and synergistically.

On one level, valuing differences is an approach to the work of affirmative action and equal employment opportunity, but it is more than that. It is a way of helping people think through their assumptions and beliefs about all kinds of differences – individual, cultural, geographical, and organizational. As such, valuing differences is an approach to both the work of personal growth and development and the work of increasing an organization's productivity.

Capitalizing on the value of differences

It is often acknowledged that differences among people and cultures are the wellspring of life's richness and excitement. But the reality is that differences create discomfort and conflict. As a result, managers and leaders in the workplace face the critical challenge to find the most effective way to help people deal with their differences. This issue is even more significant in any organization with an international work force.

Generally, people are comfortable with their sameness. Some managers insist that the best way to reduce conflict and maintain harmony is to focus on the ways in which people are alike. It is argued that people work together best if they ignore their differences.

When, however, people believe that their differences make up an essential part of who they are, they may find it difficult to see the ways in which they are alike. They may even see their sameness differently.

Having to stay focused on the similarities often means that those who recognize their differences feel left out and devalued. Ignoring differences, therefore, not only supports the fiction of a homogeneous workforce, but it leads to the potentially dangerous conclusion that differences are unacceptable.

Differences in and of themselves fuel creative energy and insight. They are the points of tension that spark alternative viewpoints and ideas and ignite the kindling forces behind creativity and innovation. They are the reference points for probing the meaning of beliefs and core values and for refining the understanding of who we really are.

Difference is intrinsically valuable to individual growth and development. Diversity, the mix and various combinations of human differences, is essential to growth and synergy in any organization. People and their differences make up the foundation of an organization's ability to develop broad perspectives and to approach business problems in new and creative ways.

This valuing differences model outlines and explains the work of helping people and their organizations learn how to capitalize on differences and reach their fullest potential. The work begins by focusing people on their differences.

If people feel that their differences make up an essential part of their worth, then they feel most valued when they believe they are seen in their fullest dimensions, both as individuals and as members of their own group(s). The central valuing differences task is learning to pay attention to people as unique individuals, while recognizing and taking into account their differences as members of particular groups. This is the real work of individualizing people; that is, learning to see them in their fullest dimensions. This work enables people to see others as equal though not the same.

VALUING DIFFERENCES: PRINCIPLES AND PROCESS

The Valuing Differences model is based on the following key principles.

1 People work best when they feel valued.
2 People feel most valued when they believe that their individual and group differences have been taken into account.
3 The ability to learn from people regarded as different is the key to becoming fully empowered.
4 When people feel valued and empowered, they are able to build relationships in which they work together interdependently and synergistically.

These principles have shaped the content and steps in a process that helps people sort through their beliefs and assumptions about others and their individual and group differences. The following are the five steps in this process.

1 Stripping away stereotypes.
2 Learning to listen and probe for the differences in people's assumptions.
3 Building authentic and significant relationships with people one regards as different.
4 Enhancing personal empowerment.
5 Exploring and identifying group differences.

These steps are involved in the work of an ongoing process of personal development and growth. The first four are not necessarily sequential and may be undertaken simultaneously. The fifth step, for reasons explained later should be undertaken after some of the other work has been done. The following discussion highlights some of the critical points in the valuing differences process.

Stripping away stereotypes

The first step in the process is to help people to lean how to identify and strip away their stereotypes, defined in this work as fixed inflexible notions about a group. In the valuing differences process, participants are encouraged to examine their prejudgments openly and, where possible, to substitute facts.

Erasing stereotypes liberates people from the need to manage their lives by force-fitting others into neat, tidy categories and roles. It is also an important step in learning to accept one's own differences. In doing so, people are better able to manage the tension of holding on to their own views, while respecting and protecting others' rights to believe differently, even in ways that appear flatly contradictory to their own values and beliefs.

Building relationships with people one regards as different

Another step in the valuing differences approach is encouraging people purposefully to do the work of building authentic and significant relationships with those they regard as different. Too often, individuals only take the time to get to know, depend on, and trust those with whom they feel most comfortable – usually people they view as most like themselves. They do not take the time to build relationships with people whose differences make them uneasy.

This is a particularly disturbing problem for personnel professionals who struggle with the question of how to achieve parity at the top of an organization. Managers in these positions, often white men, fill the positions regarded as critical only with people whom they feel they know and can trust, and on whom they can depend. A first step toward breaking this cycle is to encourage managers to go out of their way to build meaningful, authentic relationships with people they regard as different.

Relationships across the lines of group differences give people an opportunity to understand that members of different groups have been socialized into different but equally valid assumptions and ways of seeing the world. As a result, one can understand that conflicts and tension created by differences are not always irreconcilable clashes in values and principles, but sometimes are mere differences in perspective.

Developing such relationships is an important step in learning to take one another seriously and in eliminating the patronizing behavior that may occur between colleagues who are uneasy with each other. When people get to know each other, it is more likely that they will give honest feedback and even share important, unsolicited information. Although people may have some highly divergent differences, some of which they may never understand, they acquire the ability to see each other as potential allies, if not friends.

The process of bonding with people regarded as different, like building any significant relationship, is not without risks. In learning to depend on others, people risk the possibility of being let down and feeling devalued, sometimes even betrayed. Part of the valuing differences work is taking the time to put these risks in perspective.

Enhancing personal empowerment

Enhancing one's sense of inner personal power is a pivotal step in the valuing differences approach. It is at once both the means and the end of the work. The more comfortable people are in working with and learning from others regarded as different, the more empowered they become. The more empowered people are, the more open they become to learning from differences in the perspective of others.

Locked into an either/or approach to life, people become threatened by any deviation from their perceptions of the norm. They fear that others' differences mean that they must change. Therefore, they close in and join ranks with people whom they believe to be most like themselves. They respond like victims. The difference between feeling and not feeling like a victim is one's sense of personal empowerment – one's ability to accept, move toward, and even embrace different ideas and perspectives. The process of opening oneself up and becoming comfortable with others' differences is then synonymous with empowerment.

An empowered person listens and probes for differences in others' assumptions and even "tries on" different perspectives to glean others' strengths and wisdom. People like this will take risks to build authentic relationships and, though making mistakes from time to time, allow others the right to do the same.

Personal empowerment deepens the ability to trust in oneself and in the constructive potential of others. It allows one to commit to stay in the dialogue and wrestle with the complexities of issues created by differences. This sense of empowerment helps individuals accept and even anticipate change and, in some cases, figure out ways to respond productively to those who have not learned to value differences.

When people are empowered, they are more comfortable with the fundamental question underlying almost all conflict: "By whose standards shall we decide, yours or mine?" Rarely is there an easy answer to this question. However, people who have internalized the understanding that power is not a zero-sum game are more willing to share it. Sometimes they learn that the answer can be: "Ours." Personal empowerment enables an individual to accept the fact that there may be times when complex issues must be decided on the basis of others' standards. Certainly empowered people include in their search for the answer the well-being of others and the success of the whole.

Identifying group differences

The last step in the valuing differences process is working together with the people regarded as different to identify and articulate the core identity issues held by different groups. This involves probing for group differences in the assumptions and perspectives that shape people's values and views of the norm or their interpretation of what the norm should be. In some cases, a group's difference may be a shared perspective that has developed as a result of the way it has been treated by another group. In other cases, the differences may be cultural. Studying the implications of group differences regarding issues such as building relationships, sharing power, and styles of bonding is a component of this work. Understanding group differences is an important step toward developing effective strategies to help people learn how to work together interdependently.

Although this work is critical to helping people deal effectively with issues created by differences, it requires a careful approach. Whenever possible, participants in the process should be encouraged to begin by learning to recognize stereotypes. Otherwise they may find themselves working at cross purposes. The problem with focusing on identifying group differences lies in the risk of promulgating stereotypes. The question is: Can individuals talk safely about group differences without legitimizing or reinforcing stereotypes?

In the valuing differences process, participants explore together the information that the groups share about themselves in an effort to arrive at the truth about group differences.

ADDRESSING ALL DIFFERENCES

In the USA, each group protected by Equal Employment Opportunity (EEO) legislation seeks the power to influence others and to make changes consistent with its standards for a better world; non-EEO groups also seek the same power. But, traditional EEO approaches focus on protected-class groups to the exclusion of others. Consequently, there is an "us versus them" view of the work, which victimizes and disempowers everyone. It reinforces the prevailing notion that people of difference, those in the EEO groups, have no power, and those in the non-EEO groups have all the power and responsibility for making changes.

The shift in focus

Valuing differences neutralizes this disempowering approach by shifting to a view of every individual as a person of difference. To bring about meaningful and lasting change, the task is to build environments in which every person feels valued and empowered. Each one must perceive that there is an opportunity to influence the process of making the choices and tradeoffs necessary to correct the inequities imposed on victimized groups.

This will occur only when people trust that their own perspectives will be heard. Then they can be open to hearing and taking into account others' perspectives. They become willing to examine their own behaviors and may even be willing to alter their thinking about the issues of power and control in their relationships with others, including EEO-protected groups.

The word "differences" in the term "valuing differences" is all-inclusive. It applies not only to the traditional EEO differences, but also to other categories that must be dealt with effectively. Included are obvious differences, such as geographical and cultural perspectives on workstyles and ways of doing business. Included, too, are less obvious but important and more subtle differences such as thinking and learning styles, which have received little attention. Whether dealing with one end or the other of the continuum of obvious to subtle diversity, valuing differences provides an inclusive focus for working with differences in a way that opens up blocked communications between organizations and between people.

It is important to note that, in a valuing differences environment, valuing may include a wide range of positive responses to differences. At a minimum, it means recognizing and accepting the fact of difference. It may mean going as far as actually embracing the difference; that is, adopting or using it in one's own thinking or behavior. In some cases, it means caring enough about another person or group to expend energy exploring and studying the assumptions behind the difference. Or, valuing a difference may mean simply respecting and accepting it as worthwhile, without the need to understand it and certainly without giving in to any impulse to judge it.

Race and sex as metaphors

The valuing differences approach often refers to race and gender as metaphors for all differences. This reference is based on the discernment that, whatever the difference, the dynamics of the conflict or struggle created by discomfort with differences are the same. The same question underlying EEO issues also underlies issues created by other kinds of differences: "By whose standards, yours or mine?"

Raising one's level of comfort with the issues one regards as either most difficult or emotional allows one to become open to dealing effectively with issues created by any kind of difference. In the United States many people regard race and gender as two of the foremost emotional issues. The perspectives and patterns of our relationships in these areas reinforce behavior in other areas of discomfort and conflict created by differences. Accomplishing the valuing differences work in these areas may provide people with the key to opening up to thinking differently and to unlocking their rigid perspectives on the world.

MOVING BEYOND THE MULTICULTURAL APPROACH TO DIFFERENCES

The goal of the valuing differences approach is substantially broader than that of multicultural work. Multicultural programs give people the opportunity to study a wide range of specific cultures. Though these programs can be an important part of the valuing differences process, it is important to distinguish between the two. First, the differences people must learn to deal with often are not cultural in the strictest sense of the word. For example, whites, blacks, men, women, gays, and physically disabled people are not distinct cultural groups. Categorizing them so simplistically only reinforces stereotyped thinking.

Second, a strict multicultural approach to learning about differences can be impractical because it would be extraordinarily time consuming. In the United States alone, the number of cultures and subcultures is overwhelming. In effect, valuing differences is a simpler approach. It focuses primarily on helping people to develop an empowered mindset that is comfortable with differences, some of which a person may never have an opportunity to study but must still respect.

Using small groups in the valuing differences process

The work of learning to value differences is accomplished best in small, ongoing discussion groups. Small groups are laboratories in which people help each other explore the issues created by differences with others. Most people join these groups because they intuitively recognize that the honest, in-depth exploration of differences cannot be done in isolation. It must be done with others and, in most cases, with people one perceives as different. Other people make a conscious decision to join these small groups to take a disciplined approach to thinking critically about issues raised by differences.

In small group work, it is essential that people take into account how highly emotional the work of dealing with differences can be. This means that the groups' leaders should know how to help participants feel safe. When people talk openly and honestly about differences, they often feel threatened and challenged. With or without justification, they believe that they are being asked to change, and they feel the risks that come with honest self-disclosure. According to an old saying, one may accuse oneself of prevarication or theft, but seldom of prejudice.

Only when people feel safe, do they hear and learn from one another. Therefore, the first and foremost responsibility of the small group leader is to help participants establish and maintain a safe environment in which they are willing to explore the issue as peers and maintain the dialogue.

DEVELOPING HUMAN POTENTIAL AND INCREASING ORGANIZATIONAL PRODUCTIVITY

Valuing differences legitimizes a focus on people's personal needs as individuals, managers, and leaders. Given the issues and conflict created by differences, this work becomes a unique context for exploring a broad range of issues critical to personal development, including such issues as intimacy and loneliness. Because organizational productivity relates directly to effective use of human resources, development of individuals as managers and leaders is a critical outcome of the approach.

Management development

Productivity depends on how well people work together, which in turn depends on how they deal with each other's differences. Prejudice, intolerance, and insensitivity to individual differences create barriers to becoming effective managers and to being managed effectively. Valuing differences provides an opportunity for managers to learn how to work with these issues and how to tap into the strengths of all people, including those regarded as different. The valuing differences model and approach posits that paying attention to people and their differences is a principal form of valuing them. When they feel that they are valued and that their differences add value, they are motivated to do their best work.

Leadership development

The valuing differences approach allows participants in the process to work on developing leadership skills and attributes such as empathy and authenticity, as well as the ability to be forthright and to take risks. It provides an opportunity for managers to work through and refine their views and assumptions about power and the processes for empowering people.

This work helps an organization's leadership to multiply faster than it would otherwise. As more people are empowered to deal with issues created by differences and are in touch with their leadership skills and responsibilities, the organization is then in a powerful position to establish specific strategies to capitalize on its diversity and the synergy of differences as sources of collective growth, creativity, and strength.

HOW THE VALUING DIFFERENCES APPROACH EVOLVED AT DIGITAL EQUIPMENT CORPORATION

Valuing differences evolved as an approach to dealing with the issues created by differences at Digital Equipment Corporation, a Fortune 100 computer manufacturer. In part, the approach unfolded as a natural progression of the core values established when Digital was founded some 30 years ago in Maynard, Massachusetts. However, valuing differences is primarily the product of the intersection of Digital's core values and the powerful insights developed in the course of the company's Affirmative Action and Equal Employment Opportunity work.

From the start, Digital's culture was grounded in a set of strong values such as "respect for the individual" and "doing the right thing." When the company began struggling with its AA/EEO responsibilities in the mid-1970s. Digital leaders saw their primary work as identifying barriers to doing the right thing and then working to remove those obstacles.

Talking about difference

The first major problem identified was Digital's managers' reluctance to talk about the issues of race and sex. The prevailing view was that open and frank discussion, particularly in the presence of minorities and women, was taboo in polite conversation. If they couldn't talk to one another about these issues, they couldn't learn from people they regarded as different.

To help raise their level of comfort in discussing AA/EEO issues, top-level managers were encouraged to come together in small groups where they would feel "safe" and could learn how to "slow down" their emotions. As they began to talk openly and frankly in these small groups, they learned that, although pain and vulnerability came with acknowledging their racism, they were greater victims when they denied them.

They also began to explore other areas traditionally regarded as taboo in the corporate world, such as bonding, intimacy, and love. These subjects added depth and breadth and so enriched the AA/EEO discussions that managers began to regard the work as an opportunity to learn as much about themselves as about 'them' – women and minorities. They no longer feared the work as a forced guilt trip, but began to view it as personal development – an investment in their own growth.

Erasing stereotypes

Over time, other employees – Hispanics, Blacks, and white men and women at different levels in the company – joined these discussions, working with the top-level managers in small ongoing groups that eventually became known as Core Groups. Because the initial goal was to raise awareness about the issues and concerns of minorities and women, the early work in the Core Groups was focused on learning to individualize women and minorities by erasing the stereotypes about them. This focus was based on an assumption that by learning to see women and minorities as unique individuals, everyone would be able to work together better to address EEO issues. Instead, even as they erased stereotypes and raised the level of comfort and trust in talking openly and candidly – at times even confronting one another – people within the different race and gender groups continued to feel devalued. As a result, they continued to hold on to conflicting and competing views about which EEO strategies should be put in place.

Valuing all people as people of difference

Slowly, however, they began to develop the understanding that in one way or another everybody, not just women and minorities, felt victimized and disempowered by racism and sexism. Everyone is a member of some group that has a special interest in the outcome of EEO issues and, in this sense, each individual is a "person of difference." By focusing attention solely on the issues and concerns of minorities and women, they were, in effect, discounting and devaluing those in non-EEO groups and protected class groups. This approach reinforced the 'us versus them' view of the work, which made everyone feel victimized and, therefore, disempowered.

This insight led to understanding that valuing people clearly means building an environment in which all individuals – each one a person of difference – can feel their interests matter and will be taken into account. As a step toward creating such an environment, a formal distinction was made between the work of EEO and the work of learning to value all people and their differences. At this point it was recognized that the empowerment of all groups, including white males, is a critical step in the process.

Recognizing the importance of group differences

As they continued to sort through their conflicts, participants in the small groups also recognized that again and again they returned to one nagging question underlying all the dialogue. By whose standards shall we decide? Yours or mine? Stripping away the stereotypes had not stripped them of their differences, and their standards were determined by those differences.

In the effort to avoid stereotyping in order to see one another as individuals, they had made faulty assumptions about their similarities. The work designed to help people learn how to deal with different race and gender groups had not taken into account the importance of these group differences. When they ignored the differences, they argued and disagreed because they all felt devalued. This insight led to the next step in the process – focusing on group difference as well as individual differences.

Although there was a fear that the work of identifying group differences was risky because it could reinforce and even legitimize stereotypes about groups, it was recognized that this work was critical. Learning how to recognize and understand the core identity issues of different groups is an important step toward developing effective strategies to help people of difference learn how to work together interdependently.

Having begun the work of building an environment of trust and candor to help people strip away their stereotypes, participants began probing for differences in group assumptions and perspectives that shaped their values and perceptions of the norm. As a result they discovered that they held unexamined and faulty assumptions about their own group differences, which in turn led to faulty assumptions about the differences of others. With Digital as the larger context for the discussions, they studied the implications of group differences with respect to such issues as building significant relationships, sharing power, and styles of bonding in the workplace.

Valuing all differences

Participants in Core Groups began to address the full spectrum of EEO issues – not just race and gender but also issues of age, physical ability, and sexual orientation. As Core Groups spread through the company, participants from various organizational, functional, and geographical subcultures began to address a wider range of differences. It became obvious that – no matter what the difference was – the dynamic underlying the conflict and struggles was the same. The question that underlay the EEO dialogues was also at the base of the issues created by other kinds of group differences. By whose standard shall we decide? It was recognized that the process for addressing EEO issues could also be applied effectively to issues created by other kinds of differences.

This more inclusive focus – which became known as "Valuing Differences" – made it possible to address issues created by differences in assumptions between managers and subordinates as well as between staff and line. It provided a way to open up traditionally blocked communication links, such as those between manufacturing and engineering and the highly emotional one between smokers and non-smokers. It also allowed entry into discussions about the issues created by differences in Europe and Asia, where Digital managers had often become confused, if not offended, by the EEO approach of managers from the USA.

USING CORE GROUPS AND OTHER METHODS

Today Digital employees regard Core Group work as a unique opportunity for personal and leadership development. These groups usually meet at least four hours a month. They are led by participants who have attended a workshop designed to help them understand that the honest and candid exploration of assumptions and stereotypes about people and the groups to which they belong is almost always highly intense, emotional work. In this workshop, Core Group leaders develop the skills involved in "keeping people safe." They also learn how to help people identify "what's in it for them" to do the personal development work and how to lead each group in examining "what's in it for Digital"; that is, the connection between the Core Group work and Digital's productivity and profitability.

In 1985 Digital leaders institutionalized valuing differences as a written policy and as a function. As a result, numerous line organizations within the company employ full-time Valuing Differences managers, whose work is separate from that of EEO. Part of their work is leading Core Groups.

Although small discussion groups continue to be the backbone of the Valuing Differences approach, the company also uses other means of enabling employees to do the personal development work necessary in this area. The following company-sponsored activities are some examples:

1 Celebrating differences – a multicultural approach that gives people the opportunity to focus on the differences of particular groups at given times throughout the year.

2 UDD (Understanding the dynamics of differences) – a two-day course designed to introduce employees to the valuing differences concept.
3 A network of same-differences interest groups – includes a number of leadership groups that meet on a regular basis.

Chapter 21

Women in management: organizational socialization and assessment practices that prevent career advancement

Beverly Alimo-Metcalfe

Despite almost 20 years of equal opportunities legislation in Britain, the number of women in senior management positions is derisory.

If ever there was a powerful opportunity for change in the patterns of employment of women, the 1990s should be providing it.

THE CHANGING PATTERN OF WOMEN IN THE LABOUR FORCE IN BRITAIN

The most conspicuous change in the labour force in the UK in the last few years, which is expected to continue in the next decade, is the greater participation of women.

Women will be desperately needed to fill the void created by the predicted shortfall by the year 2000 of one million workers in the 16–24 years old bracket. Large organizations and major high street banks and building societies are taking urgent steps to recruit more women, and to develop the largely untapped reservoir of potential amongst their female employees. But whether their significant contribution to the UK workforce will be in areas other than those in which they currently dominate, namely low-status, low-paid, part-time, low-interest jobs, seems unlikely.

The position of women in management

In terms of the managerial population, it is difficult to establish accurate figures for the proportion of women in management in Britain since definitions of management used by different studies may vary. However, from the sources in Table 21.1, there may be some evidence that the proportion of women in management is increasing.

However, figures given for women in senior management remain negligible. One to 2 per cent is the most commonly stated figure (e.g. Hirsh and Jackson, 1990).

Management as an occupation is clearly gender-segregated. In 1985 the Labour Force Survey estimated that probably more than 50 per cent of

Table 21.1 Women in management (%)

1975	10%	(Marshall 1984)
1977	19%	Labour Force Survey 1977
1979	20%	Labour Force Survey 1979
1985	22%	Labour Force Survey 1985
1989	26%	Labour Force Survey 1989

Note: Preliminary results, *Employment Gazette*, April 1990

female managers were in office work, retail and catering. Even in organizations where women are employed in significant proportions, namely local government, education and the National Health Service (NHS), they are grossly underrepresented in senior management. In the Civil Service, for example, which comprises 50 per cent female staff mainly at lower clerical grades, only 8 per cent of principal grades are occupied by women, with only 4 per cent of women in higher positions.

With respect to primary education, 40 per cent of head teachers are female. The figures are lower if one inspects those for higher education.

Alban Metcalfe and Nicholson summarize the biographical data obtained in their study as follows:

The results show that women managers are found more in service organizations/occupations and in specialist functions. They also tend to be younger and more highly qualified than males. Women in management are much more likely to be in dual career marriages than men. All in all these results suggest that women managers have to surmount greater obstacles than men to reach equivalent positions; they require higher educational attainments and have to overcome or forego competing domestic demands.

(Alban Metcalfe and Nicholson 1984: 15)

The experiences of working as a woman manager

Most female managers have male bosses and are more likely to have female than male staff. While it is also true that they are working in traditionally 'female' functions, given the preponderance of men in the most influential and controlling positions, women managers often remark on the male dominance of the organization and on a sense of discomfort or tension, which may be experienced as a major stressor.

The work-related pressures included prejudice and discrimination. 'Compared to married male managers, married female managers were much more likely to experience higher pressures in respect of career and spouse/partner conflicts, career/home conflicts, and career and marriage/child bearing conflicts'. (Davidson 1989).

Single women managers were likely to experience pressure from colleagues who perceived them as an 'oddity' and who may exclude them from social and business events, but also they experienced the stresses of decisions relating to the form of a relationship with a partner – to marry, to live together or not to live together – and the quandary, sometimes exacerbated by pressures from others, of whether to have children, and when.

Additional sources of stress and frustration mentioned included not being taken seriously; being excluded from decision-making situations which in some way involved them; their advice not being sought despite their 'expert' knowledge; being told that they were receiving preferential treatment by virtue of being female; lack of development opportunities that were offered to male colleagues; and an overriding sense of isolation and alienation. Several women felt that they had experienced clear discrimination with respect to pay and promotion and a few mentioned that they had considered taking their case to the industrial tribunal which legislates on equal pay matters, but the price of being labelled a 'trouble-maker' would damage their future opportunities.

Women and management style

In the USA there has been substantial research conducted into management or leadership style and investigating the possibility of gender differences. Most studies have concluded that there is no greater difference between women and men than between women as a population. However, some recent research has produced new findings. An international study by Rosener (1990) of 355 members of the International Women's Forum and 101 males, matched for position, type and size of organization in a wide range of industries and sectors of employment, found significant differences in their reported leadership style.

The men in her sample were more likely to adopt 'transactional' leadership styles, that is exchanging rewards or punishment for performance. Also, men were more likely to use power that comes from their organizational position and formal authority.

Women on the other hand were more likely to use 'transformational leadership', that is motivating others by transforming their self-interest into the goals of the group, and to use 'interactive leadership' styles by encouraging participation, sharing power and information and enhancing peoples's self worth. Women were also much more likely than men to ascribe their power to personal characteristics such as charisma, interpersonal skills, or personal contacts rather than to organizational stature. Women as leaders were found to believe that people perform best when they feel good about themselves and their work, and to try to create a situation that contributes to that feeling.

Viewed in the context of the changing shape and culture of organizations (e.g. Barnham *et al.* 1988; Harrison 1987) where values of cooperation and caring, and visionary leadership are expected to be at least as important as task-orientation, one might well presume that women have qualities and styles best suited to leading them.

Organizational socialization and assessment practices

Organizational socialization is the process by which individuals are inducted into the norms, values, standards and procedures of the organizational culture. It takes place as a result of the individual crossing a variety of boundaries. In order to achieve a senior management position in an organization one has to make several boundary passages, each of which is marked by some process of assessment. These include the assessment procedure for initial selection into the organization and the subsequent assessment practices, formal and informal, both ongoing and located in specific events.

Acker and Van Houten (1974: 161) maintained that gender differences in organizational participation are related to:

1 Differential recruitment of women into jobs requiring dependence and passivity;
2 Selective recruitment of particularly compliant women into these jobs;
3 Control mechanisms for women used in organizations which reinforce control mechanisms to which they are subjected in other areas of society.

Despite the passage of time and the introduction of equal opportunities legislation, there is little evidence that any real progress has been made at either the organizational or individual level, to lead women to expect to be able to receive equal treatment to that of male colleagues. Moreover, as assessment techniques become more and more complex discrimination may be becoming subtler and less amenable to initial scrutiny.

ASSESSMENT OF POTENTIAL

The assessment of potential is a particularly complex, and often controversial procedure. Since by definition, it is concerned with prediction, it inevitably involves risk taking, and to those unfamiliar with the complex technicalities and processes involved, there exists range of potential pitfalls.

The three major stages of assessment, whether it be for selection, promotion, to identify development needs, are:

1 The identification of criteria or dimensions on which assessments are based.
2 The techniques or predictors chosen as methods of assessment.
3 The judgement or assessment by people who, using the data collected,

make a decision such as to select a candidate, promote an employee, identify an employee for an accelerated development programme, or assess performance to distribute a rating, which may or may not relate to pay bonuses.

Serious concerns arise with respect to all three stages of the assessment process in relation to women.

Stage one: what are we assessing?

Identification of the criteria or dimensions against which an individual is going to be assessed is the bedrock of any assessment process. If the job for which the individual is being assessed is a senior management job there is great reason for concern with respect to potential gender bias.

The criteria

In order to identify dimensions of assessment one seeks out job 'experts' – individuals who are very familiar with the job and its demands. Clearly, this often includes current job holders and usually their bosses. These people describe the qualities and skills involved and give examples of effective and ineffective behaviours, and this information will be used later to establish a job profile against which candidates will be assessed. In the case of senior management jobs these providers of criteria are highly likely to be male.

Much has emerged from the feminist literature on organizational theory on the subject of men's dominant position in society and the resultant construction of institutions created in their own image which utilize patriarchal power that devalues women (e.g. Calas and Smircich 1989, 1990). Most organizational theorists have omitted any mention of women, and 'central elements of bureaucracy (which organizational design has taken for granted) are founded on assumptions about the subordination of women' (Martin 1990: 2). Implicit assumptions of the value of certain concepts are made which have been summarized in Table 21.2.

As Martin remarks: 'Inspection of these columns reveals the hidden assumptions; the devalued characteristics are all traditionally more likely to be associated with women than with men' (1990: 12).

Models of career progression reflect the male pattern of continuous employment, high workload which frequently overlaps into family life, age requirements (that can only be achieved without interruptions for child rearing) and freedom to be geographically mobile (NEDO/RIPA 1990).

Given the evidence cited earlier that there are distinctions between masculine and feminine management styles, and given the fact that women are unlikely to be in senior management positions and therefore will not be

Table 21.2 Concepts and values

Valued	Devalued
Objective	Subjective
Rational	Irrational
Expert	Untrained
Abstract	Case-by-case
Dehumanized	Humane
Detached	Involved
Impersonal	Personal
Unemotional	Emotional
Authoritarian	Nurturant
Unequal	Egalitarian
Graceless	With grace
Unsympathetic	Sympathetic
Untouched by gratitude	Moved by gratitude

solicited for their views on the qualities, abilities, skills of senior management, there must be considerable concern that the criteria elicited from a solely, or predominantly, male sample are more likely to assess for qualities relating to this group or the population, and moreover gender bias will now be embedded in the assessment process.

Stage two: the techniques to be used to assess behaviour

Focusing on selection or promotion, there are a range of techniques currently being used by organizations, which include:

- The selection interview.
- Ability tests and personality scales.
- The assessment centre.

Despite its renowned reputation for poor reliability and validity, the selection interview remains the most commonly used procedure in most organizations (Robertson and Makin 1986). Suitability for a job depends largely on the selector's stereotype of the 'ideal' candidate. Being so vulnerable to the influence of subjective opinion with respect to appearance, interpersonal perception and social judgements, it is far from surprising that the selection interview has been found to be biased against females applying for 'out-of-role' jobs (e.g. engineering, computing, management, etc.). Type of dress, that is 'masculine' as opposed to 'feminine', has been shown to affect one's chances of 'success', and even the wearing of lipstick was found to influence the judgements that male assessors made of female candidates. While the effects of perceived attractiveness might increase the chances of acceptance of male candidates for managerial jobs, it has been found to jeopardize the chances of females (Iles and Robertson 1988), and it is worth remembering that it is frequently males who occupy powerful gate-keeping positions to entry to organizations (Stewart 1978: 336).

Standardized psychological tests are becoming increasingly used by organizations in Britain (Robertson and Makin 1986). While this initiative might be welcomed as another way of eliminating potential bias, it is necessary to be particularly wary that it does not in fact hide a more deeply rooted and hence less easily challenged prejudice. Gender bias may be due to the construct and content validity of the instrument as a result of the composition of the original sample from which the dimensions were derived, and the norms on which the interpretations are based.

The most recent popular advance in assessment techniques is the Assessment Centre Methodology (Thornton and Byham 1982). Although its origin dates back to the 1940s (ibid.) its growth in usage is a relatively recent phenomenon (Robertson and Makin 1986). One again needs to be wary of potential problems for women's career development.

The first stage of assessment centre design is the identification of criteria for job success and the creation of examples of behaviours that reflect different levels of competence on the various dimensions being assessed. As stated above, these may well be gender-biased.

The actual methodology of the assessment centre bringing participants together in groups can place women at a distinct disadvantage. Since assessment centres are so expensive they are typically used for elite groups in organizations or for making senior management appointments. This means that frequently women participants are in the minority. There is substantial evidence from the group dynamics literature that being a minority member of a group imposes pressures on the individual which inhibit her/his potential contribution (Rosenberg et al. 1955).

A recent field study which attempted directly to test Kanter's theory that being in a numerical minority in an unbalanced sex ratio group (i.e. unequal numbers of females and males) would inhibit performance in a group (Finnigan 1982) had results which confirmed the hypothesis for three sex ratio situations: male-dominant groups, female-dominant groups, and those in which there were equal numbers of both sexes. However, under-achievement was particularly pronounced for females in male-dominant groups. This might be due to what has been called the 'feminine modesty' effect identified by Gould and Stone (1982).

Finnigan (1982) offers three possible reasons for individuals in a minority group appearing to be inhibited from contributing to group discussion:

1 Members of this majority sex inhibit contributions of the token females by restricting their opportunities for input. Males tend to ask fewer, and only specific kinds of questions of females. Also they most frequently ask women for information rather than opinions. Consequently, the majority sex may be seen to direct the nature of the minority responses.

2 A second source of inhibition might stem from the minority's perception of the illegitimacy of their contribution. Thus, feeling that they were 'outside' may result in self-imposed inhibitions by the females. An extension of the 'modesty effect' (Gould and Stone 1982) may also be exacerbating the situation.

3 Inhibition due to cultural gender role norms. This relates to the experiences of females in male-dominant groups of not being valued for their contributions as highly as the male members.

Male members of female-dominant groups contributed actively in the leadership roles in the group and their contributions were valued as highly as those of female members. Finnigan interprets this as due to the high status attributed to males overcoming any stigma associated with being a minority member.

The assessors

As has been stated earlier, it is far more likely that males will be assessors for techniques being used to assess individual suitability for senior management. What then are the perceptions that men hold of women with respect to their suitability for management?

What do men think of women?

Two recent studies used Schein's Descriptive Index with US management students (Schein and Mueller 1990) and with British and German management students. The data may be seen as depressing, particularly for the German sample. As the researchers state:

> the results reveal that males in all three countries perceive successful middle managers as possessing the characteristics, attitudes and temperaments more commonly ascribed to men in general than to women in general. Within each country there were large and significant resemblances between the ratings of men and managers, and mean zero resemblances between ratings of women and managers.
>
> (Schein and Mueller 1990: 9)

If men do not perceive women as possessing the competencies for management this may well affect their judgements of the behaviours they are observing and assessing. Unfortunately, there appears to be no research on the subject. Until such data are collected one can only urge great care with respect to ensuring that:

1 at the stage of criteria identification as many females as male jobs encumbents and bosses are included in the sampling population;

2 criteria are scrutinized as to whether they merely reflect 'espoused' theories of management or what managers actually do;
3 the assessor panel is composed of female and male assessors in equal proportions;
4 assessor training promotes rigorous guidelines as to non-sexist assessment language to be adopted in the assessor conference;
5 groups of candidates include equal proportions of females and males.

Performance appraisal

Organizations' appraisal systems vary considerably, irrespective of whether they are primarily evaluative or developmental. Since they are concerned with reviewing performance they contain an element of assessment. They are also considered to be an important means of ensuring the creation of personal development plans and ensuring that they are monitored (e.g. Fletcher and Williams 1985). Research by Corby (1983) highlighted the different quality of appraisals for women and men in the British Civil Service. While the men generally speaking received critical feedback, the women were far more likely to receive innocuous non-specific criticism, if indeed any. This suggested the discomfort male bosses felt in relation to female subordinates. Since the quality of information exchanged in the appraisal was crucial for development purposes, and was used either intentionally or unintentionally for the purposes of making recommendations for promotion, this information exchange is not to be overlooked when investigating organizational procedures in women's career development.

GENDER AND ATTRIBUTION OF SUCCESS

Two very important themes already mentioned that have emerged from the literature are that males do not perceive the characteristics associated with success in management as being associated in any way with characteristics of females. Secondly, we have noted that there is a definite bias in the evaluation of women's behaviour in out-of-role jobs. A review by Wallston and O'Leary states:

> Data on perceived sex differences in causal attribution for performance ... suggest that the explanations offered for the success on failure of women and men differ markedly ... A man's successful performance of a task is generally attributed to skill, whereas a woman's identical performance is attributed to effort or luck. On the other hand, men's failure is attributed to (bad) luck, women's to low ability.
> (Wallston and O'Leary 1991:24)

Clearly the perceived cause of success will lead to different responses to that success. Rewards will vary depending on whether they were due to internal or external causes, as indeed will decisions such as promotion or placement. The repercussions therefore can directly affect other development opportunities. The longer-term effects of differential assessments of competence and potential for women and men may be reflected in the findings for promotion rates.

CHANGES IN ORGANIZATIONS – THE FUTURE

Organizational theorists such as Handy (1989) and Kanter (1989) maintain that large organizations will have to undergo metamorphosis to meet the considerable pace of change. They will become smaller, flatter and decentralized, relying on people working across functions in project teams, and they will require different styles of management where emphasis is on informal open communication. Managers will no longer be able to rely on the authority of status and position but will have to establish personal credibility by results, much of which will depend on their interpersonal and team-building skills. This is not simply a vision of the future, it is already a reality. Ashridge Management Centre and the Foundation for Management Education (Barnham et al. 1988) undertook a survey of leading-edge companies in Europe. Their findings paint a picture of managers as developers, encouraging openness and trust in the workplace, encouraging informal communication and adopting a participative style. Chief executives need to be visionaries who encourage change and challenge to the status quo, transforming cultures where past emphasis has been on 'doing' to 'being' values such as cooperation, belonging, caring, and receptivity. Few would not acknowledge that these were qualities more closely associated with women than men and indeed this has been found to be the case in a British study (Vinnicombe 1987).

Rosener's study of leadership style concludes that:

> (Women) are succeeding because of – not in spite of certain characteristics generally considered to be 'feminine' and inappropriate in leaders.
>
> The women's success shows that a non-traditional leadership style is well suited to the conditions of some work environments and can increase an organization's chances of surviving in an uncertain world.
>
> (Rosener 1990)

It remains to be seen whether women will be enabled to offer such resources to the organizations that desperately need them.

REFERENCES

Acker, J. and Van Houten, D. R. (1974), 'Differential recruitment and control: the sex structuring of organizations', *Administrative Science Quarterly*, 19, 152–63.

Alban Metcalfe, B. (1985), 'The effects of socialization on women's management careers,' *Management Bibliographies and Reviews*, 11, (3).

Alban Metcalfe, B. and Nicholson, N. (1984), *The Career Development of British Managers*, British Institute of Management Foundation, London.

Alimo-Metcalfe, B. and Wedderburn-Tate, C. (1993), 'Women in business in the UK,' in M. J. Davidson and C. L. Cooper (eds) *European Women in Business and Management*, Paul Chapman Publishing, London.

Barnham, K. Fraser, J. and Heath L. (1988), *Management for the Future*, Ashridge Management Research Group and the Foundation for Management Education.

Calas, M. B. and Smircich, L. (1989), 'Using the "F" word: feminist theories and the social consequences of organizational research', paper presented at the *Academy of Management Meeting August*, Washington, D.C.

Calas, M. B. and Smircich, L. (1990), 'Re-writing gender into organizational theorizing: directions from feminist perspectives', in M. I. Reed and M. D. Hughes (eds) *Rethinking Organization: new directions in organizational research and analysis*, Sage, London.

Corby, S. (1983), 'Women in the civil service: looking back or held back?' *Personnel Management*, February, pp. 28–31.

Davidson, M. J. (1989), 'Women managers and stress: profiles of vulnerable individuals', *Clinical Psychology Forum*, 22, pp. 32–4.

Finnigan, M. (1982), 'The effects of token representation on participants in small decision-making groups', *Economic and Industrial Democracy*, 3, 531–50.

Fletcher, C. and Williams, R. (1985), *Performance Appraisal and Career Development*, Hutchinson, London.

Gould, R. J. and Stone, C. G. (1982), 'The "feminine modesty" effect: a self-presentational interpretation of sex differences in causal attribution', *Personality and Social Psychology Bulletin*, 8 (3) 477–85.

Handy, C. (1989), *The Age of Unreason*, Penguin Business Books, London.

Harrison, R. (1987) *Organization Culture and Quality of Service: a strategy for releasing love in the workplace*, Association for Management Education and Development.

Hirsh, W. and Jackson, C. (1990), *Women into Management: issues influencing the entry of women into managerial jobs*, IMS Report No. 158. University of Sussex: Institute of Manpower Studies.

Iles, P. A. and Robertson, I. T. (1988), 'Getting in, getting on, and looking good: physical attractiveness, gender and selection decisions', *Guidance and Assessment Review*, 4, (3) pp. 6–8.

Kanter, R. M. (1989), *When Giants Learn to Dance*, Simon and Schuster, London.

Marshall, J. (1984) *Women Managers: travellers in a male world*, Wiley, Chichester.

Martin, J. (1990) 'Re-reading Weber: searching for feminist alternatives to bureaucracy', paper presented at the *Annual Meeting of the Academy of Management*, San Francisco, August.

National Economic Development Office/Royal Institute of Public Administration (1990) *Women Managers: the untapped resource*, Kogan Page, London.

Robertson, I. and Makin, P. J. (1986), 'Management and selection in Britain: a survey and critique', *Journal of Occupational Psychology*, 59 (1) 45–58.

Rosenberg, S., Erlich, D. E. and Berkowitz, L. (1955), 'Some effects of varying combinations of group members on groups performance measures and leadership behaviour', *Journal of Abnormal and social Psychology*, 51, 195–213.

Rosener, J. (1990) 'Ways Women Lead' *Harvard Business Review*, November–December, 119–25.

Schein, V. E. and Mueller, R. (1990), 'Sex-role stereotyping and requisite management characteristics: a cross cultural look,' paper presented at the 22nd International Congress of Applied Psychology, 22–27 July, Kyoto, Japan.

Stewart, J. (1978), 'Understanding women in organizations: toward a reconstruction of organizational theory', *Administrative Science Quarterly*, 23, 336–50.

Thornton, G. C. and Byham, W C. (1982), *Assessment Centers and Managerial Performance*, Academic Press, London.

Vinnicombe, S. (1987), 'What exactly are the differences in male and female working styles?' *Women in Management Review*, 3, (1) pp. 13–21.

Wallston, B. S. and O'Leary, V. E. (1981), 'Sex makes a difference: differential perceptions of women and men', *Review of Personality and Social Psychology*, 2, 9–41.

Chapter 22

Why executives lose their balance*

Joan R. Kofodimos

* Reprinted, by permission of the publisher, from *Organizational Dynamics*, summer 1990/
© 1990 American Management Association, New York. All rights reserved.

Executives who are effective in their jobs and successful in their careers often devote most of their time and energy to work and little to family or leisure. They stay at the office into the evening, travel frequently, entertain clients over dinner, and take full briefcases home for the weekend. Even when executives are not working, work often occupies their minds.

Typically, executives say they wish they could do a better job of balancing work and family. The issues of greatest worry to them often have to do with their personal lives – marriage, children, health, lifestyle, and values. Yet although they may be troubled about the imbalance, they rarely change the way they allocate their time and energy.

This chapter outlines a framework for understanding the causes and consequences of imbalance. It is based on findings from the Executive Development Project, a research study that we conducted at the Center for Creative Leadership from 1982 to 1988. We conducted intensive clinical case studies of about 20 executives, investigating each individual's work, personal life, and life history. By means of interviews, questionnaires, and/ or psychological instruments, we collected data not only from each executive himself, but also from co-workers and family members. In return for such in-depth access to their lives, we provided the executives with feedback and developmental counseling.

The sample consists exclusively of men. Therefore, when our discussion pertains to the implications of our own research findings, we can only speak with authority about male executives and will use the male pronoun. We expect that, although female executives face some issues similar to those of males, they face others that are quite different.

THE TIME-ENERGY IMBALANCE

Organizations pressure managers to focus a great deal of energy on work and reward them for doing so, especially during the early years of their careers.

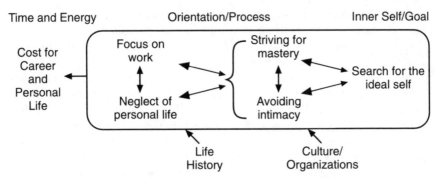

Figure 22.1 Levels of imbalance

The focus on work

Managers at this early stage often justify their extra-hard work by saying it is a temporary necessity that will allow them to advance to a secure position where they can relax a bit. But the pressures continue; long hours, repeated relocation, and frequent travel are treated as proof of commitment and loyalty throughout the manager's career. Conversely, reluctance to make these trade-offs is thought to reflect a lack of dedication.

Hard work is encouraged not only by the organizational reward system, but also by the values of the manager's colleagues. If the manager does accept the implicit contract for life on the fast track, he is likely to reap the rewards of his hard work and dedication. These rewards – praise, respect, power, money, and achievement – provide an incentive to spend even more energy working. With advancement and increasing responsibility, the pressures only mount.

The spiraling imbalance

The executive's responsiveness to organizational pressures affects his personal life. As work expands to dominate his time and energy, neglected family relationships degenerate and become increasingly unsatisfying. Career rewards may become especially appealing by contrast. Soon the executive is trapped in a cycle: He turns more and more to work for gratification, and as the investment in work versus family becomes increasingly lopsided, the two areas provide increasingly discrepant levels of affirmation and reward.

As personal life becomes more impoverished, hard work can become an escape from, or even a substitute for, an unhappy personal life.

The executive's tendency to use the workplace to meet his relationship and leisure needs is facilitated by the nature of his job. Playing golf with clients, discussing projects with colleagues over drinks, or attending meetings in exotic locations may satisfy desires for affiliation, recreation, or excitement and provide the illusion of a rich personal life.

Office romances can result when the workplace becomes the primary source of personal relationships.

Imbalance may reach a marked level in executives' lives before they acknowledge that it has developed. They may justify it in terms of the need to provide for their families or put children through school. Or they may insist that they do attend to their families and circumscribe their hours at work – a claim with which their friends and family disagree. Sometimes friends try unsuccessfully to express their concern.

A major crisis can shock managers into facing an imbalance and its harmful consequences. Crisis may come in the form of a marriage breakup, children's emotional difficulties, or personal health problems such as an early heart attack. These events cause executives to realize what they stand to lose as a result of their overwhelming focus on work, and subsequently they may make major changes in their allocation of time and energy.

The love of work

Why are executives so reluctant to recognize the imbalance? Why does it frequently take a crisis for them to see that it exists? One answer may be that because they do care about their families, they want to avoid the pain of confronting the family problems to which they have contributed. They also might be unwilling to give up the gratifications of work if forced to choose between a successful career and a satisfying personal life.

Executives accommodate themselves to organizational pressures because they love their work. To have a job that one truly enjoys is enviable. But it becomes a problem when a person loves his work so much that it is all he wants to do, even at the cost of his family and his health. What is it about the satisfaction of success in work that, for some people, transcends the potential satisfaction of success in personal life?

THE INNER IMBALANCE

Executives love their work because it satisfies fundamental inner needs. Work is a vehicle for creative expression and personal growth. Work and achievements are key elements defining a person's identity. Through work, one enacts one's values, displays and contributes one's unique gifts to the world, carries out one's purpose in life. And work allows one to fulfill a central urge: the drive for mastery.

The drive for mastery

Mastery is the experience of developing and exercising an ability. Theorists describe the striving for mastery as a basic and universal human process. Attaining mastery helps individuals to clarify their identity, enhance their self-esteem, and feel pleasure and joy. For some people, however, striving for mastery is a more central driving force than it is for others. Executives have a particularly strong "need to master." We refer to a dominant striving for mastery as "expansiveness." Expansiveness provides the impetus which, in combination with talent, leads people to seek and achieve high executive positions. Once they reach such positions, expansiveness helps them excel at fulfilling the requirements of those positions, such as setting goals and standards, mobilizing large groups of people, exercising power and influence in the service of organizational objectives, and making logical and thoughtful decisions.

The lure of mastery is compelling, and often an individual who has experienced the satisfactions of mastery increasingly defines his identity and purpose in terms of the mastery drive. He spends increasing amounts of time on a quest for mastery, focusing primarily on his career and work, which are prime sources of the mastery experience.

The expansive person, whose being is dominated by the striving for mastery, also experiences a more subtle form of imbalance. Mastery entails an approach toward life and the world that is oriented toward developing and exercising one's abilities. To this end, the individual relies on intellect and rationality, takes an active posture, focuses on future goals, seeks productivity, exerts discipline over self and others, maintains distance from others, and values individuality. The expansive person is likely to take this approach not only in his job but also in his personal life. Frequently, the consequence is an inability to relax and enjoy leisure; there also may be a consequent health risk.

The individual who seeks mastery in all areas of his life also faces a risk to his family life. Certainly the quest for mastery has its place in the family; the family has tasks to be accomplished and goals to be met. Yet a fulfilling family and personal life also involves the ability to build and maintain intimate and harmonious relationships, and to be sensitive to others' needs and feelings – an ability that does not generally contribute to the feeling of mastery.

The executive's capacity for intimacy can be squeezed out by the over-dominant striving for mastery. But another force adds to an executive's difficulty in achieving intimacy: active avoidance of it.

The avoidance of intimacy

Many executives are uncomfortable with the experience and expression of emotion, the vulnerability and dependency involved in being intimate, and the confrontation with their inner selves which can occur during times of idleness. Their frequent choice of co-workers as friends is one manifestation of this avoidance. The focus on workplace relationships allows the individual to circumvent the intimacy that might be expected in a relationship outside the workplace.

Of course, expansive individuals do indeed have feelings, needs for love and nurturance, and fears of rejection and loss of esteem – but they hide these needs and fears from themselves and others. Hard work thus serves not only the constructive purpose of striving for mastery, but also the defensive purpose of avoiding intimacy. Working focuses attention outside oneself, onto "safe" areas such as future goals, productive activities, rational thoughts, and analyses.

The role of work as a defense mechanism is especially visible during a life crisis. Although pain seems necessary to a reevaluation of one's life, it is not sufficient. Some executives who are going through such crises as divorce become more intensely involved than usual in their work. Instead of finding an opportunity to restructure their lifestyles, they become vociferous in their affirmation of work and their denial of guilt or regret.

By avoiding intimacy, the executive ironically is unequipped to deal with relationship problems. Thus he faces two sets of forces contributing to imbalance:

1 The rewards of the job versus the unfulfilling nature of personal life.
2 The joy of mastery versus the threat of intimacy.

Work provides the executive with esteem and affirmation that family and leisure do not and, at the same time, work helps the executive to avoid the painful dynamics present in family and leisure. "Workaholism," the addiction to work, is rooted in this combination of pressures.

A person who works hard and loves his work is not necessarily a work addict; some people work hard, love their work, and are happy that way. But the work addict, denying his addiction like any other kind of addict and arguing that he works because he enjoys it and could stop any time, will in fact work even when it costs him his health, well-being, and relationships with friends and family.

CHILDHOOD ORIGINS OF STRIVING FOR MASTERY AND AVOIDING INTIMACY

A powerful force works to make striving for mastery and avoiding intimacy so compelling: the natural and universal human wish for self-esteem.

Healthy self-esteem comes from accepting and respecting one's real self – strengths and foibles alike. But most of us are not completely happy with our real selves; we have ideals for ourselves, and our self-esteem can become dependent on how closely we live up to these ideals. For expansive people such as executives, mastery fulfills these ideals, while intimacy threatens them. This phenomenon comes about as a result of two influences:

1 life history, especially childhood;
2 organizational pressures and values.

Psychoanalytic theorists have shown that the origins of the search for mastery lie in the process of child-rearing. When parents bring a child into the world, they invariably hold particular desires for him or her. They seek to shape the child's behavior by rewarding evidence of desired qualities with tenderness and affection and by punishing evidence of undesired qualities with anger and anxiety. For example, a child with ambitious and doting parents may be rewarded for her talents and achievements – for winning games, coming out tops in class, being the best at whatever she pursues. In contrast, the child for perfectionistic and dominating parents may be criticized for not achieving highly enough or for not being popular or athletic enough.

Consequently, the child comes to learn that certain behaviors are "good" and others are "bad." But, more important, the child receives an implicit message from parents: We will love you if you are a "good" child and reject you if you are a "bad" child. As a result, the child develops the belief that some aspects of himself are "good" and that others are "bad." The child begins to understand that love and approval are forthcoming from his parents only if he becomes the "good" person they want him to be. The child adjusts behavior and expression of feelings to conform to the parents' wishes.

Although parents may consciously believe that punishing unwanted qualities and instilling new ones in this way is "for the child's own good," their underlying motive is more likely to be their own need that the child become a certain type of person or their need to feel that they have been good parents. Their behavior does not meet the child's need, crucial in the development of a stable identity, to be understood and respected by the parents for the "real" self he or she is and the inner feelings he or she experiences. Since the child's sense of security depends on the parents' love, and since the child suffers from disapproval for being "bad," he or she learns to hide the "bad."

A wide range of family circumstances can produce a person driven by striving for mastery. But the strategies children devise for coping with the pressures of parents and other authorities have a common intent: to gain self-esteem by creating and displaying a desired image of self, a "persona" as Carl Jung called it, which includes the "good" elements (strong, rational, invulnerable) and excludes the "bad" (emotional, dependent, vulnerable). The characteristics defined as "bad," (which Jung calls the "dark side") are repressed from consciousness, as if wishing them gone could make them vanish. But the child's inner reality cannot be changed by mandate; the dark side will continue to exist and exert its influence. In times of stress or emotion it will pop up, unbidden, into consciousness or behavior.

Effects of the dark side

A person pursuing an ideal self-image must maintain the delusion of possessing the qualities of that ideal – but since the ideal self is an incomplete picture of one's real self, the self-esteem that depends on possessing these qualities is fragile. Maintaining it requires the use of protective strategies geared toward modifying behavior and perceptions so that one can see oneself, and be seen by others, as living up to the idealized imaged.

For example, an individual will attribute evidence contradicting the ideal image to outside forces or will create phony weaknesses to cover the real ones. These flaws may be consistent with the individual's persona, such as being bad at details or being naïve, shy, or absentminded, and they allow a denial of dark-side weaknesses such as selfish, insecure, ruthless, or angry feelings and impulses. The individual will reconstruct memories of childhood so that it was perfectly happy with perfectly loving parents. Modifying feelings to correspond with how the individual should feel may also occur. The emphasis is not on being, but on appearing.

Intimacy threatens the ideal image

Avoiding intimacy serves the purpose of protecting the ideal image. Intimacy threatens to allow inner dark-side feelings to seep through to consciousness and force the individual to confront his own dark side. Intimacy also threatens to allow others to discover that dark side, thus providing the reason that the individual comes to prefer relationships centered in the workplace: It is the perfect setting for the illusory gratification of self-ideals. Here, competence and mastery are salient, and intimacy is de-emphasized. The person can gain respect and admiration for his authority, position, intellect, and achievements, while the intimate details of his self and his life remain unknown.

In addition, a person who is striving for his ideal self, and has been alienated from his own wishes, will come to experience others' wishes as his own, as he did with his parents' wishes. Subordinating his own needs to those of the organization, he will value loyalty, obedience, and duty. He will develop a value system which makes suppression of his own wishes in the service of his duty a virtue.

Striving for mastery, avoiding intimacy, and questing for the ideal self are such powerful drives in an executive's adult life that continuing influences must reinforce these phenomena. Childhood experience can provide only the groundwork. Institutions such as schools, the military and, particularly, work organizations build upon that groundwork.

HOW ORGANIZATIONS REINFORCE STRIVING FOR MASTERY AND AVOIDING INTIMACY

Organizations continue to shape the individual by creating their own idealized image for the individual to live up to. This image happens to match the expansive profile perfectly. Expansive people are selected and promoted in organizations because they fit the accepted requirements of the managerial role. Once they are placed in these roles, their expansive tendencies are strengthened by work demands and reward systems. Appropriate qualities for the managerial role include intellect, technical knowledge, and planning and problem-solving ability. By contrast, qualities such as emotional depth, sensitivity, caring for others, and self-awareness are seen as being irrelevant, even as creating impediments to the work.

Consequently, the individual who predominates in the organization is detached from emotions, especially from uncomfortable feelings and thoughts that would conflict with his conscious attitude of confidence and enthusiasm about organizational life. To compete and win, he must be detached from compassion for the losers. To devote himself to career success, he must be insulated from loneliness, guilt, or regret regarding sacrifices in his personal life. Thus the executive who strives for mastery and avoids intimacy is exactly what the organization wants.

Because the value placed on organizational success is so deeply embedded in our culture, people who want successful careers are faced with a dilemma: to succeed, they may have to adopt the necessary mastery type values, attitudes, and behavior, even though doing so might involve compromising themselves and subordinating some of their needs and values to those of the organization.

ADDRESSING THE IMBALANCE

If imbalance is indeed so deeply rooted and firmly reinforced, what are the possibilities for change? How might an executive establish more balance in his life? And what changes would need to be made in organizational and cultural practices and norms? There is no easy answer, no recipe for success. The solution must reflect the complex dimensions of the imbalance problem (see Figure 22.1).

A manager trying to achieve balance typically addresses only the behavioral level of imbalance by making an effort to devote more time and energy to family and leisure. But since he has not changed his assessment of the greater rewards to be gained by mastery than by intimacy, he is likely to use this time to strive for mastery in his personal life. Although he tries to enjoy leisure time, he is likely to feel guilty, uncomfortable, and wasteful if he cannot make that time productive. For example, one executive now allows himself to watch football games on television on Sunday afternoon, but he reads business magazines at the same time. Another executive takes his briefcase along to his son's soccer games.

Similarly, the executive trying to attend more closely to parenting is likely to apply a mastery-oriented approach. In short, when managers try to balance their work lives and their personal lives solely by equalizing the amount of time and energy they devote to each, they address only part of the problem. Striving for mastery carries over into their personal lives: They "manage" their children by means of standards for achievement and by reward and control systems. They rely on intellectual and analytical approaches to family issues. They approach leisure activities with perfectionistic and goal-oriented expectations; and they remain emotionally distant from their families.

This approach to improving family life is likely to be unfulfilling and short-lived. Frustrated in his attempt to gain the rewards of mastery from the chaotic and emotional setting of family life, the manager will figure out that work is a much easier place to pursue the satisfactions of mastery. The reallocation of time and energy can, however, be a useful element of change if the manager does not try to be too "masterful" about it. He might, for example, set aside unstructured time with his family or give himself permission to goof off in his own favorite way.

Getting to deeper levels

A more lasting approach to balance requires addressing the deeper levels involved in imbalance (see Figure 22.2). This approach recognizes that the imbalanced relationship between inner-personality drives underlies the imbalance in life structure and that, therefore, addressing imbalance involves moderating the drive for mastery and encouraging the capacity for intimacy. Our culture assumes that these yearnings are mutually incompatible; the conflict between individual achievement and close attachments is a popular theme. In contrast, Eastern philosophies hold that such polarities are incomplete and meaningless without each other. There is tension between mastery and intimacy, but it may be helpful to look at that tension as necessary, healthy, and constructive.

Striving for mastery is incompatible with intimacy when mastery is based on the ideal image and thus needs to be buffered from the intimacy which threatens to expose the dark side. In order to allow oneself the experiences of both mastery and intimacy, one must accept and value one's real self,

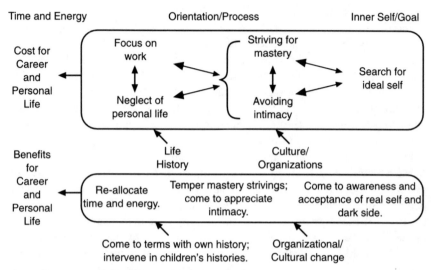

Figure 22.2 Levels of intervention

recognize the illusions in the ideal image, and allow the suppressed aspects of self back into consciousness. One may discover that these dark-side elements are not so terrifying when they are faced, and that indeed they can be given constructive expression. For example, if the individual can become aware of the anger he had hidden, he can turn it into furious work on a pet project.

What balance involves

Thus balance ultimately involves resurfacing one's real self and achieving the natural unity between persona and dark side. This deep endeavor requires looking at those forces that have shaped us, coming to terms with personal history, seeing parents as human and imperfect, feeling grief and resentment for the painful aspects of upbringing, and then getting on with life. Balance means being able to step back and critically look at the influence of the organization in which one lives.

This is not a task one might leap to undertake, but the challenge of such development is likely to emerge of its own accord, particularly at mid-life, when it is common to reevaluate lifestyle, direction, and past choices. Formerly neglected issues such as spirituality and life mission present themselves to be addressed. Formerly neglected aspects of self demand attention. For men at mid-life, the more feminine side of self emerges, bringing introspection and the need and capacity for nurturance and play. One can skip right through mid-life ignoring these issues, but at the peril of continuing growth and development.

One force against this kind of inner development, however, is the power of inertia and past success. Executives have been successful in many respects just the way they are. And to reinforce this success, they have built up a value system that ranks their strengths and areas of success (work and mastery) higher than their weaknesses and areas of failure (personal life and intimacy). Furthermore, organizations reward executives for being just the way they are – so the very aspects of striving for mastery that create problems at home are the same characteristics that apparently make executives effective and successful at work.

Does this mean that a fulfilling personal life is inconsistent with work effectiveness? If an executive wants to grow in areas constructive to career success, will he impede his personal development and harm his personal life? Conversely, if he tries to express all sides of himself, will his career be compromised? On the contrary: if a manager continues to neglect imbalance as long and severely as we see managers neglecting it, then crisis is likely to erupt. Then the time and energy involved in repairing personal life (recovering from a heart attack, going through a divorce, dealing with delinquent children) will surely be subtracted from career investment. A manager is much better off preventing such problems from occurring.

Furthermore, inner imbalance can directly hamper work effectiveness. The common performance problems executives exhibit can, in fact, be traced to an overdominant striving for mastery, the avoidance of intimacy, and the underlying quest for the idealized self.

THE RELATIONSHIP BETWEEN LIFE BALANCE AND WORK EFFECTIVENESS

An executive who is unaware of his own emotional life is likely to be insensitive to the emotional life of co-workers – their needs, their feelings, and the things that motivate them. Thus lacking empathy and compassion, he is unlikely to receive their wholehearted support and commitment. An executive who is uncomfortable expressing feelings might fail to provide needed positive feedback, encouragement, or appreciation. An executive who denies doubts or vulnerabilities might not seek advice or help when it is needed. An executive who is reluctant to own up to weaknesses or mistakes might resist critical feedback and delay taking corrective action. An executive who needs to be perfect and therefore to handle and control every issue facing his unit might be unwilling to delegate responsibility to others. An executive who is overly demanding of others (as he is of himself) might intimidate them into hiding their problems from him. An executive who fears failure might be reluctant to take risks and therefore be overly slow and analytical in his decision making. So inner imbalance can compromise the very success and achievement it was intended to further.

Conversely, inner balance can enhance managerial effectiveness. Attuned to his own inner emotions and needs, a manager can better understand and appreciate the key role of such emotions and needs in organizational life and handle their inevitable emergence in himself and others more effectively. He will recognize that people bring their own inner lives, values, and fears to the job and that these intangibles influence the way they approach their work. He will further recognize that the treatment people receive on the job also has consequences for their work performance. He will have an increased capacity for compassion and nurturance and a decreased need for personal power; he will be better able to play a mentoring role with younger people and subordinates; he will take pleasure in others' successes and not need all the glory for himself. He will be able to empathize with others' feelings and needs, to listen to and motivate them. He will be able to own up to his mistakes, failures, and uncertainties.

The essence of the relationship between balance and work effectiveness is this: an executive who strives for mastery and avoids intimacy in an attempt to pursue the ideal image is, by definition, unconscious of his own dark side, and thus by definition unconscious of many of the motives and needs driving him. Therefore, he is likely to make decisions, take actions, and approach problems in ways intended to serve his inner needs rather than organizational requirements. Furthermore, his behavioral repertoire is restricted by the inability to engage in emotion or intimacy.

By contrast, the more an executive can consciously see and accept all aspects of himself, the more he becomes able to recognize how his inner needs are influencing his preferences for making decisions, taking actions, and solving problems. With this recognition he can better set aside the demands of his own needs when they conflict with the organization's interests. He can also utilize his capacity for emotion and intimacy in the service of his role.

It would be unfair – and ineffectual – to put all the pressure on executives to change. Organizations must also change. By instituting such policies as flexitime, day care, and maternal/paternal leave, a number of organizations have addressed balance issues, and they have demonstrated consequent productivity improvements. For an organization to address comprehensively balance would involve system-wide intervention into organizational values, structures, and processes that reward inner imbalance.

Inner and outer balance can and should be consistent with career success and managerial effectiveness. A manager should be able to have both a successful career and a satisfying personal life.

Chapter 23

Management development in Europe

Mel Berger and Paul Watts

The Single European Market offers great opportunities for businesses to expand their markets and raise profitability. In many cases realizing this potential will necessitate liaison with European partners through joint projects, joint venture activities and concurrent activity with partners. Key criteria for the success of such operations include: effective communications across national and international boundaries in both bilateral and multilateral arrangements; the ability to bridge cultural differences without recourse to cultural stereotypes and thereby the ability to negotiate successfully with European partners and clients.

This chapter analyses one mechanism for building international awareness – the use of a training programme. The analysis will be of a bilateral training programme between France and the UK, which has run for two years at the time of writing in 1992, with 108 delegates having attended the programme.

For some mysterious reasons, in the face of differences or misunderstandings, we humans tend to read the most negative interpretations into the behaviour of others – they are inefficient, they are not helpful, they are deliberately making us look bad. Mistakes and changing priorities become excuses to 'blame and complain'. When cultural differences are added into the 'human equation', potential for distortion increases. Culture is associated with national difference, but in its broadest sense can be applied to different professional disciplines, status levels, age groups, genders and regions.

These issues are complex enough in bilateral arrangements. Now consider how these complexities will expand exponentially when negotiating, planning and team working in a multinational context. Organizations in the field of management development have a key role to play in helping companies to tackle and to overcome some of the interpersonal complexities that act as barriers to effective business procedures. In seeking to do this it is first necessary to analyse the psychological elements of intercultural dealings. We suggest that there are four major elements each of which must be addressed in order to achieve full collaboration.

Language

It is commonplace to misunderstand communication even when there are close work relationships and a common language. This can be a result of using words with different meanings or of politeness in not questioning to clarify ambiguous messages. Many cultures have strong norms against openness and confrontation, so miscommunication is less likely to be detected. A similar problem of language can also occur between different departments of the same company or between different regions of the same country. We have all attended meetings where technical experts appear to be speaking a foreign language!

Tolerance

Faced with different customs, perceptions and language, the most common human tendency is to stereotype the other party in a negative way. They may have made an innocent mistake, but are likely to be seen as being deliberately obstructive or, at best, as being incompetent. Tolerance is based on understanding different cultures, and not judging who is 'better', 'best', or most 'clever'. At an organizational level one department often blames the other.

Teamwork

Effective problem solving is the result of blending different attitudes and skills. It can be an uncomfortable process in which people are prepared to adopt a give-and-take approach and to work with others whose differences are complementary. It is most comfortable to work with people who think like yourself, but this generally does not lead to a synergistic blend of ideas or to identifying potential flaws. At an international level it is likely that certain cultures tend to be more focused on creative design while others may be more oriented to precision implementation.

Another 'psychological' process for dealing with differences is that of 'oppression'. That is, 'I will attempt to control you by creating and enforc-ing the view that I am superior or better or fit to rule'. Oppression may be institutionalized (e.g. apartheid, or simply implemented through shared attitudes, 'we don't promote ... because they are ...'. Where one of the parties in a negotiation believes that they have more power and that they can gain by being in control, oppression is a common result.

National values

Basic values cut across all aspects of a given culture and will exert a strong influence over work customs and practice. The crucial perception here is knowing what to look for and thoroughly researching the characteristics of a culture before conducting business. Hofstede[1] identified four basic values which differentiate cultures:

1 Power Distance (preferred leadership style);
2 Uncertainty Avoidance (need for structure);
3 Individualism/Collectivism;
4 Masculinity/Femininity (competitiveness versus caring).

These four psychological/cultural elements, which we have briefly described – communication, tolerance, teamwork and values – are sequential. Accurate communication is the foundation for understanding and tolerance. Tolerance is a prerequisite of team work. To begin to tackle these issues people must have the opportunity to meet and interact, but just being together does not automatically result in close collaboration. Unless explicit efforts are made to bridge the gap, cooperation will not ensue. Some people can do this intuitively, most others need some framework and guidelines. Research has shown that those who have the knack of reaching across cultural differences are often those whose upbringing had an international dimension, such as having lived in different countries or of having parents and friends of different national backgrounds.[2]

THE TRAINING NEED

In 1989 we were approached by an Anglo-French company to join in designing a programme for its commercial people. The new programme was to be based on an existing course, which had been run solely for the French. The programme was to be in English, because that was the official language of the company and the most generally used business language. The goals were to:

1 Provide training in presentation and negotiation skills.
2 Develop awareness of cross-cultural differences and increase skills of collaboration.
3 Build the corporate identity through contact between managers based in different sites and of different nationalities.

A design team was established by French and British personnel specialists from the company. To achieve a cultural balance in the facilitation of the programmes, two trainers whose professional experience bridged a number of cultures were invited to collaborate. We believed that cultural awareness, tolerance and skill are best developed from an exploration of real here-and-now experiences of people with different nationalities having to work together. The programmes were seen by the participants as very successful. The types of key learning points reported by them are presented in Table 23.1.

Table 23.1 Examples of reported learning

Presentation
  Preparing for a presentation.
  Structuring a talk.
  Use of gestures and non-verbal techniques.
  A good strategy for handling 'trick questions'.
  The importance of correct interpretation of words.
  The necessity of adapting one's speech pace and content to the audience's
    level of English comprehension.

Negotiation
  Preparation of strategy.
  Use of questions to establish the position of the other party.
  A more detached view of the process, stages and signs to look for in a
    negotiation.
  Review of exercises by means of TV, identifying personal impact.
  Managing conflict and deadlocks and how they vary across different cultures.

Cross-cultural
  In all international situations to consider different cultures and to prepare
    accordingly.
  Cultural differences are more than stereotypes.
  Working with French and Germans brought out different approaches, values
    and ethics more clearly.

International team work
  To live and cooperate with people of another culture.
  The differences between us (Europeans) are primarily those of personality
    rather than of culture.
  The importance and usage of visual aids, particularly in a multinational setting.

COURSE DESIGN

The course concentrated on persuasive presentation for the first one-and-a-half days, on negotiation skills for the next two-and-a-half days, and on direct applications to the work environment during the final day. The specific design was built around the four intercultural elements.

Level one: language

The first two days were focused on building accurate communication and learning 'international', or 'offshore' English.[3] Those delegates for whom English was not their mother tongue took about a day to tone their ears to a continual flow of English. There was a similar 'running-in' factor for the native English speakers. Learning 'offshore' English means speaking slower, pronouncing words with more care (and an open mouth), and using simpler words. For many this was difficult, particularly those with strong regional accents.

Each delegate had three opportunities to make persuasive presentations.

After each, the question of clarity and understanding was put to the listeners, of different nationalities. The obvious lesson is that it is relatively easier for the native English speaker to adjust from complex to simpler language usage than it is for the non-British to adjust from simple to complex.

We continued to ask about the level of comprehension across the national divide throughout the week. Understanding increased considerably by Tuesday and Wednesday, though a few people with very quiet voices or strong regional accents continued to struggle to make themselves clear. During the competitive negotiation exercises, there was a tendency to forget the conscious language control and revert to one's normal speed and word usage.

The learning was on an individual basis. Each delegate was given comprehensive feedback on what he did well and coached in areas for improvement. Attention was given to language usage, non-verbal communication, logical structuring and visual aids. Particularly in the international arena, all these areas must be in concert in order to reinforce the intended message.

Level two: tolerance

Tolerance and the awareness of differences was tackled directly in the middle of day two. The starter question to the French was to 'characterize the typical presentation style of the British'; and to the British it was to 'characterize the style of the French'. The common elements were that the French were generally seen as flamboyant, expressive in voice and gestures and verbose. The British were seen as formal, methodical and reserved. There were interesting exceptions. On one programme, the French were seen as indirect in getting to their main point. In another programme the British were seen as expressive.

Having shared stereotypes, the groups discussed the effect of these perceptions on business relationships. For example, if the British are seen as impersonal, does this hinder the development of trust? Similarly, if the French are seen as flamboyant, does this reduce their credibility?

Level three: teamwork

The negotiation part of the course was aimed at the development of communication and negotiation skills and at identifying and practising different negotiation styles.

The presentation sessions helped people to put across ideas, that is, to send communication. Equally important for negotiations are the skills of listening and questioning for information, that is receiving communication. A full morning was given to the art of questioning with special emphasis given to developing the ability to act neutrally and avoid arguing while seeking information. We also looked at how to run an effective meeting based on listening, questioning and summarizing, and agenda management.

These skills are particularly important in the international setting where careful listening and drawing out information can build bridges of understanding. Within the context of a structured meeting, each party can have its say, which goes a long way towards preventing the native English speakers from dominating the airspace. Those for whom English is not their mother language will take longer to formulate and express their ideas. Additionally, most Anglo cultures place value on the taking of initiatives and self-expression, rather than 'politely' drawing out ideas from others. Those cultures which are naturally assertive need to exercise self-control when dealing with more polite cultures.

Key learning points were to encourage the French to feel that it is reasonable and acceptable to speak slowly, to question for clarification and to stop others from interrupting them. The British were encouraged to take more care in drawing out the views of others, testing for understanding and not letting time pressure overtake order, politeness and consensus building.

Throughout the negotiation sessions we examined various styles of handling differences of ideas, positions and opinions. Using a questionnaire (designed by Thomas and Kilmann) we helped delegates to focus on five distinct styles of negotiating:

1 Competition: desiring to win or dominate, even at the other's expense (win-lose).
2 Collaboration: looking for the best possible mutual acceptable solution (win-win).
3 Accommodation: preparedness to give ground or to make concessions in order to reach an agreement (lose-win).
4 Compromise: giving and taking so that each pair wins a little and loses a little (half-win-half-win; half-lose-half-lose).
5 Avoid: deciding not to negotiate (lose-lose).

HOW TO USE DIFFERENCES CREATIVELY

We were interested to find out whether there were cultural differences of style as measured by the questionnaire. There were two notable but slight differences. According to the delegate's self-perception, the French are slightly more likely to 'avoid' while the British were slightly more likely to 'collaborate'. When we asked delegates to describe how they saw one another the only difference was that the British were seen as more competitive.

Another aspect of style was looked at in terms of how people deal with the inevitable deadlocks which occur during the life of a negotiation. Here the results were dramatic. The British approach is predominantly behavioural or tactical – they threaten, concede, tell a joke or call a recess.

The French, by contrast, are more analytic. They like to analyse the situation, identify root causes of differences, seek further basic information or summarize areas of agreement and disagreement.

The Germans and Swiss took a different stance, which was more structural. They like working parties, bringing in mediators, referring back to head office and changing the team composition.

An important implication of this finding is that one's natural approach to negotiating is likely to be at odds with the natural approach taken by someone of another culture.

These differences are undoubtedly a reflection of basic values and education. This argues for the need to be aware of cultural differences and to tolerate and accommodate them. In the international arena, you are unlikely to change people, you can only hope to understand one another and to find common acceptable ground. Table 23.2 presents this information in detail.

Level four: national values

On day five we wanted to provide a general map for conceptualizing cultural values and how they influence negotiation. Hofstede's research[1] highlights values that should be clearly reflected in organizational and commercial behaviour. We asked delegates to identify examples of how the values affect negotiating behaviour (see Table 23.3) and to draw up guidelines for dealing with cultures which differ markedly from their own. These guidelines were:

1 Select your team to include people whose own values match the characteristics of the other culture, or who have a sincere appreciation of the culture.
2 Assess the extremeness (rigidity) of the other culture. The culture whose values are moderate are likely to have to conform most. If your bargaining position is poor and you are in their country, you will probably have to conform to the other.
3 Respect the customs and practices of the other and do not expect them to change.
4 Negotiations will be slower than you are probably used to because of differences in language, culture and commercial practices. Patience and politeness are essential.

Table 23.2 Ways to break a deadlock

1 *Samples of British responses (mentioned by two or more groups):*
- **Behavioural** (relationship)
  Take time out to reassess (e.g. recess, coffee break).
  Change tactics (e.g. firm–conciliatory, friendly–distant, patient–impatient).
  Offer concessions.
  Break for social interaction.
  Introduce a new personality.
  Threaten them, become aggressive.
  Walk away!

- **Analytic**
  Reassess the position within the meeting, recap and clarify.

- **Procedural** (within meetings)
  Make a counterproposal.
  Change subject or agenda.

- **Structural** (external to meeting)
  Seek arbitration, a third party with an independent viewpoint.

2 *Samples of French responses (mentioned by two or more groups):*

- **Behavioural**
  Take a break (coffee, lunch, tea).
  Break to give both sides time to review.

- **Analytic**
  Summarize the situation – identify points of agreement and disagreement
  and minute the agreement.
  Reformulation of the disagreement.
  Identify the causes of deadlocks on both sides.
  Review the targets.

- **Procedural** (within meeting)
  Restart negotiation process on a different point.

- **Structural** (external to meeting)
  Call for a third party or an expert.

3 *Samples of German/Swiss responses (mentioned by two or more groups):*

- **Behavioural** (relationship)
  Suggest a break (ten minutes).

- **Analytic**
  Reformulation to get to the real issues.

- **Procedural** (within meeting)
  Defer the critical item to a later stage.

- **Structural** (external to meeting)
  Transfer the critical subject to a task force.
  Depart and meet if there is any change.
  Break to get more information/opinion from own organization.
  Define the issue, establish a task force.

Table 23.3 Values which affect negotiating strategy

When dealing with a high Power Distance culture: Status differences are very important and must be respected.	*When dealing with a low Power Distance culture:* Status differences matter less than technical expertise and one's role on the specific project.
Authority will remain with the most senior person; it is essential to clarify who is the key decision-maker.	Authority will be delegated to middle levels of the organization.
If you influence the most senior person you will succeed.	You will need to influence many people in order to succeed.
When dealing with a high Uncertainty Avoidance culture: Talks about procedures and agenda are essential; once agreed, they will be rigidly adhered to.	*When dealing with a low Uncertainty Avoidance culture:* It is preferable to be flexible about the agenda; it will be relatively easy to adapt and respond as you work.
You need to prepare in great detail and have relevant experts at hand; credible documentation is essential.	You need to prepare in general terms, and not in detail! Overdocumentation could be seen as too restricting.
Strict procedures and methods demonstrate credibility.	Flexibility and openness help to build trust.

CONCLUSION

The bottom line of cross-cultural training is whether delegates become more aware, tolerant and adaptable. Within the context of one's own organization, people are often told to be themselves, to be natural. In an international setting, however, being natural may be offensive and may cost you business. It is important to recognize when your natural tendencies need to be held in check. It is also essential to remember that what is natural in one country, or region, may not be natural in another.

Based on our experience we have developed a checklist of skills which are important in cross-cultural settings. These are summarized in Table 23.4.

Table 23.4 Intercultural effectiveness skills checklist

Communication skills
   Using simple, jargon-free words, speaking clearly and concisely.
   Voice level, intonation, speed and rhythm.
   Non-verbal gestures and movement to emphasize points.
   Structuring a talk or input.
   Signalling and summarizing to maintain clarity and interest of audience.
   Use of relevant visual aids and back-up material.
   Interpreting non-verbal behaviour of others.
   Ability to adapt one's style to the audience, e.g. knowing how and when to
      be personal versus technical versus commercial.

Awareness of cultural differences
   Judging how your 'cultural style' is likely to be perceived.
   Knowing how 'values' of a country affect its people's approach to negotiation.
   Awareness of your own tendencies to stereotype and how to keep them from
      'biasing' the relationship.
   Accepting cultural differences of others without judgement.

Teamwork skills
   Listening and questioning with an enquiring attitude (without argument).
   Debate and dialogue, finding ways to build bridges of understanding between
      all parties.
   Structuring and managing meetings.
   Problem solving, dealing with different views and opinions.

Selection of a team
Putting together complementary cross-cultural teams.
   Assessing which people are most likely to adapt in order to work
      collaboratively with people from other cultures.

REFERENCES

1 Hofstede, G. (1991), *Cultures and Organizations*, McGraw-Hill, Maidenhead, Berkshire.
2 Saxton Bamp Fylde International (1989), *The Search for the Euro-Executive*, London.
3 Guy, V. and Mattock, J. (1991), *The New International Manager*, Kogan Page, London.

Acknowledgements

Chapter 1 Senge, P. M. (1990) *Sloan Management Review*, Fall, pp. pp. 7–23, edited version. Reprinted by permission of the *Sloan Management Review*. © 1990 the Sloan Management Review Association.

Chapter 2 Dale, M. (1993) *Developing Management Skills*, Kogan Page, London, edited version of chapter 9, pp. 219–51.

Chapter 3 Salaman, G. and Butler, J. (1990) *Management Education and Development*, Vol. 21, 3, pp. 183–91. Reprinted by permission of Sage Publications Ltd. © 1990 Sage Publications Ltd.

Chapter 4 Leonard-Barton, D. (1992) *Sloan Management Review*, Fall, pp. 23–38, edited version. Reprinted by permission of the *Sloan Management Review*. © 1992 the Sloan Management Review Association.

Chapter 5 Sparrow, P. R. and Bognanno, M. (1993) *International Journal of Selection and Assessment*, Vol. 1, 1, pp. 50–8, edited version.

Chapter 6 Cockerill, T. (1989) *Personnel Management*, Vol. 21, 9, September, pp. 51–54, edited version. Reprinted by permission of Personnel Publications Ltd.

Chapter 7 Mumford, A. (1991) *Industrial and Commercial Training*, Vol. 23, 6, pp. 24–31, edited version.

Chapter 8 Gratton, L. and Pearson, J. (1993) *Occupational Psychology Conference, Brighton, January 1993, edited version.*

Chapter 9 Margerison, C. J. (1989) *Journal of Management Development*, Vol. 7, 5, pp. 43–53, edited version.

Chapter 10 Fletcher, C. (1986) *Journal of Management Development*, Vol. 5, 3, pp. 3–12, edited version.

Chapter 11 Mabey, C. and Iles, P. A. (1994). Chapter developed from article in *British Journal of Management* (1993), Vol. 4, 3, pp. 103–11.

Chapter 12 Burdett, J. O. (1991) *Industrial and Commercial Training*, pp. 10–23, edited version.

Chapter 13 Kolb, D., Lublin, S., Spoth, J. and Baker, R. (1986) *Journal of Management Development*, Vol. 5, 3, pp. 13–24, edited version.

Chapter 14 Pedler, M. (1987) *Conference Report*, September, edited version.

Chapter 15 Wellins, R. S. (1992) *Training and Development*, December, pp. 24–8, edited version. Reprinted with permission. © 1992 the American Society for Training and Development. All rights reserved.

Chapter 16 Moss Kanter, R. (1982) *The Change Masters: corporate entrepreneurs at work*, Allen & Unwin, edited version of chapter 9, pp. 255–64.

Chapter 17 Jaques, E. (1991) *The World & I*, October, News World Communications Inc., pp. 535–42, edited version.

Chapter 18 Marchington, M. (1992) *Managing the Team: a guide to successful employee involvement*, M. Marchington (ed.), Blackwell, Oxford, edited version of chapter 6, pp. 114–123, 189–98.

Chapter 19 Anderson, N., Hardy, G. and West, M. (1990) *Personnel Management*, September. Reprinted by permission of Personnel Publications Ltd.

Chapter 20 Walker, B. A. (1991) in M. A. Smith and S. J. Johnson (eds) *Valuing Differences in the Workplace*, University of Minnesota/American Society for Training and Development, pp. 7–17, 115–19, edited version. © 1991 the American Society for Training and Development. Reprinted with permission. All rights reserved.

Chapter 21 Alimo-Metcalfe, B. (1993) *International Journal of Selection and Assessment*, Vol. 1, 2, April, pp. 68–83, edited version.

Chapter 22 Kofodimos, J. R. (1991) *Organizational Dynamics*, Vol. 19, pp. 58–73, edited version.

Chapter 23 Berger, M. and Watts, P. (1992) *Journal of European Industrial Training*, Vol. 16, 6, pp. 13–21, edited version.

Index